2027

A Book of Grace-Filled Days

JOE PAPROCKI

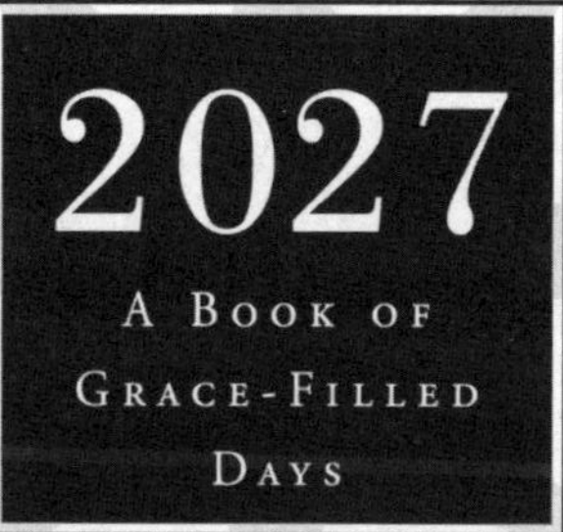

LoyolaPress.
A Jesuit Ministry

LOYOLA PRESS.
A JESUIT MINISTRY
www.loyolapress.com

Cover and interior design by Kathy Kikkert.

ISBN: 978-0-8294-5854-1

Published in Chicago, IL
Printed in Canada.
26 27 28 29 30 31 32 33 34 35 MQS 10 9 8 7 6 5 4 3 2 1

Introduction

Back in high school, I was part of a pilot program that involved Jesuit priests providing spiritual direction to students. Fr. Terry, who was also my chemistry teacher, kept telling me to listen for God's voice. So I would go home and, in a household of eleven people, try to find a quiet place to listen for God's voice. Alas, I never heard anything.

I went back to Fr. Terry and told him I was going to drop out of the program because it wasn't working. He asked what I meant by that. "I keep trying to hear God's voice," I said, "but I'm not hearing anything." He smiled and said, "Ah, that's because you're listening with your ears. I have to teach you how to listen with your heart."

Fr. Terry then went on to explain that God speaks to us in subtle ways that we need to pay attention to—through our thoughts, desires, hopes, fears, joys, memories, and feelings.

And, of course, God does use words from time to time. The words through which God reveals himself to us have been recorded in sacred Scripture. *A Book of Grace-Filled Days* is an invitation for you to listen to God speaking to you through those words and through Scripture, and then to listen again to God speaking to your heart.

May this year, indeed, be filled with grace-filled days!

Sunday NOVEMBER 29

• FIRST SUNDAY OF ADVENT •

Oh, that you would rend the heavens and come down.
—ISAIAH 63:19B

Too often we find ourselves feeling like poor little E.T. (from the movie)—abandoned here on earth and seeking a way to make contact with a distant home in order to be rescued. God seems far away from us. At such times, we echo the words of Isaiah, calling on the Lord to "rend the heavens and come down" to be in our midst. Advent reminds us that God has done just that! God has ruptured the separation between heaven and earth and come down to us. During the Advent season, we call out to Emmanuel—God with us—and we practice the virtue of confident hope that sustains us and assures us of his nearness.

Isaiah 63:16b–17, 19b; 64:2–7
Psalm 80:2–3, 15–16, 18–19 (4)
1 Corinthians 1:3–9
Mark 13:33–37

Monday

NOVEMBER 30

• ST. ANDREW THE APOSTLE •

At once they left their nets and followed him.
—MATTHEW 4:20

Saying yes to something or someone requires saying no to something else. Anytime we make a new commitment, it leaves less time and energy for previous commitments. Peter and Andrew were committed to lives as fishermen. But when the opportunity to follow Jesus came along, they left their nets behind and followed him. During this Advent season, we take time to reflect on our priorities. Are we giving sufficient time and energy to the most important commitments in our lives? What do we need to relinquish to more deeply embrace our priorities? In his book *The Freedom of Missing Out*, Fr. Michael Rossmann, SJ, reminds us that there is great freedom in saying no to many things so that we can say yes to the particular path God is calling us to take.

Romans 10:9–18
Psalm 19:8, 9, 10, 11
Matthew 4:18–22

Tuesday

DECEMBER 1

Turning to the disciples in private he said, "Blessed are the eyes that see what you see."
—LUKE 10:23

I find it odd that there are TV shows and magazine articles entitled "Secrets of the Bible," which is the opposite of what the Bible is: revelation! In today's Gospel, Jesus rejoices that God has revealed himself to those who wish to see. God does not keep secrets! During this Advent season, we take time to pray with God's revealed word in Scripture so that we may grow in our relationship with the Lord. Likewise, we take time to look around and reflect on all of the ways that God is revealing himself to us and pray for the grace to reveal God's mercy, compassion, and love to others through our words and actions so that they too may experience the nearness of God.

Isaiah 11:1–10
Psalm 72:1–2, 7–8, 12–13, 17
Luke 10:21–24

Wednesday

DECEMBER 2

"My heart is moved with pity for the crowd, for they have been with me now for three days and have nothing to eat."
—MATTHEW 15:32

Compassion and empathy are closely related, but they are not the same thing. Empathy is the ability to recognize that someone is suffering and feel what they feel. That, however, can be done from a distance. Compassion is when we feel another's suffering so strongly that we are compelled to alleviate it through some course of action. Empathy is felt in the heart, but compassion is felt in the gut. Jesus experienced empathy for the hungry people, but he did not stop there. His compassion moved him to feed them. May this Advent be a time of moving beyond empathy and practicing compassion in imitation of Jesus.

Isaiah 25:6–10a
Psalm 23:1–3a, 3b–4, 5, 6
Matthew 15:29–37

Thursday

DECEMBER 3

• ST. FRANCIS XAVIER, PRIEST •

"Not everyone who says to me, 'Lord, Lord,' will enter the Kingdom of heaven, but only the one who does the will of my Father in heaven."
—MATTHEW 7:21

While words are important, it is also true that talk is cheap. We say, "Don't just talk the talk; walk the walk." In his book *Praying with Our Feet*, Ansel Augustine, DMin, reminds us, "As we preach about a just society and the dignity of humans within the walls of our church, it is up to all of us to pray with our feet. To step out. To create the conditions where justice is within reach." This Advent season, may we pray as Dr. Augustine suggests—with our feet—as we work to reveal God's mercy and compassion to those most in need.

Isaiah 26:1–6
Psalm 118:1 and 8–9, 19–21, 25–27a
Matthew 7:21, 24–27

Friday

DECEMBER 4

• ST. JOHN OF DAMASCUS, PRIEST AND DOCTOR OF THE CHURCH •

*That I may gaze on the loveliness of the LORD
and contemplate his temple.*
—PSALM 27:4B

Simply put, we are drawn to beauty. Beauty helps us to transcend the merely physical and material and leads us to an experience of the spiritual or mystical. And we cannot help but think that what is authentically beautiful somehow also possesses mystery. Unfortunately, in our quest to encounter authentic beauty, we too often settle for shortcuts that lead us to encounter beauty's imposters. As this Advent season progresses, let us pray for the grace we need to set aside those imposters and gaze on that which is truly lovely: God's face, which we behold when we seek God's presence. And to be in the mystery of God's presence is an intensely beautiful experience.

Isaiah 29:17–24
Psalm 27:1, 4, 13–14
Matthew 9:27–31

Saturday

DECEMBER 5

"Without cost you have received; without cost you are to give."
—MATTHEW 10:8

In college, my best high school friend and I took a theology course together. The Jesuit priest who taught it, recently arrived from Italy, had a heavy Italian accent. One day in class, he blurted out with glee, "Life is a gift!" which came out as "Life is a geeft!" My friend and I chuckled, and as time went on, we found ourselves occasionally (and perhaps a bit irreverently) saying, "Life is a geeft!" at happy moments. Years later, with decades of life's ups and downs behind us, my friend and I still find ourselves, at moments of deep gratitude, quietly and reverently saying to each other, "He was right. Life *is* a geeft!" Advent is a good time to reflect on our blessings with deep gratitude, and to generously share our gifts with others.

Isaiah 30:19–21, 23–26
Psalm 147:1–2, 3–4, 5–6
Matthew 9:35—10:1, 5a, 6–8

Sunday

DECEMBER 6

• SECOND SUNDAY OF ADVENT •

A voice cries out:
In the desert prepare the way of the LORD!
—ISAIAH 40:3

It's no coincidence that in today's first reading and the Gospel we hear of a voice crying out in the desert. It is in this place of desolation—the desert—that we are to prepare the way of the Lord. Like the Jewish people who encountered God in their desert experience, we often encounter God in the midst of our desolation. In Ignatian spirituality, desolation is not only those moments when our lives are falling apart, but can refer to any moment when we feel distant from God or are experiencing sadness or emptiness in our prayer and spiritual life. On this Second Sunday of Advent, we are urged to bring a message of hope to those in our lives who are experiencing desolation in whatever form that may be: anxiety, despair, loneliness, doubt, confusion, anger, loss, or emptiness.

Isaiah 40:1–5, 9–11
Psalm 85:9–10, 11–12, 13–14 (8)
2 Peter 3:8–14
Mark 1:1–8

Monday

DECEMBER 7

• ST. AMBROSE, BISHOP AND DOCTOR OF THE CHURCH •

A highway will be there,
called the holy way.
—ISAIAH 35:8A

In the years preceding the advent of the Internet, advocates for this new online tool referred to it as an "information highway." The phrase conjures images of vehicles moving at high speeds with no obstacles slowing them down. In today's first reading, Isaiah promises that a highway will be found in the desert: a clear path even in the midst of the most barren and challenging circumstances. In today's Gospel, a group of people clear a path by removing obstacles to bring a paralyzed man to Jesus. The message to us is clear: We are called to create a highway for those whose access to God is being blocked by obstacles such as despair, grief, illness, unemployment, broken relationships, and more. May this Advent season inspire us to set aside our own needs and lift up the needs of others.

Isaiah 35:1–10
Psalm 85:9ab and 10, 11–12, 13–14
Luke 5:17–26

Tuesday

DECEMBER 8

• THE IMMACULATE CONCEPTION OF THE BLESSED VIRGIN MARY (PATRONAL FEAST DAY OF THE UNITED STATES OF AMERICA) •

"Behold, I am the handmaid of the Lord. May it be done to me according to your word."
—LUKE 1:38

Like all Marian feasts, today's celebration of the Immaculate Conception is not primarily about Mary! In fact, the Blessed Virgin Mary's great Magnificat prayer proclaims that it is the Lord who is to be magnified. The Marian feasts are ultimately about Mary's Son, Jesus. This reality is captured in many icons and paintings that depict Mary holding her child, such as William-Adolphe Bouguereau's *Madonna of the Lilies* (1899). Often, Jesus's face eclipses the face of his mother, and Mary's eyes are humbly cast downward, saying in essence, "It's not about me." Like Mary, we are called to hold Jesus up to the world—not to draw attention to ourselves but to turn people's attention to the face of God.

Genesis 3:9–15, 20
Psalm 98:1, 2–3ab, 3cd–4
Ephesians 1:3–6, 11–12
Luke 1:26–38

Wednesday

DECEMBER 9

• ST. JUAN DIEGO CUAUHTLATOATZIN, HERMIT •

They that hope in the LORD will renew their strength,
they will soar as with eagles' wings.
—ISAIAH 40:31

St. Juan Diego played a significant role in the evangelization of the Americas as a result of his encounter with Our Lady of Guadalupe. The experience of this humble man led to the widespread conversion of indigenous people to Catholicism. He knocked on the doors of the powerful to bring attention to the needs of the downtrodden. Today's feast challenges us in one of two ways. If we are among the more affluent, we are challenged to believe that we can learn something from those less fortunate. If we are among those less affluent, we are challenged to overcome any sense of inadequacy that society has placed on us and ask God for the strength of Juan Diego to proclaim to those in power that God wants things to be different.

Isaiah 40:25–31
Psalm 103:1–2, 3–4, 8 and 10
Matthew 11:28–30

Thursday

DECEMBER 10

"Whoever has ears ought to hear."
—MATTHEW 11:15

In today's world, we are exposed to multiple voices telling us what to believe, what's important, what's good, what's evil, how to be happy, and more. Unfortunately, we don't always know whether the voices we are listening to can be trusted. Sometimes, we end up listening because they are telling us precisely what we want to hear. As we approach the halfway point of Advent, this would be a good time to tune out the myriad voices that bombard us and tune into the voice of Jesus, who speaks God's truth and urges us to heed carefully what we hear. What we hear from Jesus is often in contrast to what we hear from the voices of today's world. Jesus often challenges us to step outside of our comfort zones and follow him to the margins where God's mercy is needed most.

Isaiah 41:13–20
Psalm 145:1 and 9, 10–11, 12–13ab
Matthew 11:11–15

Friday

December 11

• ST. DAMASUS I, POPE •

"But wisdom is vindicated by her works."
—MATTHEW 11:19

The fourth-century reign of Pope Damasus was mired in bitter divisions. For a time, Damasus even had to contend with a rival who also claimed the Chair of St. Peter. This shows that acrimonious polarization, whether in the church or in politics, is not a new phenomenon. In today's world, we are often overwhelmed by hateful polarization that sometimes causes us to question the very people we thought were trustworthy. Jesus experienced this as well in the criticisms that came from both ends of the spectrum. His advice about wisdom being vindicated by her works continues to speak to us today. During this Advent season, we lift our voices and sing, "O come, O Wisdom from on high . . . / to us the path of knowledge show / and teach us in her ways to go."

Isaiah 48:17–19
Psalm 1:1–2, 3, 4 and 6
Matthew 11:16–19

Saturday

DECEMBER 12

• OUR LADY OF GUADALUPE •

"My soul proclaims the greatness of the Lord;
my spirit rejoices in God my savior."
—LUKE 1:46–47

Several different translations of this verse reveal a variety of interpretations including "My soul glorifies the Lord" and "My soul magnifies the Lord." The word *glorify* also means to magnify or to enlarge or make greater or draw attention to something's or someone's greatness. Mary does not draw attention to herself; instead, she points to God. For this reason, we refer to her great prayer as the Magnificat. During Advent, and on this Feast of Our Lady of Guadalupe, we can ask ourselves, What do *we* magnify? What do we focus our attention on and make greater than it really should be? Is it popularity? Possessions? Status?

Zechariah 2:14–17 or Revelation 11:19a; 12:1–6a, 10ab
Judith 13:18bcde, 19
Luke 1:26–38 or 1:39–47

Sunday

DECEMBER 13

• THIRD SUNDAY OF ADVENT •

Rejoice always. Pray without ceasing. In all circumstances give thanks, for this is the will of God for you in Christ Jesus.
—1 THESSALONIANS 5:16–18

Wow! St. Paul packed a lot into a few short sentences! We are to rejoice always, never cease praying, and render constant thanks. While it sounds like he's asking a lot, St. Paul tells us that this is God's will for us. The three imperatives are intimately connected: To pray without ceasing is to always be aware of God's nearness. That's something to give thanks for and something that brings us joy. To rejoice always is not to glibly say, "Don't worry, be happy!" or "Put on a happy face!" It is a deep-down gladness: a disposition we carry with us when we know with full confidence that God is near to us at all times and we can't wait to share this good news with everyone.

Isaiah 61:1–2a, 10–11
Luke 1:46–48, 49–50, 53–54
1 Thessalonians 5:16–24
John 1:6–8, 19–28

Monday

DECEMBER 14

• ST. JOHN OF THE CROSS, PRIEST AND DOCTOR OF THE CHURCH •

Your ways, O LORD, make known to me;
teach me your paths.
—PSALM 25:4

In the *Star Wars* spinoff *The Mandalorian*, some inhabitants of the planet Mandalore belong to a tribe of warriors who follow a specific way of life guided by a code of conduct. Their creed is summed up by the phrase "This is the way." Ignatian spirituality also speaks of a "way of proceeding," meaning that as followers of Jesus, we should have a different way of thinking, acting, and speaking. In today's Responsorial Psalm, we pray, "Your ways, O Lord, make known to me." As we utter these words, we must be careful what we ask for: God's ways are not our ways. To learn God's ways is to relinquish some ways that we thought were sound but in reality are selfish. In contrast, God's ways are selfless, placing the well-being of others before our own.

Numbers 24:2–7, 15–17a
Psalm 25:4–5ab, 6 and 7bc, 8–9
Matthew 21:23–27

Tuesday

DECEMBER 15

"Amen, I say to you, tax collectors and prostitutes are entering the Kingdom of God before you."
—MATTHEW 21:31

It is no coincidence that we begin the Mass by acknowledging our brokenness and publicly state that we are sinners: in our thoughts, in our words, in what we have done, and in what we have failed to do. It is this very brokenness that is the key to our salvation, for without acknowledgment of our brokenness we remain impenetrable to God's grace; the soil of our hearts and minds remains compacted. When we embrace our brokenness, we become vulnerable, and through the "cracks" in our being the grace of God can and will enter. This is precisely why Jesus says the sinners are closer to the kingdom of God. Their "cracks" allow in grace that is inaccessible when we conceal or deny our own flaws.

Zephaniah 3:1–2, 9–13
Psalm 34:2–3, 6–7, 17–18, 19 and 23
Matthew 21:28–32

Wednesday

DECEMBER 16

"Go and tell John what you have seen and heard."
—LUKE 7:22

When someone takes the witness stand in a court of law, they are called upon to credibly share what they have seen and heard. Based on their testimony, the jury will reach a verdict. When John's disciples ask Jesus if he is "the one who is to come," Jesus tells them to go tell John what they have seen and heard: "The blind regain their sight, the lame walk, lepers are cleansed." We too, as followers of Christ, are called upon to give witness to the marvelous deeds that the Lord has done in our own lives and in the lives of others. To proclaim the gospel is to tell others about what we have seen and heard so they too may come to believe that Jesus is, indeed, "the one who is to come."

Isaiah 45:6c–8, 18, 21c–25
Psalm 85:9ab and 10, 11–12, 13–14
Luke 7:18b–23

Thursday

DECEMBER 17

The book of the genealogy of Jesus Christ, the son of David, the son of Abraham.
—MATTHEW 1:1

At first glance, today's Gospel—the genealogy of Jesus—may not strike you as the most inspiring reading. However, if you think about this Scripture passage as a peek into Jesus's family album, you will find the richness of this Gospel reading. Among the many pictures in this album, you will find both heroes (Abraham and David) and villains; great people and a few n'er-do-wells (adulterers and foreigners). In essence, a family album tells a story that is made up of many smaller stories, some glorious and some a bit messy. The beauty of Jesus's family tree is that it reveals how God's grace brings about salvation through imperfect people. This reminds us that, even in the chaos of our own lives, God is quietly but relentlessly guiding us to the arrival of his Son, Jesus Christ.

Genesis 49:2, 8–10
Psalm 72:1–2, 3–4ab, 7–8, 17
Matthew 1:1–17

Friday

DECEMBER 18

This is the name they give him:
"The LORD our justice."
—JEREMIAH 23:6

Each morning, as we awaken, we have a hoped-for vision of how the upcoming day should unfold. The presentation I am giving will go flawlessly. The time I spend visiting my mother will be free of any conflict. The person who wronged me yesterday will apologize today and all shall be well. If only everything would be as it should be! The truth is, God has a vision for how the world should be, and because we humans often fail to live up to that plan, God comes to us with *justice*. In Scripture, justice is neither revenge nor punishment but a notion of setting things right—making things the way they should be. Today's first reading reminds us that justice is not just a side hustle for God. Justice is God's *name*. We pray for justice in our world and in our lives.

Jeremiah 23:5–8
Psalm 72:1–2, 12–13, 18–19
Matthew 1:18–25

Saturday

December 19

"But now you will be speechless and unable to talk until the day these things take place, because you did not believe my words."
—Luke 1:20

It is not easy to trust. Zechariah, the father of John the Baptist, found it difficult to trust the angel Gabriel's message that he and his wife Elizabeth would have a son, despite their advanced ages. As a result, he is made mute until the child is born. While this may seem harsh, the meaning is clear: We are not to spread doubt or a lack of faith. Unlike Mary, who would ask how the impossible could be possible, Zechariah is seeking certainty or proof: "How shall I know this?" The message for us is to resist the temptation to desire certainty in all things. Faith is not about proof. It is about trusting the evidence placed before us.

Judges 13:2–7, 24–25a
Psalm 71:3–4a, 5–6ab, 16–17
Luke 1:5–25

Sunday
DECEMBER 20

• FOURTH SUNDAY OF ADVENT •

"The Holy Spirit will come upon you, and the power of the Most High will overshadow you."
—LUKE 1:35

At the heart of being filled with the Spirit is the notion of experiencing a transformation. When people's outward behavior changes, we sometimes ask, "What's come over you?" In fact, it is a change of behavior—for the better—that is considered to be evidence that one has been filled with the Holy Spirit and is no longer living by the power of an ordinary human spirit. In today's Gospel, Mary is overcome by the Holy Spirit and transformed from a simple peasant girl into the Mother of God. During this last week of Advent, we pray to be overcome by the Holy Spirit so that people who encounter us acting with compassion, mercy, and generosity might ask, "What's come over you?"

2 Samuel 7:1–5, 8b–12, 14a, 16
Psalm 89:2–3, 4–5, 27, 29 2a
Romans 16:25–27
Luke 1:26–38

Monday

DECEMBER 21

• ST. PETER CANISIUS, PRIEST AND DOCTOR OF THE CHURCH •

Mary set out in those days and traveled to the hill country in haste to a town of Judah, where she entered the house of Zechariah and greeted Elizabeth.
—LUKE 1:39–40

A good way to discern if a stirring that you're experiencing is from God is to watch to see if it makes you turn inward or outward. After Mary's encounter with the angel Gabriel, she did not retreat into herself. In fact, despite her own pregnancy, she proceeded "in haste" making the difficult journey to the hill country to care for her cousin Elizabeth who, because of her advanced years, would need assistance in her pregnancy. When God touches our hearts, the movement is always outward—not withdrawing from the world but plunging ever more deeply into it, carrying the word of God within us, so that those we encounter may also feel a stirring within at our greeting.

Song of Songs 2:8–14 or Zephaniah 3:14–18a
Psalm 33:2–3, 11–12, 20–21
Luke 1:39–45

Tuesday

December 22

"He has cast down the mighty from their thrones and has lifted up the lowly."
—LUKE 1:52

With the explosion of social media, many people now feel the need to take a stand on topics ranging from politics to religion to sports, and everything in between. In today's Gospel, the words of Mary's Magnificat remind us that taking the right stand is not as important as standing in the right place. Mary proclaims that her life is an example of where God stands: with the lowly. She proclaims that God has "scattered the proud in their conceit," "lifted up the lowly," and "filled the hungry with good things," while "the rich he has sent away empty." In just a few days, we will celebrate the birth of Jesus in a lowly manger, visited by poor shepherds. We will find God where he stands: with those at the margins.

1 Samuel 1:24–28
1 Samuel 2:1, 4–5, 6–7, 8abcd
Luke 1:46–56

Wednesday

DECEMBER 23

• ST. JOHN OF KANTY, PRIEST •

Lo, I am sending my messenger
to prepare the way before me.
—MALACHI 3:1

A "messiah complex" is one thing that John the Baptist did *not* have. Even while others questioned if he was "the one who is to come," John insisted that his role was simply to prepare the way of the Lord. Predisposition is important. In fact, I would venture to say that our primary role as followers of Christ is simply to predispose people—to influence or put people in the frame of mind to be receptive to the Good News of Jesus Christ. And we don't do this by doing all the talking. We don't argue people into following Christ. Rather, we can lay the groundwork for persuading people to follow Christ through active listening, showing empathy, and performing works of mercy that bring hope to those experiencing despair, cynicism, or emptiness.

Malachi 3:1–4, 23–24
Psalm 25:4–5ab, 8–9, 10 and 14
Luke 1:57–66

Thursday

December 24

In the tender compassion of our God
the dawn from on high shall break upon us.
—LUKE 1:78

We usually place our trust in those who have shown previously that they will be true to their word. For this reason, many of the prayers and pleas of people in Scripture, especially in the Old Testament, begin with a litany of the wonderful deeds of the Lord. The message is clear: Because God has been faithful throughout salvation history, he will be faithful again. Zechariah's canticle recalls how the Lord has saved his people throughout history. In essence, the message is: If you've seen the sun come up every morning of your life, you can trust it will happen again tomorrow. May our Christmas celebrations remind us that the Lord will not let us down when we need him most. He is Emmanuel: God with us.

2 Samuel 7:1–5, 8b–12, 14a, 16
Psalm 89:2–3, 4–5, 27 and 29
Luke 1:67–79

Friday

DECEMBER 25

• THE NATIVITY OF THE LORD (CHRISTMAS) •

All who heard it were amazed by what had been told them by the shepherds.
—LUKE 2:18

What is so amazing about a baby being born? The idea of a child being divine would not be astonishing to people familiar with Roman and Greek mythologies in which gods masquerading as humans visited Earth. What is astonishing is that God loves us so much that he chose to dwell among us in Jesus. The nearness or immanence of God is blasphemous to those who think of God solely as transcendent. This child is truly Emmanuel: God with us. This uniting of heaven and earth is the reason we celebrate this day with joy!

VIGIL:
Isaiah 62:1–5
Psalm 89:4–5, 16–17, 27, 29 (2a)
Acts 13:16–17, 22–25
Matthew 1:1–25 or, for shorter form,
Matthew 1:18–25

NIGHT:
Isaiah 9:1–6
Psalm 96:1–2, 2–3, 11–12, 13
Titus 2:11–14
Luke 2:1–14

DAWN:
Isaiah 62:11–12
Psalm 97:1, 6, 11–12
Titus 3:4–7
Luke 2:15–20

DAY:
Isaiah 52:7–10
Psalm 98:1, 2–3, 3–4, 5–6 (3c)
Hebrews 1:1–6
John 1:1–18 or, for shorter form,
John 1:1–5, 9–4

Saturday

DECEMBER 26

• ST. STEPHEN, THE FIRST MARTYR •

As they were stoning Stephen, he called out,
"Lord Jesus, receive my spirit."
—ACTS 7:59

How sobering that on the second day of the Christmas season we recall the martyrdom of St. Stephen. We do so because it was on this date in 415 AD that St. Stephen's tomb and relics, which had been lost and forgotten for centuries, were recovered. While it might seem like a killjoy to focus on a martyr the day after we celebrate the birth of Christ, the message is clear: Christ was born to lay down his life for others. Followers of Christ are called to do the same. The laying down of our life may not involve actual martyrdom, but it does involve setting aside our own needs to put the needs of others first, even when that involves great sacrifice. Sounds like the Christmas spirit to me.

Acts 6:8–10; 7:54–59
Psalm 31:3cd–4, 6 and 8ab, 16bc and 17
Matthew 10:17–22

Sunday

DECEMBER 27

• THE HOLY FAMILY OF JESUS, MARY, AND JOSEPH •

The child grew and became strong, filled with wisdom; and the favor of God was upon him.
—LUKE 2:40

We all would like to make the world a better place for our children in hopes that they will do the same for others. The best vehicle for shaping a child into the kind of person who can contribute to this goal is the family. Families, not laws and policies, stand the best chance of transforming minds and hearts and teaching virtues. Pope Francis referred to the family as a "school of human values" (*Amoris Laetitia*). It is within families that children can learn about mutual giving and receiving, forgiveness, resolving conflict, unity and diversity, stability, responsibility, service, sacrifice, and the distinction between right and wrong. On this Feast of the Holy Family, may God give each of our families the grace to become change agents in a world where so many of the above virtues are lacking.

Genesis 15:1–6; 21:1–3 or Sirach 3:2–6, 12–14
Psalm 105:1–2, 3–4, 5–6, 8–9 (7a, 8a) or Psalm 128:1–2, 3, 4–5
Hebrews 11:8, 11–12, 17–19
Colossians 3:12–21 or, for shorter form, Colossians 3:12–17
Luke 2:22–40

Monday

December 28

• THE HOLY INNOCENTS, MARTYRS •

[Herod] ordered the massacre of all the boys in Bethlehem and its vicinity two years old and under, in accordance with the time he had ascertained from the magi.
—MATTHEW 2:16

Herod's massacre of innocent children is a stark reminder of the contrast between earthly kingdoms and the kingdom of God ushered in by the birth of Jesus. Leaders like Herod who are desperate to hold on to power and dominance will trample anyone they see as a threat. Their strategy is to convince others that their tyranny is actually necessary severity to protect against those threats. Jesus, on the other hand, came to establish a kingdom of justice and selflessness. In the Ignatian tradition, this is called living as a "person for others." As Christians, no matter where we live, we are citizens of the kingdom of God and thus are subject to God's will, which is to be done on earth as it is in heaven.

1 John 1:5—2:2
Psalm 124:2–3, 4–5, 7b–8
Matthew 2:13–18

Tuesday

DECEMBER 29

• ST. THOMAS BECKET, BISHOP AND MARTYR •

Whoever claims to abide in him ought to walk just as he walked.
—1 JOHN 2:6

An old legend tells of a handsome prince who had a crooked back that kept him from achieving his full potential. That is, until the king hired a sculptor to create a statue of the prince that portrayed him not with a crooked back but with a straight back. Whenever the prince gazed at it, he got excited. As time went by, people began to talk about how the prince seemed to be standing up straighter. This encouraged the prince, who then studied the statue day and night until one day he was able to walk perfectly upright. Each one of us is made in the image and likeness of God, but our sinfulness prevents us from becoming the person God wants us to be. We achieve our full potential by imitating Christ and by walking just as he walked.

1 John 2:3–11
Psalm 96:1–2a, 2b–3, 5b–6
Luke 2:22–35

Wednesday

DECEMBER 30

She gave thanks to God and spoke about the child to all who were awaiting the redemption of Jerusalem.
—LUKE 2:38

Throughout the Gospels, people who encounter Jesus can't seem to help but tell others about their experience! The very first visitors to Jesus, the shepherds, went forth from their encounter sharing their story with anybody who would listen. In today's Gospel, just days after Jesus was born, the prophetess Anna encounters the newborn king and, we are told, "talked about the child to all who looked forward to the deliverance of Jerusalem." St. Pope Paul VI famously wrote that "it is unthinkable that a person should accept the Word and give himself to the kingdom without becoming a person who bears witness to it and proclaims it in his turn" (*Evangelii Nuntiandi*). Like Anna, we seek to tell others about how, in Jesus, we find deliverance from all that afflicts and oppresses us.

1 John 2:12–17
Psalm 96:7–8a, 8b–9, 10
Luke 2:36–40

Thursday

DECEMBER 31

• ST. SYLVESTER I, POPE •

Every lie is alien to the truth.
—1 JOHN 2:21

In the early 2000s, a political advisor told journalist Ron Suskind (*The New York Times*) that journalists were living in "the reality-based community"—a worldview that he insisted was obsolete since "we create our own reality." A decade or so later, another political advisor famously coined the phrase "alternative facts." We increasingly live in a world in which it is more and more difficult to find the truth. The Word made flesh, whom we celebrate on this seventh day in the Octave of Christmas, would go on to refer to himself as "the Way, the Truth, and the Life." St. John reminds us in today's first reading that "every lie is alien to the truth." As followers of Jesus, we are called to live in the light of truth, not in the shadows and darkness of untruths.

1 John 2:18–21
Psalm 96:1–2, 11–12, 13
John 1:1–18

Friday
JANUARY 1

• SOLEMNITY OF MARY, THE HOLY MOTHER OF GOD •

So you are no longer a slave but a son, and if a son then also an heir, through God.
—GALATIANS 4:7

Thanks to Mary, the Mother of God, we are heirs to God's abundant kingdom. It was her yes that allowed God's only Son, Jesus, to enter into the human race as our brother. The Good News of Jesus Christ is that we are heirs to the abundant riches (graces) of God's kingdom and that we are called to begin sharing in this inheritance *now*. We are literally called to start a new life filled with riches. This is the essence of discipleship: to live as an heir of God's kingdom and to invite others to share in its abundant riches. This new life also calls us to respond in a particular manner: We are called to emulate the One who bestows this gift upon us.

Numbers 6:22–27
Psalm 67:2–3, 5, 6, 8 (2a)
Galatians 4:4–7
Luke 2:16–21

Saturday

JANUARY 2

• ST. BASIL THE GREAT AND ST. GREGORY NAZIANZEN, BISHOPS AND DOCTORS OF THE CHURCH •

Who is the liar? Whoever denies that Jesus is the Christ.
—1 JOHN 2:22

In today's readings, and throughout the Christmas season, we are reminded that Jesus is more than a great teacher, a wise philosopher, a miracle worker, or an all-around swell fella. He is the Christ. He is our Savior. We stretch our celebration of this feast of Christmas over a season to celebrate the fact that Jesus has come to save us because we are incapable of saving ourselves from sin. Anyone participating in a twelve-step program knows this all too well: The first steps toward healing are to stop lying to oneself, admit powerlessness, and rely on a power beyond oneself for healing. Because of the birth of Jesus Christ, we are thankfully "in recovery" and we joyfully commit ourselves to "work the program" through a life of discipleship, knowing full well that it is the grace of Christ that sustains us.

1 John 2:22–28
Psalm 98:1, 2–3ab, 3cd–4
John 1:19–28

Sunday

JANUARY 3

• THE EPIPHANY OF THE LORD •

And having been warned in a dream not to return to Herod, they departed for their country by another way.
—MATTHEW 2:12

The narrative of the Magi is rich, complex, and contains many layers of meaning. Perhaps one of the most significant passages in this account is often overlooked: the last sentence that says the Magi departed for their country "by another way." In that short phrase, we are taught that this is what happens when one encounters the Lord: We return to the journey of our lives, but "by another way." This echoes a Zen Buddhist proverb: "Before enlightenment, chop wood and carry water. After enlightenment, chop wood and carry water." In other words, we return to our everyday lives and routines but in a different way. Like the Magi, may we be guided and inspired to live "by another way"—a way that leads us to encounter our Lord Jesus at every turn.

Isaiah 60:1–6
Psalm 72:1–2, 7–8, 10–11, 12–13
Ephesians 3:2–3a, 5–6
Matthew 2:1–12

Monday

JANUARY 4

• ST. ELIZABETH ANN SETON, RELIGIOUS •

From that time on, Jesus began to preach and say,
"Repent, for the Kingdom of heaven is at hand."
—MATTHEW 4:17

Our brains are designed to form and hold onto habits. Through repetition, the brain strengthens neural pathways, enabling us to respond to situations "automatically," or without much conscious effort. Jesus calls us to repent, which means to change our way of thinking so that we no longer think as man thinks, but rather, as God thinks. Since the brain does not like to let go of old habits, our efforts at repentance must be ongoing. We must strive each day to put on the mind of Christ and to respond to the world around us in a Christlike manner. Through the repetitive practice of Christian virtues, we gradually develop new habits to replace the old ones. Repentance is a lifelong process and commitment.

1 John 3:22–4:6
Psalm 2:7bc–8, 10–12a
Matthew 4:12–17, 23–25

Tuesday JANUARY 5

• ST. JOHN NEUMANN, BISHOP •

In this way the love of God was revealed to us.
—1 JOHN 4:9

It's strange that there are so many books and TV programs about "secrets" of the Bible when the Bible is totally about revelation, which is the complete opposite of a secret. God keeps no secrets. All of salvation history is the story of God striving to reveal himself to us through his words and actions, which always boil down to mercy, compassion, justice, and love. Our work as disciples of Jesus Christ is not to debate people into following Jesus. Rather, our work is to reveal God's mercy, compassion, justice, and love to the world, in both words and deeds. The traditional Christian hymn is not "they will know we are Christians by our apologetics," but rather, "they will know we are Christians by our love." Through Works of Mercy—both Corporal and Spiritual—God's love is revealed to each generation.

1 John 4:7–10
Psalm 72:1–2, 3–4, 7–8
Mark 6:34–44

Wednesday

JANUARY 6

• ST. ANDRÉ BESSETTE, RELIGIOUS •

In this is love brought to perfection among us, that we have confidence on the day of judgment.
—1 JOHN 4:17

We sometimes visualize Judgment Day as looking and feeling like the experience of Dorothy and her companions approaching the Wizard of Oz—with great fear and trembling. And yet, throughout Scripture, we hear the words, "Do not fear!" In today's Gospel, Jesus approaches the apostles during a storm, walking on the water. He does not sneak up on them and say, "Boo!" Rather, Jesus says, "It is I, do not be afraid." Pope Benedict XVI asserted that we should not approach our judgment with terror, but rather, should think of it as an image of hope grounded in God's love, justice (which is absolute fairness, not revenge), and mercy. Fear of God is not about shaking in our boots before him, but about fear of doing that which causes us shame in the face of God's complete goodness.

1 John 4:11–18
Psalm 72:1–2, 10, 12–13
Mark 6:45–52

Thursday
JANUARY 7

• ST. RAYMOND OF PENYAFORT, PRIEST •

If anyone says, "I love God," but hates his brother, he is a liar.
—1 JOHN 4:20

In today's first reading, John does not mince words. The message is clear: Love of God and love of neighbor cannot be separated. In his encyclical, *Deus Caritas Est*, Pope Benedict XVI reminded us, "In a world where the name of God is sometimes associated with vengeance or even a duty of hatred and violence, this message is both timely and significant." In fact, this passage reminds us that one of the primary ways we show love of God is precisely through love of neighbor. This means that when discussing, advocating for, or formulating policies that affect groups of people such as immigrants, those who are poor or vulnerable, the unborn, the elderly, those who are incarcerated, to name a few, love of neighbor must always shape our response.

1 John 4:19—5:4
Psalm 72:1–2, 14 and 15bc, 17
Luke 4:14–22

Friday

JANUARY 8

"Lord, if you wish, you can make me clean." Jesus stretched out his hand, touched him, and said, "I do will it. Be made clean."
—LUKE 5:12–13

We all desire to be made whole. And yet, by our very nature as human beings, we are wounded and incomplete. Much like the leper in today's Gospel, some of our woundedness is caused by factors beyond our control such as an illness or an event that harms us. Many times, however, we wound ourselves (and others) by our thoughts, words, and actions. The message of today's Gospel is that in order for us to be made whole—to be made clean—we need a power beyond ourselves. Ultimately, we are incapable of saving ourselves or making ourselves whole. Like the leper, we humbly approach Jesus and ask him to make us whole, confident that this indeed is God's will.

1 John 5:5–13
Psalm 147:12–13, 14–15, 19–20
Luke 5:12–16

Saturday

JANUARY 9

For the LORD loves his people.
—PSALM 149:4

Today's Responsorial Psalm tells us that the Lord takes delight in his people. This is a preview of what we will hear in tomorrow's Gospel when Jesus, freshly baptized by John, emerges from the waters of the Jordan to a voice expressing delight in him. Few things mean more to children than to see their parents delight in them. Whenever children accomplish a new task, they inevitably call out to their parents, "Mommy, Daddy, look!" The job of the parents is simply to look upon their child with delight. This is what it means to bless someone: to look upon them with delight. As you go through your day today, remember that God delights in you. In turn, as you encounter others, strive to express your delight in them through kind words and actions, including something as simple as a friendly smile.

1 John 5:14–21
Psalm 149:1–2, 3–4, 5 and 6a and 9b
John 3:22–30

Sunday

JANUARY 10

• THE BAPTISM OF THE LORD •

It happened in those days that Jesus came from Nazareth of Galilee and was baptized in the Jordan by John.
—MARK 1:9

By all accounts, the Jordan River is a mucky, murky, and muddy body of water. Yet, it is a life-giving body of water for the desert region of the Jordan Valley. Because the area where John baptized is situated in a desert region, it took some effort to get to. Jesus's baptism in the Jordan reminds us of the lengths to which God is willing to go to be with his people. Jesus, the Word made flesh, was willing to enter into the muck of humanity . . . he was indeed fully human without loss of his divinity. True leaders do not separate themselves from those they lead. Rather, they get into the trenches and get their fingernails dirty. By entering into the muck of humanity, Jesus brings us new life.

Isaiah 55:1–11
Isaiah 12:2–3, 4bcd, 5–6 (3)
1 John 5:1–9
Mark 1:7–11
Alternative readings Isaiah 42:1–4, 6–7 and/or Acts 10:34–38 may be used.

Monday

JANUARY 11

Then they abandoned their nets and followed him.
—MARK 1:18

The notion that Simon and Andrew "abandoned their nets and followed him" is inspiring. At the same time, it is daunting and intimidating. Few of us are ready to change careers in order to follow Jesus more closely. As a result, many of us feel as though we are disappointing failures when it comes to responding to the Lord's call. Unfortunately, this is due to a misinterpretation of the account. Jesus tells Simon and Andrew that, while they will remain in the same career, they will be seeking a new catch. We are called not to change careers, but to abandon any nets that are gathering too much debris in favor of nets that will gather life-giving graces. Jesus is calling us to reexamine what it is that we consider to be a good catch.

Hebrews 1:1–6
Psalm 97:1 and 2b, 6 and 7c, 9
Mark 1:14–20

Tuesday

JANUARY 12

"I know who you are—the Holy One of God!"
—MARK 1:24

Throughout much of Mark's Gospel, people react to Jesus's miracles and teachings with amazement but also with confusion, asking, "Who can this be?" Strangely, however, the demons and the unclean spirits seem to know exactly who Jesus is. In today's Gospel, a man with an unclean spirit appears in the synagogue and shrieks, "I know who you are—the Holy One of God!" The demons recognize who Jesus is, and yet they refuse to embrace his life-giving power and authority, preferring instead to hold on to whatever power they possess. The climax of Mark's Gospel will be the testimony of the Roman centurion at the foot of the cross, looking upon the powerless form of the crucified Christ and proclaiming, "Truly this man was the Son of God!" (Mark 15:39). It is in the giving and emptying of ourselves that others will truly recognize Christ.

Hebrews 2:5–12
Psalm 8:2ab and 5, 6–7, 8–9
Mark 1:21–28

Wednesday

JANUARY 13

• ST. HILARY, BISHOP AND DOCTOR OF THE CHURCH •

Because he was himself was tested through what he suffered, he is able to help those who are being tested.
—HEBREWS 2:18

Participants in twelve-step programs have the help of a sponsor to navigate the steps of the program leading to recovery. Make no mistake, however: Sponsors are themselves addicts who are in recovery. The whole wisdom behind having a sponsor is to be able to turn to someone who knows what you're going through and who has been there themselves. Today's first reading assures us that in Jesus, we find someone who has been there and understands what we are going through. Jesus had a full share in our humanity and, as we state firmly in the Nicene Creed, he "suffered death and was buried." During our times of suffering and despair, who better to turn to than the One who has defeated sin and death and now offers new life?

Hebrews 2:14–18
Psalm 105:1–2, 3–4, 6–7, 8–9
Mark 1:29–39

Thursday

JANUARY 14

Encourage yourselves daily while it is still "today," so that none of you may grow hardened by the deceit of sin.
—HEBREWS 3:13

I keep a cartoon on my desk at home that shows a mechanic leaning over a car engine while his boss stands looking over his shoulder, asking, "Did I tell you that you're doing a good job?" The mechanic replies, "No," to which the boss responds, "I didn't think so." The truth is, many of us go through our lives, day after day, without receiving much affirmation or encouragement for our efforts. Unfortunately, affirmation and encouragement are underrated. To affirm someone is to bless that person! It is a way of letting people know that their efforts are recognized, appreciated, and validated. How lucky we are to be affirmed by our God each time we are sent forth from the Mass with his blessing. May we go forth and do the same for others.

Hebrews 3:7–14
Psalm 95:6–7c, 8–9, 10–11
Mark 1:40–45

Friday

JANUARY 15

After they had broken through, they let down the mat on which the paralytic was lying. When Jesus saw their faith, he said to him, "Child, your sins are forgiven."
—MARK 2:4–5

In Charles Dickens's *A Christmas Carol*, Ebenezer Scrooge tells the ghost of his deceased partner, Jacob Marley, "You were always a good man of business." The ghost screams back, "Mankind was my business! The common welfare was my business; charity, mercy, forbearance, benevolence, were all my business." Indeed, as followers of Christ, we are called to make others' business our own. This is what the four people in today's Gospel did for the paralyzed man: They made it their business to bring him to Jesus. The paralyzed man never says a word, but we are told that Jesus "saw *their* faith" and healed him. As followers of Jesus, may we make other people's business our own, especially when they face obstacles to grace.

Hebrews 4:1–5, 11
Psalm 78:3 and 4bc, 6c–7, 8
Mark 2:1–12

Saturday

JANUARY 16

So let us confidently approach the throne of grace to receive mercy and to find grace for timely help.
—HEBREWS 4:16

Quite often, the higher a person is on the corporate ladder, the less approachable they are. Corporate executives tend to be surrounded by gatekeepers who control access to these higher-ups. Access to those in power is often difficult, if not impossible. Today's first reading refers to Jesus as our High Priest—the one person who had direct access to the divine presence in the temple. We are told, however, that this High Priest is approachable . . . we have direct access to the Divine Presence in and through Jesus Christ! And, unlike Dorothy and her companions who approached the *Wizard of Oz* with great fear and trembling, we are told to approach the throne of grace "confidently," where we will find help in time of need.

Hebrews 4:12–16
Psalm 19:8, 9, 10, 15
Mark 2:13–17

Sunday

JANUARY 17

• SECOND SUNDAY IN ORDINARY TIME •

Jesus turned and saw them following him and said to them, "What are you looking for?" They said to him, "Rabbi"—which translated means Teacher—"where are you staying?" He said to them, "Come, and you will see."
—JOHN 1:38–39

Invitations are powerful. They make the invitee feel special, affirmed, honored, wanted, accepted, noticed, part of a relationship, and part of something bigger than themselves. Personal invitations can change lives because they can change the way we think and feel about ourselves and others, which means that they serve as a critical tool in the process of conversion, which is the call to change how we think, feel, and act. In today's Gospel, Jesus extends an invitation to two disciples of John the Baptist. Jesus does not invite them into a belief system or a set of doctrines. He invites them to "come" and "see" where he stays: an invitation to a relationship that will change them.

1 Samuel 3:3b–10, 19
Psalm 40:2, 4, 7–8, 8–9, 10 (8a, 9a)
1 Corinthians 6:13c–15a, 17–20
John 1:35–42

Monday

JANUARY 18

No one pours new wine into old wineskins. Otherwise, the wine will burst the skins, and both the wine and the skins are ruined. Rather, new wine is poured into fresh wineskins.
—MARK 2:22

We tend to have a hard time letting go of doing things the way we've always done them. While many traditions are worth treasuring, we also benefit from letting go of those things in our lives that are no longer life-giving. In a daily Mass homily (on February 2, 2021), Pope Francis said, "We cannot remain stuck in nostalgia for the past, or simply keep repeating the same old things, complaining every day. We need patience and courage to keep progressing and exploring new paths, discovering what the Holy Spirit prompts." Jesus makes all things new, including especially our minds and hearts. New experiences can make us anxious. However, they can also breathe much-needed new life into us and bring about renewal.

Hebrews 5:1–10
Psalm 110:1, 2, 3, 4
Mark 2:18–22

Tuesday

JANUARY 19

This we have as an anchor of the soul, sure and firm, which reaches into the interior behind the veil, where Jesus has entered on our behalf as forerunner.
—HEBREWS 6:19–20

As a lifelong die-hard Chicago Cubs fan, I participated in the 108-year period of hoping for the Cubs to win a World Series (57 years of my own life), which finally happened in 2016. I realized along the way, however, that this was not really hope that I was feeling. It was wishful thinking. I had absolutely no confidence that the Cubs would ever win. Hope and wishful thinking are not the same. Our hope in God is a confident hope—a hope in something that we know is going to happen. In today's first reading, we are reminded that our hope in Jesus is like an anchor, "sure and firm." This anchor—this hope—gives us the stability and security we need to stay afloat in the midst of life's turbulent storms.

Hebrews 6:10–20
Psalm 111:1–2, 4–5, 9 and 10c
Mark 2:23–28

Wednesday

JANUARY 20

• ST. FABIAN, POPE AND MARTYR * ST. SEBASTIAN, MARTYR •

Looking around at them with anger and grieved at their hardness of heart, Jesus said to the man, "Stretch out your hand." He stretched it out and his hand was restored.
—MARK 3:5

The Gospels repeatedly show that Jesus experienced great frustration with the Pharisees, who were seeking to trap him. Since Jesus did not fit their narrative, they had closed their minds to him. Jesus was doing a wonderful thing—healing a man with a shriveled hand. However, because Jesus performed this miracle on the Sabbath, the Pharisees with their closed minds saw only a violation of rules and rubrics. Although we are told that Jesus looked at them "with anger," we are also told that he was "grieved at their hardness of heart." This word suggests that Jesus viewed them with compassion and desired greatly that their hearts and minds would open up to him. As we experience and encounter closed-mindedness, may we react with compassion, striving always not to defeat but to open minds.

Hebrews 7:1–3, 15–17
Psalm 110:1, 2, 3, 4
Mark 3:1–6

Thursday

JANUARY 21

• ST. AGNES, VIRGIN AND MARTYR •

Hearing what he was doing, a large number of people came to him.
—MARK 3:8

In the world of marketing, "creating a buzz" refers to creating excitement and hype to generate interest and brand awareness. This type of "buzz" is artificially manufactured. Some buzz, however, happens without any help. Today's Gospel tells us that huge crowds came to Jesus because they had been "hearing what he was doing." With no social media to assist in those days, we can conclude that this buzz was created by word of mouth. This passage reminds us of a highly effective strategy for evangelization: simply passing along information about something exciting related to the gospel. It could be a retreat, an inspirational book or article, a sacred concert, a parish mission, a diocesan conference, a podcast, or a video series. We need not go full apologetics with every person we meet. Sometimes we just need to generate some buzz.

Hebrews 7:25—8:6
Psalm 40:7–8a, 8b–9, 10, 17
Mark 3:7–12

Friday

JANUARY 22

• DAY OF PRAYER FOR THE LEGAL PROTECTION OF UNBORN CHILDREN •

He appointed Twelve, whom he also named Apostles, that they might be with him and he might send them forth to preach.
—MARK 3:14

Jesus formed a movement, which is simply defined as bringing together a group of people to collectively work toward a shared vision. The movement began with the Twelve, and the vision that was to be shared and worked toward was the kingdom of God: a reality in which God's will reigns. Two things jump out from verse 14. First, he called the apostles "that they might be with him." At the heart of this movement is a relationship with Jesus Christ, who is the embodiment of the kingdom of God. Second, he sent them forth to preach. Their goal was not to create an insular group that withdrew from the world. Rather, Jesus sent them forth into the world. As followers of Jesus, we are to "be with him" so that we too might be sent forth.

Hebrews 8:6–13
Psalm 85:8 and 10, 11–12, 13–14
Mark 3:13–19

Saturday

JANUARY 23

• ST. VINCENT, DEACON AND MARTYR * ST. MARIANNE COPE, VIRGIN •

When his relatives heard of this they set out to seize him, for they said, "He is out of his mind."
—MARK 3:21

When we refer to someone as being out of their mind, we are suggesting that they are acting irrationally, foolishly, or even insanely. It is not a compliment. Why would Jesus's family think that he was out of his mind? Perhaps it is because of what has come to be known as the trilemma posed by C. S. Lewis in his book *Mere Christianity*: For Jesus to present himself as the Son of God, he had to be either a lunatic, a liar, or Lord. Ironically, those of us who proclaim that Jesus is indeed Lord are often viewed as lunatics and liars for spreading such supposed malarkey. And yet, we are called to proclaim Jesus as Lord and to live as people who are out of their minds since our quest is to put on the mind of Christ.

Hebrews 9:2–3, 11–14
Psalm 47:2–3, 6–7, 8–9
Mark 3:20–21

Sunday JANUARY 24

• THIRD SUNDAY IN ORDINARY TIME •

"This is the time of fulfillment. The kingdom of God is at hand. Repent, and believe in the gospel."
—MARK 1:15

Many people are remembered for their last words. Truth is, we can also learn a lot about a person from their first words. In today's Gospel, Jesus bursts on the scene, fresh from his forty days in the desert, and he announces that the reign of God—anticipated for centuries—is at hand and that in response to God's reign, we should reform our lives. These first words of Jesus are filled with urgency: The time is now, and this new reality requires action. To reform our lives is not just to give up a few bad habits. It is to reshape our priorities to allow God to truly reign in our lives. That's what the words, "thy will be done" mean, and Jesus is here to show us how to make that a reality.

Jonah 3:1–5, 10
Psalm 25:4–5, 6–7, 8–9 (4a)
1 Corinthians 7:29–31
Mark 1:14–20

Monday

JANUARY 25

• THE CONVERSION OF ST. PAUL THE APOSTLE •

He fell to the ground and heard a voice saying to him, "Saul, Saul, why are you persecuting me?"
—ACTS 9:4

In his own conversion, St. Paul was transformed from a persecutor of Christians into a missionary for Christ. Needless to say, his conversion was more dramatic than the ones most of us experience. It does, however, provide a kind of template for how conversion occurs. In essence, Paul is shaken from his complacency (perfectly satisfied with the direction of his life) by being thrown a curveball—an unexpected upheaval of his entire belief system. That experience is followed by four more C's—confusion (blindness), counsel (Ananias's help), course correction (a new direction in life), and conversion (a new identity: Saul becomes Paul). If you find yourself feeling complacent at the moment, be on guard: A curveball leading to conversion may be coming your way!

Acts 22:3–16 or 9:1–22
Psalm 117:1bc, 2
Mark 16:15–18

Tuesday

JANUARY 26

• ST. TIMOTHY AND ST. TITUS, BISHOPS •

I am grateful to God,
whom I worship with a clear conscience as my ancestors did,
as I remember you constantly in my prayers,
night and day.
—2 TIMOTHY 1:3B

These days, we are surrounded by numerous and loud voices that spread fear about "others" who are not like us, urging us to close off those circles and build walls. Jesus, on the other hand, continually widens those circles, referring to those who do the will of God not only as friends but as brother, sister, and mother. Just as St. Paul embraced Timothy and Titus, who were shunned because of their Gentile heritage, may we expand our circles to embrace those who are shunned because they are different.

2 Timothy 1:1–8 or Titus 1:1–5
Psalm 40:2 and 4ab, 7–8a, 10, 11
Mark 3:31–35

Wednesday

JANUARY 27

• ST. ANGELA MERICI, VIRGIN •

"But those sown on rich soil are the ones who hear the word and accept it and bear fruit thirty and sixty and a hundredfold."
—MARK 4:20

In today's Gospel, Jesus urges us to plant our lives "on rich soil." When soil gets compacted, seeds cannot take root. Unless the soil is loosened, air, water, and nutrients cannot penetrate, and those seeds that do germinate cannot break through the surface. In a similar way, the seeds of God's word cannot take root in our hearts if they have been hardened. We need to plant ourselves in good rich soil, meaning that we situate our lives within a context that allows God's word to penetrate, removes obstacles that compete for nutrition, and allows faith to take root and break through the surface and transform the world. What obstacles are competing for nutrition in your life? What causes the soil of your heart to become compacted?

Hebrews 10:11–18
Psalm 110:1, 2, 3, 4
Mark 4:1–20

Thursday

JANUARY 28

• ST. THOMAS AQUINAS, PRIEST AND DOCTOR OF THE CHURCH •

We must consider how to rouse one another to love and good works.
—HEBREWS 10:24

Many people take to social media for the sole purpose of riling up those they perceive as opponents, whether political, religious, or sports related. This practice can be highly reinforcing, especially when it is rewarded by likes and shares. Today's first reading, however, urges us to "consider how to rouse one another to love and good works." Letting our virtues shine through naturally (as opposed to "virtue signaling" or calling attention to oneself) is what Jesus urges in the Gospel when he tells us to put our light "on a lampstand" and not "under a bushel basket." It is in this spirit that we seek to "rouse one another to love and good works"—not by being preachy, but by living in a manner that allows the light of God's grace to shine forth and draw others to follow in the Lord's footsteps.

Hebrews 10:19–25
Psalm 24:1–2, 3–4ab, 5–6
Mark 4:21–25

Friday

JANUARY 29

We are not among those who draw back and perish, but among those who have faith and will possess life.
—HEBREWS 10:39

So many things occurring in our lives and in our world can bring us to the point of despair—a pervading sense of hopelessness. We find ourselves asking if our efforts to be good people and to make the world a better place really and truly make a difference. In today's first reading, the Letter to the Hebrews addresses this reality and urges us, "Do not throw away your confidence; it will have great recompense." In the Gospel, Jesus tells us that even the smallest mustard seed grows into a large, life-giving shrub. We need such messages of hope and encouragement, and we in turn must do all we can to bring reassurance to those who are on the brink of despair. This is what faith is all about.

Hebrews 10:32–39
Psalm 37:3–4, 5–6, 23–24, 39–40
Mark 4:26–34

Saturday

JANUARY 30

A violent squall came up and waves were breaking over the boat, so that it was already filling up. Jesus was in the stern, asleep on a cushion.
—MARK 4:37–38

One blessing of being hard of hearing is that when I take my hearing aids out to go to sleep, I can't hear a thing! I can sleep through the noisiest of storms. Today's Gospel tells us that Jesus comfortably slept through a storm while accompanying his disciples on a boat ride. Jesus's sleep, however, was not due to him being oblivious. Rather, it was due to his confidence. When he awakened, he chastised his disciples for fearing the storm when, all along, they were accompanied by One whom the wind and the sea obey. At times, we feel as though Jesus is asleep in the midst of our storms. May we confidently call on the One who says, "Quiet! Be still!" to the turbulence in our lives.

Hebrews 11:1–2, 8–19
Luke 1:69–70, 71–72, 73–75
Mark 4:35–41

Sunday JANUARY 31

• FOURTH SUNDAY IN ORDINARY TIME •

"A prophet like me will the LORD, your God, raise up for you from among your own kin; to him you shall listen."
—DEUTERONOMY 18:15

Being a prophet is not a very lucrative or attractive job. Throughout salvation history, those called to be prophets responded with hesitancy, claiming they were too old, too young, didn't speak well, had an unclean tongue, and so on. Jonah, in fact, originally simply declined the invitation. To be a prophet is to speak God's truth, which is becoming much more difficult in a world where everyone claims to have their own truth. We are called to discern those voices that truly proclaim God's words of mercy, compassion, justice, and charity. We, ourselves, are called to share in the prophetic ministry of Jesus, calling others to hear and embrace God's truth, even in the midst of rejection and ridicule.

Deuteronomy 18:15–20
Psalm 95:1–2, 6–7, 7–9 (8)
1 Corinthians 7:32–35
Mark 1:21–28

Monday

FEBRUARY 1

[Jesus said] "Go home to your family and announce to them all that the Lord in his pity has done for you."
—MARK 5:19

There are many ways of following Jesus. The example that is often held up as the model for following Jesus is the disciples who dropped their nets, left their boats, and immediately followed him. In today's Gospel, a man cured of possession asks Jesus if he can do likewise. Surprisingly, Jesus does not grant his request but tells him to go home to his family and tell them about the Lord's great mercy. This is actually how most of us follow Jesus: We focus on our family and those around us—our sphere of influence. It is laudable to leave behind one's profession and go forth to distant lands to proclaim the gospel. Yet today's Gospel reminds us that if we are busy raising a family, we are right where God wants us to be.

Hebrews 11:32–40
Psalm 31:20, 21, 22, 23, 24
Mark 5:1–20

Tuesday

FEBRUARY 2

• THE PRESENTATION OF THE LORD •

[Simeon said] "Now, Master, you may let your servant go
in peace, according to your word,
for my eyes have seen your salvation,
which you prepared in the sight
of all the peoples:
a light for revelation to the Gentiles,
and glory for your people Israel."
—LUKE 2:29–32

If today's readings bring about a sense of déjà vu, don't be surprised—we are basically celebrating Christmas once again! In fact, some Christian traditions recognize February 2, the Feast of the Presentation of the Lord, as the official end of the Christmas season, and some people leave their decorations up until this day. This day is also known as Candlemas, a day on which candles—symbols of the light of Christ—are blessed. The revealing light of Christ illuminates our path from birth to death and beyond.

Malachi 3:1–4
Psalm 24:7, 8, 9, 10
Hebrews 2:14–18
Luke 2:22–40

Wednesday

FEBRUARY 3

• ST. BLASE, BISHOP AND MARTYR • ST. ANSGAR, BISHOP •

So he was not able to perform any mighty deed there, apart from curing a few sick people by laying his hands on them. He was amazed at their lack of faith.

—MARK 6:5–6

For years, I have calmed the nerves of people preparing for the sacraments by reminding them that in the sacraments, God does all the work. The only thing we need to do is receive. In today's Gospel, Jesus is met by closed minds and hearts. He was unable to perform any miracles there because the Lord does not force his grace upon anyone. He offers it. He invites us. Our job is to be predisposed to receive. This may sound easy. However, in order to receive, we need to let go of what we are clutching: possessions, anger, guilt, self-righteousness, self-centeredness, addictions, desires, indifference, and so on. Perhaps the most powerful prayer to begin each day is to lift open hands to God.

Hebrews 12:4–7, 11–15
Psalm 103:1–2, 13–14, 17–18a
Mark 6:1–6

Thursday

FEBRUARY 4

Jesus summoned the Twelve and began to send them out two by two and gave them authority over unclean spirits.
—MARK 6:7

Western civilization has a fascination with the lone hero, an individual who stands apart from society and defeats challenges through his or her own strength and ingenuity. Today's Gospel offers us a different model of heroism: Jesus sends his apostles out in pairs—not alone—to proclaim the gospel. Not only does this emphasize the collegial nature of the church and shared effort in ministry, but it also reinforces the biblical principle that two witnesses are needed to affirm the truthfulness of any statement. Likewise, it is very clear that the apostles go forth with power and authority that is not of their own doing but rather comes from the Lord. May we go forth, as followers of Christ, with our brothers and sisters in faith and ministry.

Hebrews 12:18–19, 21–24
Psalm 48:2–3ab, 3cd–4, 9, 10–11
Mark 6:7–13

Friday

FEBRUARY 5

• ST. AGATHA, VIRGIN AND MARTYR •

Do not neglect hospitality, for through it some have unknowingly entertained angels.
—HEBREWS 13:2

In our world, we sometimes underemphasize hospitality. Very simply, hospitality is characterized by generously and warmly welcoming and receiving others. This is something we can and should do at home, at work, in social situations, when we're shopping, when we're commuting—in just about any situation. Hospitality is a way of connecting with others, of putting the needs of others before our own, and of making space for others. Hospitality opens doors to the possibility of relationship. We are called to practice hospitality not just when meeting people for the first time, but each time we encounter them. All three of the great Abrahamic religions—Judaism, Christianity, and Islam—view hospitality and civility as a minimum requirement, as encapsulated in the account of Abraham and Sarah welcoming the three strangers (angels) in Genesis 18.

Hebrew 13:1–8
Psalm 27:1, 3, 5, 8b–9abc
Mark 6:14–29

Saturday

FEBRUARY 6

• ST. PAUL MIKI AND COMPANIONS, MARTYRS •

When Jesus disembarked and saw the vast crowd, his heart was moved with pity for them, for they were like sheep without a shepherd; and he began to teach them many things.
—MARK 6:34

This verse from today's Gospel perhaps best captures Jesus's compassionate stance toward others. The Gospels, and all of Scripture for that matter, teach us that compassion is not just some warm and fuzzy feeling that God gets every so often but is a divine attribute. This means that to be a disciple of Christ, compassion is nonnegotiable. Each of us will become more recognizable as a child of God, made in God's image and likeness, if we show compassion, especially for those in need. It is important for us to remember that, while empathy is felt in the heart, compassion is felt in the gut. A truly compassionate response is visceral: It is felt so deeply that it moves us to action.

Hebrews 13:15–17, 20–21
Psalm 23:1–3a, 3b–4, 5, 6
Mark 6:30–34

Sunday FEBRUARY 7

• FIFTH SUNDAY IN ORDINARY TIME •

He heals the brokenhearted
and binds up their wounds.
—PSALM 147:3

In today's readings, we encounter a good deal of brokenheartedness. Job is in the midst of his suffering and despair. St. Paul talks about the pressures he faces in proclaiming the gospel. Jesus encounters many people who are sick with various diseases. In the midst of these readings, however, we joyfully sing Psalm 147: "Praise the Lord, who heals the brokenhearted." While it is part of the human condition to experience despair, it is not God's will. God's will for us is to be "safe from all distress" in the words of the priest at Mass after the Lord's Prayer. As followers of the Lord, we welcome his healing into our own lives and share in his mission of healing the brokenhearted whom we encounter. This healing often begins simply by being present to those in despair and reminding them that they are not alone.

Job 7:1–4, 6–7
Psalm 147:1–2, 3–4, 5–6
1 Corinthians 9:16–19, 22–23
Mark 1:29–39

Monday

FEBRUARY 8

• ST. JEROME EMILIANI, PRIEST * ST. JOSEPHINE BAKHITA, VIRGIN •

Then God said, "Let there be light," and there was light.
—GENESIS 1:3

Some words we speak are efficacious, which means that speaking the words achieves the desired effect that the words represent. Saying, "I do" at a wedding seals the marriage relationship. Saying, "I'm sorry" enables forgiveness to happen. Saying, "I love you" conveys love to another person. Today's first reading about creation reminds us that God's word is efficacious: God spoke and it was done. In fact, the Gospel tells us that God's word is so efficacious that people simply needed to touch the tassel of Jesus's cloak to be healed. Jesus is, of course, the Word made flesh. As we come forward to receive him in Holy Communion, we say, "Lord, I am not worthy that you should enter under my roof, but only say the word and my soul shall be healed," knowing that he is as good as his word.

Genesis 1:1–19
Psalm 104:1–2a, 5–6, 10 and 12, 24 and 35c
Mark 6:53–56

Tuesday

FEBRUARY 9

[Jesus responded] "You disregard God's commandment but cling to human tradition."
—MARK 7:8

Research reveals that consumers today are seeking to purchase authentic products from genuine people rather than settling for something fake from someone who's phony. Authenticity is harmony between who one is and what one does and says. If we claim to be followers of Christ, people will justifiably watch us to see if there is a consistency between what we say, how we act, and how we live. Jesus reminds us in today's Gospel that we cannot hide behind religious practices and traditions and then disregard God's commandment to love and respect others. Pope Francis taught that while traditions root us in the past, they are intended to move us forward "where the old and the new converge to create a new humanism" (Audience, June 1, 2022).

Genesis 1:20–2:4a
Psalm 8:4–5, 6–7, 8–9
Mark 7:1–13

Wednesday FEBRUARY 10

• ASH WEDNESDAY •

Behold, now is a very acceptable time;
behold, now is the day of salvation.
—2 CORINTHIANS 6:2

A sense of urgency is a hallmark of success. Great leaders know how to create, instill, and sustain a sense of urgency in their followers. In his book *Leading Change*, leadership guru John P. Kotter explains that transformation is difficult in groups where complacency runs high. St. Paul speaks to us on this Ash Wednesday with a sense of urgency: "*Now* is the acceptable time!" Complacency has no place in discipleship. Without a sense of urgency, we can easily allow our attention to be diverted to trivial things. Ultimately, that is what the deadly sin of sloth is all about—paying attention to trivial things instead of to what is urgent for the health of our soul. Urgency need not mean that we act with speed, but rather, that we pay immediate attention to what deserves our undivided attention.

Joel 2:12–18
Psalm 51:3–4, 5–6ab, 12–13, 14 and 17
2 Corinthians 5:20—6:2
Matthew 6:1–6, 16–18

Thursday

FEBRUARY 11

• THURSDAY AFTER ASH WEDNESDAY • OUR LADY OF LOURDES •

Then he [Jesus] said to all, "If anyone wishes to come after me, he must deny himself and take up his cross daily and follow me."
—LUKE 9:23

Too often, we cling to our possessions as if they identify us, and we have a hard time letting go. Organizing expert Marie Kondo, however, recommends that if a possession does not spark joy, we should discard it. It is this letting go that frees us from being owned by our material things. The self-denial we practice during the season of Lent is done not to punish ourselves but to lead to joy. To deny ourselves something that we think defines us is to "die," to experience the death of a false self. Through self-denial, we can die to our false self and embrace the new life that the Risen Christ—our true source of happiness and the One who defines us—offers us.

Deuteronomy 30:15–20
Psalm 1:1–2, 3, 4 and 6
Luke 9:22–25

Friday

FEBRUARY 12

• FRIDAY AFTER ASH WEDNESDAY •

This, rather, is the fasting that I wish:
releasing those bound unjustly,
untying the thongs of the yoke;
Setting free the oppressed,
breaking every yoke;
Sharing your bread with the hungry,
sheltering the oppressed and the homeless;
Clothing the naked when you see them,
and not turning your back on your own.
—ISAIAH 58:6–7

Spiritual wisdom tells us that any attempt to follow God more closely requires discipline, focus, and willpower. Before attempting to master one's intangible spiritual desires, it makes sense to master some tangible physical desires, including hunger. Our Lenten fasting is not an end in itself. Rather, it is a means to an end. Fasting is intended to draw us deeper into prayer while also drawing us closer to those who are in need, opening our hearts to greater generosity.

Isaiah 58:1–9a
Psalm 51:3–4, 5–6ab, 18–19
Matthew 9:14–15

Saturday

FEBRUARY 13

• SATURDAY AFTER ASH WEDNESDAY •

Jesus said to them in reply, "Those who are healthy do not need a physician, but the sick do. I have not come to call the righteous to repentance but sinners."

—LUKE 5:31–32

Jesus insists that healthy people do not need a doctor, but sick people do. His next point cuts deep because he is warning us that no one is exempt from the illness of sin. Those of us who think we are exempt are in the deepest trouble. Self-righteousness is the denial of our human condition of imperfection and brokenness. In his song *Anthem*, the late Canadian singer-songwriter Leonard Cohen sang about how there is a crack in everything but emphasized that this is how the light gets in. This is why the Mass begins with a Penitential Act, inviting us to leave any trace of self-righteousness at the door and instead confess our sinfulness. That's how the light gets in.

Isaiah 58:9b–14
Psalm 86:1–2, 3–4, 5–6
Luke 5:27–32

Sunday

FEBRUARY 14

• FIRST SUNDAY OF LENT •

The Spirit drove Jesus out into the desert, and he remained in the desert for forty days, tempted by Satan.
—MARK 1:12

Thank goodness for back scratchers that enable us to reach those itches we have in hard-to-reach places! In our everyday lives, we sometimes get an itch—a restlessness—and we seek ways to scratch it that may not be very healthy. We call these moments temptations, and no human being is immune from the lure of temptations . . . not even Jesus. On the first Sunday of Lent, we hear about how Jesus was led by the Spirit into the desert where he was tempted. As we prepare to enter into the first week of Lent, we can use this as an opportunity to reflect on everyday temptations and how we can deal with them by recognizing limits, praying for strength, being honest with ourselves, practicing charity and self-sacrifice, and developing new and healthier habits that leave no room for temptations to unhealthy behaviors.

Genesis 9:8–15
Psalm 25:4–5, 6–7, 8–9
1 Peter 3:18–22
Mark 1:12–15

Monday

FEBRUARY 15

And the king will say to them in reply,
"Amen, I say to you, whatever you did for one of these least brothers of mine, you did for me."
—MATTHEW 25:40

The Ten Commandments are about relationships. Have you ever noticed that only three are about our relationship with God, while seven are about relationships with our neighbors? This reveals something critically important about God: God is most interested in how we love one another and insists that love of God and love of neighbor cannot be separated. God is saying that the greatest way to show our love for him is by showing love for our neighbor, and today's Gospel emphasizes that at the core of love of neighbor is mercy for those most in need. In fact, today's parable suggests that showing mercy to those in need will be the litmus test for entrance into eternity with God and is an authentic and direct way to encounter God.

Leviticus 19:1–2, 11–18
Psalm 19:8, 9, 10, 15
Matthew 25:31–46

Tuesday

FEBRUARY 16

So shall my word be
that goes forth from my mouth;
It shall not return to me void,
but shall do my will,
achieving the end for
which I sent it.
—ISAIAH 55:11

We spend much of our time and energy exerting our will. We want things to be done or to unfold in a certain way, and sometimes we bump heads with those whose vision is different or even opposed to our own. In today's readings, we hear about God's will. Through Isaiah, God reminds us that his word will not return to him empty but will achieve his will. At the heart of the words that Jesus teaches us to pray—the Our Father—are the words, "thy will be done." This prayer goes against the grain because it requires us to surrender our will and embrace God's will. When our will aligns with God's will, we find peace.

Isaiah 55:10–11
Psalm 34:4–5, 6–7, 16–17, 18–19
Matthew 6:7–15

Wednesday

FEBRUARY 17

• THE SEVEN FOUNDERS OF THE ORDER OF SERVITES •

A clean heart create for me, O God,
and a steadfast spirit renew within me.
—PSALM 51:10

Our goal for Lent is to become converts. Often, we use this word to refer to someone who is changing denominations. Today's readings, including the responsorial, focus on true conversion, which is simply a change of heart. How exactly do our hearts need to change? They need to soften. A hardened heart, like dried out clay, is inflexible. When our hearts become inflexible, we find ourselves becoming abrasive, curt, impatient, irritable, intolerant, and overly critical. A renewed heart is capable of mercy, compassion, forgiveness, understanding, kindness, and charity—actions and dispositions that, when practiced, soften our hearts. This is why, in addition to prayer, we engage in fasting and almsgiving—actions that soften and renew our hearts.

Jonah 3:1–10
Psalm 51:3–4, 12–13, 18–19
Luke 11:29–32

Thursday

FEBRUARY 18

"Do to others whatever you would have them do to you. This is the law and the prophets."
—MATTHEW 7:12

In today's world, we love soundbites: short, easily remembered comments around ten to fifteen seconds long. While Jesus was capable of delivering long sermons, he was a master of the soundbite as well. Today's Gospel is a good example as Jesus summarizes the entire "law and the prophets" by reminding us to treat others as we would have them treat us. So short. So to-the-point. And yet, this remains difficult for us to put into practice. We tend to view other people as competitors and obstacles instead of seeing them as Thomas Merton and others have taught: as other selves. When we recognize our shared humanity as a starting point, we become capable of seeing our interconnectedness, which enables us to practice solidarity and work for the common good.

Esther C:12, 14–16, 23–25
Psalm 138:1–2ab, 2cde–3, 7c–8
Matthew 7:7–12

Friday

FEBRUARY 19

If you bring your gift to the altar, and there recall that your brother has anything against you, leave your gift there at the altar, go first and be reconciled with your brother, and then come and offer your gift.

—MATTHEW 5:23–24

One of the by-products of the explosion of social media is the corresponding explosion of opinions. Gone are the days when experts shared opinions through public venues while the rest of us kept to ourselves or shared with others over a meal or a drink. Now, we all have our own platforms that enable us to share our thoughts and opinions with the world, even when no one has asked. The anonymity of social media also emboldens us to speak more harshly and uncivilly with others. Today's Gospel reminds us to handle conflicts in private rather than airing them in public. As we journey through Lent in an increasingly digital world, let us not forget to examine our behavior in cyberspace.

Ezekiel 18:21–28
Psalm 130:1–2, 3–4, 5–7a, 7bc–8
Matthew 5:20–26

Saturday

FEBRUARY 20

Today you are making this agreement with the LORD: he is to be your God and you are to walk in his ways and observe his statutes, commandments and decrees, and to hearken to his voice.
—DEUTERONOMY 26:17

When a sports team signs a highly coveted free agent, they host a press conference to introduce their new star and then with great fanfare present the team jersey to be donned for all to see. The message is clear: "You're one of us now!" and the player is contractually expected to represent the spirit and tradition of that team. Through our baptism, each of us has been "contracted" to represent the ways of God to the world. This covenant requires us to walk in God's ways and to hearken to his voice. May we renew this covenant each and every day of our lives so others may recognize that the ways of God are life-giving.

Deuteronomy 26:16–19
Psalm 119:1–2, 4–5, 7–8
Matthew 5:43–48

Sunday

FEBRUARY 21

• SECOND SUNDAY OF LENT •

A cloud came, casting a shadow over them; from the cloud came a voice, "This is my beloved Son. Listen to him."
—MARK 9:7

In today's Gospel, Peter, James, and John had a mystical experience—a moment when God's presence burst through the ordinary to reveal the extraordinary. You and I have mystical experiences—fleeting glimpses of God—in our everyday lives. Such mystical experiences can transform us by enabling us to pause and see things with clarity and from a new perspective. We become capable of seeing beyond present realities to recognize possibilities. Catching a glimpse of God compels us to remain in his presence and worship him—to give him our undivided attention so we can hear him speak to us. As followers of Jesus, we strive to make sure that, through our words and actions, the people we encounter—especially those in despair—will catch a glimpse of God and be transformed.

Genesis 22:1–2, 9a, 10–13, 15–18
Psalm 116:10, 15, 16–17, 18–19 (116:9)
Romans 8:31b–34
Mark 9:2–10

Monday

FEBRUARY 22

• THE CHAIR OF ST. PETER THE APOSTLE •

And so I say to you, you are Peter, and upon this rock I will build my Church, and the gates of the netherworld shall not prevail against it.
—MATTHEW 16:18

Each time we face a challenge, it is good to know that, in addition to the Holy Spirit, we are surrounded by a network of saints who support us, inspire us, guide us, and encourage us. At the forefront of the communion of saints is St. Peter, the rock upon whom Jesus built his church. In the Gospels, St. Peter is so relatable. One moment, he is doing or saying something that's right on target, and then the next moment, he is doing or saying something boneheaded! And yet, Jesus chose him to lead his church. St. Peter serves as a reminder that God chooses people who are quite obviously flawed: thus the phrase, "God doesn't call the qualified; he qualifies the called."

1 Peter 5:1–4
Psalm 23:1–3a, 4, 5, 6
Matthew 16:13–19

Tuesday

FEBRUARY 23

• ST. POLYCARP, BISHOP AND MARTYR •

Come now, let us set things right.
—ISAIAH 1:18

When typing on a computer, we have four choices in how to align the text: left align, right align, center, and justify. Justified text is distributed evenly between the margins and creates clean, crisp edges that make a document appear to be in proper condition with no rough or ragged borders. When Isaiah says, "Come now, let us set things right," he is calling each of us to be restored to our proper condition: to the way things should be—the way God intended. This call assumes that we need correction. Just as text on a paper cannot justify itself but must rely on the author at the keyboard, we are incapable of setting things right. We do not justify ourselves, but rather we are justified by God's forgiveness. This Lent may our ragged edges be smoothed out and our lives restored to proper condition.

Isaiah 1:10, 16–20
Psalm 50:8–9, 16bc–17, 21 and 23
Matthew 23:1–12

Wednesday

FEBRUARY 24

[Jesus said] "Whoever wishes to be great among you shall be your servant; whoever wishes to be first among you shall be your slave."
—MATTHEW 20:26–27

Today's Gospel makes it clear that "it's not about you." Your life is not so much about you as it is about what God is doing through, with, and in you. We mistakenly think that we are the stars of a show in which God makes an occasional cameo appearance whenever we invite him in. The truth is, God is the writer, producer, director, and star of an epic drama that is unfolding about all of creation, and he invites each of us to discover our very special and integral role within that drama. Jesus calls us to humility—a virtue that manifests itself in service to others. During this Lenten season, may we strive to be of service to those we encounter.

Jeremiah 18:18–20
Psalm 31:5–6, 14, 15–16
Matthew 20:17–28

Thursday

FEBRUARY 25

Lying at his door was a poor man named Lazarus, covered with sores, who would gladly have eaten his fill of the scraps that fell from the rich man's table.
—LUKE 16:20–21

In the musical *Chicago*, there's a lovable but pathetic character named Amos who, despite his best efforts, is ignored and goes unnoticed by everyone. At one point in the musical, Amos launches into a song in which he sadly sings that his name should have been Mr. Cellophane, since everyone seems to look right through him and walk right by him as if he were invisible. In our society, too many people are invisible—pushed to the margins and forgotten or dismissed. Jesus reminds us today that no human being should be invisible as the beggar Lazarus was to the rich man. Spend some time this Lent reflecting on the invisible people in our society, and commit to seeing them and responding to their needs.

Jeremiah 17:5–10
Psalm 1:1–2, 3, 4 and 6
Luke 16:19–31

Friday

FEBRUARY 26

Finally, he sent his son to them, thinking, "They will respect my son."
—MATTHEW 21:37

Throughout salvation history, God has sent messengers to his people, culminating in the sending of his only Son, Jesus. Unfortunately, humanity's track record when it comes to receiving these messengers is not very good. Today's first reading as well as the parable we hear in today's Gospel reveals how those with a prophetic message are too often treated. Upon hearing today's readings, we are invited to reflect on the various messengers that God has sent into each of our lives to speak his truth to us. Whose voice have we listened to? Whose voice have we rejected? Who in our lives may be speaking God's truth to us right now, and how receptive are we to hearing God's truth? If you are longing to hear God's voice, be sure not to tune out those closest to you who may very well be God's messengers for you.

Genesis 37:3–4, 12–13a, 17b–28a
Psalm 105:16–17, 18–19, 20–21
Matthew 21:33–43, 45–46

Saturday

FEBRUARY 27

Now the older son had been out in the field and,
on his way back, as he neared the house,
he heard the sound of music and dancing.
—LUKE 15:25

I've often thought that what has come to be known as the Parable of the Prodigal Son is mistitled. In reality, this parable should be known as the Parable of the Older Brother. While the first two-thirds of the story provide a heartwarming message about God's unconditional love, the last third of the story challenges us to examine the extent to which we are just going through the motions and expecting a reward for doing the minimum. The parable is left without an ending: We don't know if the older brother joins the festivities. It remains up to us to decide if we can fathom such generous mercy that enables God to celebrate those whom we see as less worthy.

Micah 7:14–15, 18–20
Psalm 103:1–2, 3–4, 9–10, 11–12
Luke 15:1–3, 11–32

Sunday FEBRUARY 28

• THIRD SUNDAY OF LENT •

Many of the Samaritans of that town began to believe in him because of the word of the woman who testified.
—JOHN 4:39

In a courtroom, witnesses are called to testify, sharing what they have seen, heard, and experienced and offering that as evidence to persuade the jury. This is how the gospel is spread as well. Like the woman who encountered Jesus at the well, we are called to testify—to talk about what it is like to encounter Jesus. This can take the form of subtle references to our faith in everyday conversations such as, "When I was at Mass on Sunday . . ." or "I was just reading a very inspiring book . . ." or "When I was praying last night . . ." Whether in person or on social media, we can do the same as the woman at the well: invite others to begin to believe because of our testimony.

Exodus 20:1–17 or, for shorter form, Exodus 20:1–3, 7–8, 12–17
Psalm 19:8, 9, 10, 11 or 95:1–2, 6–7, 8–9 (8)
1 Corinthians 1:22–25 or Romans 5:1–2, 5–8
John 2:13–25 or 4:5–42

Monday

MARCH 1

Help us, O God our savior,
because of the glory of your name;
Deliver us and pardon our sins
for your name's sake.
—PSALM 79:9

As much as we strive to handle things on our own, there are moments when we recognize our deep need for help. In today's psalm, we hear a humble plea: "Help us, O God our savior." The psalmist, trusting in God's goodness and the glory of his name, calls not only for deliverance but also for mercy. This prayer reminds us that turning to God is not a last resort but a source of hope and renewal. During this season, take time to ask for God's help with a sincere heart—trusting that he hears you, forgives you, and gently draws you back into the embrace of his saving love.

2 Kings 5:1–15ab
Psalm 42:2, 3; 43:3, 4
Luke 4:24–30

Tuesday MARCH 2

[Jesus answered] "So will my heavenly Father do to you, unless each of you forgives your brother from your heart."
—MATTHEW 18:35

Catholics do not believe in the concept of karma, nor do we believe that entering into eternity begins with the immediate washing clean of one's slate. Our belief in an experience of purgation can be described as coming face-to-face with God as together we review how we dealt with others in life. This is not a punishment but rather an experience of purgation that, for many of us, may be painful in the same way that it hurts our eyes to go from darkness to bright light. Jesus makes it clear that the forgiveness of our sins at the time of our judgment will in some manner require us to recall the extent to which we forgave others from the heart. Lent is a time to experience that purgation, our reconciliation with God, now.

Daniel 3:25, 34–43
Psalm 25:4–5ab, 6 and 7bc, 8 and 9
Matthew 18:21–35

Wednesday

MARCH 3

• ST. KATHARINE DREXEL, VIRGIN •

Observe them carefully, for thus will you give evidence of your wisdom and intelligence to the nations, who will hear of all these statutes and say, "This great nation is truly a wise and intelligent people."

—DEUTERONOMY 4:6

We sometimes hear or get involved in discussions about what makes a nation great. In today's first reading, we find that Moses told the people that their greatness would not be measured by the strength of their military, their economic superiority, or their geographic dominance. Rather, he told them that others would be in awe of their faithful observance of their laws and statutes, given to them by God to ensure justice for all. The commandments are not designed to achieve power and prestige but rather wisdom and intelligence. We do well, this Lent, to examine our consciences in light of the Ten Commandments and pray for the wisdom and intelligence to follow God's law of love.

Deuteronomy 4:1, 5–9
Psalm 147:12–13, 15–16, 19–20
Matthew 5:17–19

Thursday

MARCH 4

• ST. CASIMIR •

[Jesus said] "Whoever is not with me is against me, and whoever does not gather with me scatters."
—LUKE 11:23

One time, on social media, a friend of mine was being challenged by a conspiracy theorist. After a heated debate, the conspiracy theorist typed, "Agree to disagree," to which my friend, who had facts on his side, responded, "If the sky is partly cloudy, we can agree to disagree. But if the sky is green, golf ball-sized hail is falling, and 100 mph winds are blowing cows across the sky, I'm not interested in debating whether or not there's a tornado." Today's readings point out that speaking God's truth to people has never been easy, especially when people are confronted with truths that do not fit their narrative. Even when Jesus was driving out demons, some people refused to believe in him. During this Lenten season, let us strive to let go of our own biases and embrace God's truth.

Jeremiah 7:23–28
Psalm 95:1–2, 6–7, 8–9
Luke 11:14–23

We shall say no more, "Our god,"
to the work of our hands.
—HOSEA 14:4

We tend to think that the first commandment, "I am the Lord your God, you shall have no other gods before me," is a bit outdated and intended for people who carved golden idols to worship. The truth is, we have more difficulty with this commandment than we think. The prophet Hosea tells the people that when they repent, they should say to God, "We shall say no more, 'Our god,' to the work of our hands." In other words, we need to repent from the notion that we are self-sustaining. Lent began with ashes on our foreheads to remind us that without God, we are nothing. Today's readings invite us to reprioritize our lives and make sure that we place God at the center as we acknowledge that he alone sustains us.

Hosea 14:2–10
Psalm 81:6c–8a, 8bc–9, 10–11ab, 14 and 17
Mark 12:28–34

Saturday MARCH 6

But the tax collector . . . beat his breast and prayed, "O God, be merciful to me a sinner."
—LUKE 18:13

These humble and heartfelt words of the tax collector in today's Gospel are among some of the most famous and most-loved words of the entire Bible. Over time, these words took the shape of what we now refer to as "the Jesus Prayer": "Lord Jesus Christ, Son of God, have mercy on me, a sinner." This prayer is sometimes described as the perfect prayer because in it, we honor the name of Jesus, we proclaim that Jesus is the Son of God, we pray for the divine mercy that we desperately need, and, finally, we confess our sinfulness. This is indeed the perfect prayer for the season of Lent as we humbly acknowledge our sinfulness and invite the Lord's healing mercy into our lives. Praying these powerful words can facilitate our repentance, which is at the heart of the Lenten season.

Hosea 6:1–6
Psalm 51:3–4, 18–19, 20–21ab
Luke 18:9–14

Sunday

MARCH 7

• FOURTH SUNDAY OF LENT •

[Jesus said to Nicodemus] "But whoever lives the truth comes to the light, so that his works may be clearly seen as done in God."
—JOHN 3:21

The hymn *Amazing Grace* is one of the most beloved hymns in all of Christianity. What's interesting is how, without hesitation, we make the words of the hymn our own: "I once was lost, but now am found; was blind but now I see." On this fourth Sunday of Lent, we do well to reflect more deeply on these words, asking the Holy Spirit to help us recognize the ways in which we are presently lost and need to be found as well as the ways in which we are experiencing blindness and need our sight restored. Along with the catechumens preparing for baptism, today we are invited to scrutinize our hearts, asking God to remove any obstacles to our ability to see his amazing grace in our everyday lives.

2 Chronicles 36:14–16, 19–23 or 1 Samuel 16:1b, 6–7, 10–13a
Psalm 137:1–2, 3, 4–5, 6 (6ab) or 23:1–3a, 3b–4, 5, 6 (1)
Ephesians 2:4–10 or 5:8–14
John 3:14–21, John 9:1–41 or, for shorter form, John 9:1, 6–9, 13–17, 34–38

Monday MARCH 8

• ST. JOHN OF GOD •

Jesus said to him, "You may go; your son will live." The man believed what Jesus said to him and left.
—JOHN 4:50

We use the phrase "they're as good as their word" to describe someone who is trustworthy and reliable, who will do what they have promised. In today's Gospel, Jesus tells a man to return home where he will find his son healed from an illness. We are told that the man "believed what Jesus said to him." This is what faith is all about: placing our trust in the words of Jesus Christ, knowing that he is trustworthy and keeps his promises. It is crucial, then, that we read, reflect on, and pray with God's word in Scripture. During this Lenten season, spend time with Scripture and get to know Jesus through his words and actions, and pray for the grace to trust him in all things.

Isaiah 65:17–21
Psalm 30:2 and 4, 5–6, 11–12a and 13b
John 4:43–54

Tuesday

MARCH 9

• ST. FRANCES OF ROME, RELIGIOUS •

The man went and told the Jews that Jesus was the one who had made him well.
—JOHN 5:15

Today's Gospel is a good example of evangelization by sharing one's story. The man cured by Jesus went off and told people that Jesus was the one who had cured him. We are called to do the same: We are to share stories of how our lives have been transformed by the mercy and love of Christ. Such stories need not be overly dramatic but may simply point out ways that Jesus has helped you, healed you (physically, emotionally, and spiritually), rescued you, restored you, and reassured you. For example, if someone were to ask how you got through a difficult situation, you might respond by explaining how the Lord brought you reassurance. That's a story, and it may be enough to pique the curiosity of others about faith in Jesus. What's your story?

Ezekiel 47:1–9, 12
Psalm 46:2–3, 5–6, 8–9
John 5:1–16

Wednesday MARCH 10

Can a mother forget her infant,
be without tenderness for the child of her womb?
Even should she forget,
I will never forget you.
—ISAIAH 49:15

One of the advantages of being a grandparent in the digital age was receiving a constant stream of pictures of our newborn grandchildren from my daughter and daughter-in-law when each of their kids were born. Both moms seemed capable of catching every mood on their infants' faces, whether they were sleeping like angels, screaming like banshees, or anything in between. What impresses me most is that in order to do this, both moms needed to have their gaze constantly fixed on their infants so as not to miss any expression on their faces. But this is what mothers do: They fix their gaze on their children. No one knows the face of a child like his or her mother. Today, Isaiah offers us this motherly image to help us know God's intimate love for each one of us.

Isaiah 49:8–15
Psalm 145:8–9, 13cd–14, 17–18
John 5:17–30

Thursday

MARCH 11

They have soon turned aside from the way I pointed out to them, making for themselves a molten calf and worshiping it, sacrificing to it and crying out, "This is your God, O Israel, who brought you out of the land of Egypt!"
—EXODUS 32:8

The term "spiritual amnesia" refers to the very real problem we humans have with remembering the good things that God has done for us. This is one of the crucial reasons worship is so important to our spiritual health because in worship we recall the great deeds of the Lord and give thanks. In addition to the Scripture readings that recall God's saving deeds, the Eucharistic Prayer includes a segment referred to as the *anamnesis*, or the calling to mind of the Paschal mystery of Christ's passion, death, resurrection, and ascension. This remembering makes these events present to us in the here and now, lest we forget that we owe everything to God.

Exodus 32:7–14
Psalm 106:19–20, 21–22, 23
John 5:31–47

Friday MARCH 12

The LORD is close to the brokenhearted;
and those who are crushed in spirit he saves.
—PSALM 34:19

Life has a way of disappointing us. Despite our best efforts, hopes, and dreams, our hearts are sometimes broken. That crack in our hearts enables despair to enter to do its dirty work of robbing us of hope. Even in the midst of despair, however, that crack remains open and enables hope to reenter and bring about healing. Today, the psalmist reminds us that our Lord is close to the brokenhearted; saving those who are crushed in spirit. If you are brokenhearted, turn to the Lord who is near to you and ask him for healing. We in turn are sent forth to seek out those who are brokenhearted and suffering from a crushed spirit to reassure them that the Lord is near to them also and that his grace mends broken hearts.

Wisdom 2:1a, 12–22
Psalm 34:17–18, 19–20, 21 and 23
John 7:1–2, 10, 25–30

Saturday

MARCH 13

Nicodemus, one of their members who had come to him earlier, said to them, "Does our law condemn a person before it first hears him and finds out what he is doing?"
—JOHN 7:50–51

It is quite common these days for pundits and talking heads to pose questions, without any evidence, asking whether a public figure or celebrity may have done wrong. Within moments, the question spreads through social media and becomes accepted fact to many, resulting in a "guilty until proven innocent" scenario. The voice of Nicodemus in today's Gospel reminds us that this is not the way of God. The *Catechism of the Catholic Church* teaches us that *rash judgment* (assuming as true, without sufficient evidence, someone's moral failing) and *calumny* (harming others' reputation by spreading falsehoods about them) are violations of the eighth commandment, which calls us to honor truth. This Lent, may we repent from our participation in such practices.

Jeremiah 11:18–20
Psalm 7:2–3, 9bc–10, 11–12
John 7:40–53

Sunday MARCH 14

• FIFTH SUNDAY OF LENT •

Those who are in the flesh cannot please God.
But you are not in the flesh;
on the contrary, you are in the spirit,
if only the Spirit of God dwells in you.
Whoever does not have the Spirit of Christ does not belong to him.
—ROMANS 8:9

Even when we feel burdened by our limitations, we are reminded in Jesus that our lives are no longer defined by the flesh alone. In today's reading, Saint Paul speaks of the Spirit dwelling within us. This indwelling presence is not abstract; it is active and it shapes how we think, act, make decisions, and love. To belong to Christ is to live from that Spirit, allowing it to guide us in ways both subtle and weighty. As we spend more time with Jesus in thought and prayer, we begin to sense his spirit unfolding within us, quietly bearing fruit in ways we may not have expected.

Jeremiah 31:31–34 or Ezekiel 37:12–14
Psalm 51:3–4, 12–13, 14–15 (12a) or 130:1–2, 3–4, 5–6, 7–8 (7)
Hebrews 5:7–9 or Romans 8:8–11
John 12:20–33 or John 11:1–45 or, for shorter form, John 11:3–7, 17, 20–27, 33b–45

Monday

MARCH 15

[Jesus said] "Let the one among you who is without sin be the first to throw a stone at her."
—JOHN 8:7

How do we balance Jesus's admonition not to cast stones unless we have no sin with the Spiritual Work of Mercy that calls us to "admonish the sinner"? While we are warned against passing judgment on people, the truth is, we make judgments all the time about whether certain people are the kind of people that we want in our lives or in the lives of our children or loved ones. This type of discernment is necessary in life. The kind of judgment we are warned against is rash, superficial, unforgiving, self-righteous, and hypocritical judgment as well as public judgment or "throwing stones." Jesus calls us today to self-reflection and self-examination and, when necessary for the well-being of another, to discreet and private correction done in a spirit of charity.

Daniel 13:1–9, 15–17, 19–30, 33–62 or 13:41c–62
Psalm 23:1–3a, 3b–4, 5, 6
John 8:1–11

Tuesday

MARCH 16

So Jesus said to them, "When you lift up the Son of Man, then you will realize that I AM, and that I do nothing on my own."
—JOHN 8:28

When Moses asked God his name. God replied, "I AM." Our God cannot be pigeonholed by a name such as the "god of fire" or the "god of rain." Our God is not a supreme being among other lower beings. Our God is the very essence of being: God is the great "I AM." In today's Gospel, Jesus identifies himself as the great I AM, indicating that he and the Father are one. Jesus is not simply a great man, a wonderful teacher, a wise philosopher, or an impressive miracle worker: He is God, the great "I AM." We proclaim this in the Nicene Creed when we describe Jesus as "God from God, Light from Light, true God from true God, begotten, not made, consubstantial with the Father."

Numbers 21:4–9
Psalm 102:2–3, 16–18, 19–21
John 8:21–30

Wednesday MARCH 17

• ST. PATRICK, BISHOP •

Jesus answered them, "Amen, amen, I say to you, everyone who commits sin is a slave of sin."
—JOHN 8:34

People reacted angrily to Jesus telling them that they must be set free, insisting that they were slaves to no one. This is classic denial. "I can stop (name addictive behavior here) anytime I want." Franciscan writer and speaker Fr. Richard Rohr has long insisted that we are all addicted to certain habits and patterns of behavior and that addiction is simply the more modern and honest way to name what the Bible calls sin. Twelve-step programs are mainly about honesty and truth. Jesus tells us today that the truth will set us free. Today, we ask ourselves, "What habits or patterns of behavior am I in denial of?" And since we are typically blind to our own addictions, perhaps we can seek help from a spiritual companion to help us name any sin that has us enslaved.

Daniel 3:14–20, 91–92, 95
Daniel 3:52, 53, 54, 55, 56
John 8:31–42

Thursday

MARCH 18

• ST. CYRIL OF JERUSALEM, BISHOP AND DOCTOR OF THE CHURCH •

I will maintain my covenant with you and your descendants after you throughout the ages as an everlasting pact, to be your God and the God of your descendants after you.
—GENESIS 17:7

In any relationship, the first person to express love and commitment is taking a big risk. If such a declaration goes unreciprocated, it is, in the words of comedian Jerry Seinfeld, "a pretty big matzo ball hanging out there." God, however, does not hesitate. He declares to Abraham that he will maintain his covenant "throughout the ages." In return, he asks that we love him by loving our neighbors. God has remained steadfastly faithful to his promise. On this Lenten Thursday, we pause to give thanks to God for his everlasting love and ask for the grace we need to reciprocate by remaining true to our end of the deal: loving our neighbors as ourselves.

Genesis 17:3–9
Psalm 105:4–5, 6–7, 8–9
John 8:51–59

Friday MARCH 19

• ST. JOSEPH, SPOUSE OF THE BLESSED VIRGIN MARY •

When Joseph awoke, he did as the angel of the Lord had commanded him.
—MATTHEW 1:24

In Scripture, dreams were often seen as a form of communication from God, and they indicated spiritual healthiness: Nighttime was when a spiritually healthy person listened for the sound of God's voice. Joseph, the husband of Mary, was the beneficiary of several dreams in which an angel of the Lord spoke to him. In other words, Joseph made sure that each night he discerned God's will for him. We, too, can do as Joseph did and make sure that at the end of each day we review our thoughts, words, and actions and ask God to speak to us about how we can align our will with his. The Daily Examen, often done at the end of the day, is a valuable tool for opening our minds and hearts to hear God's voice in the night as Joseph did.

2 Samuel 7:4–5a, 12–14a, 16
Psalm 89:2–3, 4–5, 27 and 29
Romans 4:13, 16–18, 22
Matthew 1:16, 18–21, 24a or Luke 2:41–51a

Saturday

MARCH 20

Now the Passover of the Jews was near, and many went up from the country to Jerusalem before Passover to purify themselves. They looked for Jesus.
—JOHN 11:55–56

In the Old Testament, one of the most profound effects of sin is scattering: The sins of Adam and Eve, Cain and Abel, and the folks who attempted to build the Tower of Babel—to name just a few—resulted in the scattering of people and the breaking of relationships. In today's first reading, Ezekiel proclaims an end to the scattering and the promise to gather God's people into one. In today's Gospel, people from all over are gathering for the Passover in Jerusalem, where, in just a few days, Jesus will draw all people to himself as our Passover sacrifice. As we stand on the doorstep of Holy Week, may we recommit ourselves to gathering rather than scattering.

Ezekiel 37:21–28
Jeremiah 31:10, 11–12abcd, 13
John 11:45–56

Sunday

MARCH 21

• PALM SUNDAY OF THE LORD'S PASSION •

He sent two of his disciples and said to them, "Go into the village opposite you, and immediately on entering it, you will find a colt tethered on which no one has ever sat."

—MARK 11:1–2

Jesus's triumphant entrance into Jerusalem was not accidental. This was a completely choreographed event—a campaign stop, if you will, along Jesus's route leading to his ultimate destination, Jerusalem. Mark's Gospel tells us that Jesus made specific preparations to enter in this manner, thus proclaiming himself the long-awaited king. This was Jesus's "coming out" event. We, in turn, place blessed palms in our homes, not as a sentimental decoration, but as a proclamation that Jesus is our Lord and King and that his kingdom reigns in our homes and in our hearts.

PROCESSION:
Mark 11:1–10 or John 12:12–16

MASS:
Isaiah 50:4–7
Psalm 22:8–9, 17–18, 19–20, 23–24 (2a)
Philippians 2:6–11
Mark 14:1–15:47 or, for shorter form, Mark 15:1–39

Monday
MARCH 22

• MONDAY OF HOLY WEEK •

I, the LORD, have called you for the victory of justice,
I have grasped you by the hand;
I formed you, and set you
as a covenant of the people,
a light for the nations,
To open the eyes of the blind,
to bring out prisoners from confinement,
and from the dungeon, those who live in darkness.
—ISAIAH 42: 6–7

When speaking of salvation, we often tend to focus on what we are being saved *from*: sin, death, and hell. Today's first reading reminds us of what we are being saved *for*: the victory of justice. Our salvation is not something that we passively await to enjoy once this earthly life is over. On the contrary, we are called to bask in the celebration of the victory of justice in the here and now, and to bring that good news to those who are confined by the darkness of despair and injustice.

Isaiah 42:1–7
Psalm 27:1, 2, 3, 13–14
John 12:1–11

Tuesday MARCH 23

• TUESDAY OF HOLY WEEK •

Jesus answered, "Will you lay down your life for me? Amen, amen, I say to you, the cock will not crow before you deny me three times."
—JOHN 13:38

One of the most persuasive and convincing features of the authenticity of the Gospels' events is their reporting of the glaring failure of Jesus's closest friends and followers, the apostles. It's hard to imagine that people would make up stories that paint themselves in poor light. And yet, Jesus's apostles proclaimed a story in which they had failed miserably. In today's Gospel, we hear Jesus predict Peter's cowardly actions that would occur shortly after Jesus's arrest. These painfully honest accounts of the events leading up to Jesus's death on the cross invite us to look truthfully at ourselves and to admit our own failures, knowing that the mercy, compassion, and forgiveness of the Risen Christ will lead us to new life.

Isaiah 49:1–6
Psalm 71:1–2, 3–4a, 5ab–6ab, 15 and 17
John 13:21–33, 36–38

Wednesday

MARCH 24

• WEDNESDAY OF HOLY WEEK •

He is near who upholds my right;
if anyone wishes to oppose me,
let us appear together.
Who disputes my right?
Let him confront me.
See, the Lord GOD is my help;
who will prove me wrong?
—ISAIAH 50:8–9

At many press conferences, it is common to see the person speaking surrounded by colleagues who do not speak but simply form a backdrop. The message is clear: These people have the speaker's back. In today's first reading, Isaiah "approaches the microphone" but does not stand alone: God is at his side. This is the constant message of the events of Holy Week: Jesus does not act alone. May each of us remember that even in the darkest moments, we are not alone—God, our strength, is with us.

Isaiah 50:4–9a
Psalm 69:8–10, 21–22, 31 and 33–34
Matthew 26:14–25

Thursday

MARCH 25

• THURSDAY OF HOLY WEEK (HOLY THURSDAY) •

[Jesus said] "If I, therefore, the master and teacher, have washed your feet, you ought to wash one another's feet."
—JOHN 13:14

Most books on leadership will tend to be confined to three areas: business, sports, and politics. Unfortunately, such books don't translate well to the world of Christian leadership, which is characterized by service. Jesus's style of servant leadership, epitomized in today's Gospel, calls for us to be compassionate, willing to walk with broken people, and able to serve as loving parents do for their children. Servant leaders recognize the sacredness and reaffirm the image of God in each person, putting the needs of the other before their own. To follow Christ is to wash feet.

CHRISM MASS:
Isaiah 61:1–3ab, 6a, 8b–9
Psalm 89:21–22, 25 and 27
Revelation 1:5–8
Luke 4:16–21

EVENING MASS OF THE LORD'S SUPPER:
Exodus 12:1–8, 11–14
Psalm 116:12–13, 15–16bc, 17–18
1 Corinthians 11:23–26
John 13:1–15

Friday
MARCH 26

• GOOD FRIDAY OF THE LORD'S PASSION •

[Jesus said] "For this I was born and for this I came into the world, to testify to the truth. Everyone who belongs to the truth listens to my voice." Pilate said to him, "What is truth?"
—JOHN 18:37–38

In today's proclamation of the Passion according to John, Pontius Pilate asks one of the most famous questions of all time: What is truth? Ironically, the answer to his question is staring him in the face: Jesus is the Truth, but Pilate is unable to see or hear him. From our distant perch, we may be tempted to scoff at Pilate's foolishness. Yet today's solemn liturgy challenges us to ask ourselves if we are hearing the voice of truth speaking to us. Jesus and the truth cannot be separated. We are called not only to believe the truth, but to live in the truth of Christ, which means to embody Christ, reflecting his love and character in our words and actions.

Isaiah 52:13—53:12
Psalm 31:2, 6, 12–13, 15–16, 17, 25
Hebrews 4:14–16; 5:7–9
John 18:1—19:42

Saturday
MARCH 27

• HOLY SATURDAY •

Are you unaware that we who were baptized into Christ Jesus were baptized into his death?
—ROMANS 6:3

When it comes to baptism, we tend to focus on the aspect of new life, emphasizing the life-giving, cleansing properties of the baptismal waters while overlooking one important reality: We cannot survive under water. Baptism by immersion, which resembles drowning, celebrates new life made possible by dying to an old self and to sin. On this Holy Saturday, as we celebrate the baptisms of new Catholics and renew our own baptismal promises, may we once again embrace new life in the Risen Christ.

VIGIL:
Genesis 1:1—2:2 or 1:1, 26–31a
Psalm 104:1–2, 5–6, 10, 12, 13–14, 24, 35 (30) or 33:4–5, 6–7, 12–13, 20–22 (5b)
Genesis 22:1–18 or 22:1–2, 9a, 10–13, 15–18
Psalm 16:5, 8, 9–10, 11
Exodus 14:15—15:1
Exodus 15:1–2, 3–4, 5–6, 17–18 (1b)
Isaiah 54:5–14
Psalm 30:2, 4, 5–6, 11–12, 13 (2a)
Isaiah 55:1–11
Isaiah 12:2–3, 4, 5–6 (3)
Baruch 3:9–15, 32—4:4
Psalm 19:8, 9, 10, 11
Ezekiel 36:16–17a, 18–28
Psalm 42:3, 5; 43:3. 4 or Isaiah 12:2–3, 4bcd, 5–6 (3)or Psalm 51:12–13, 14–15, 18–19 (12a)
Romans 6:3–11
Psalm 118:1–2, 16–17, 22–23
Mark 16:1–7

Sunday MARCH 28

• EASTER SUNDAY * THE RESURRECTION OF THE LORD * THE MASS OF EASTER DAY •

This is the day the Lord has made; let us rejoice and be glad.
—PSALM 118:24

Whenever he heard the phrase "This is the day the Lord has made," a friend of mine with a corny sense of humor would ask, "If this is the day the Lord has made, who made all the other days?" The answer, of course, was right before his eyes: Every day is a gift from the Lord! On this Easter Sunday, we celebrate the newness of life in the Risen Lord—a newness that makes every day a brand-new day and another opportunity to start fresh and leave the past behind. A day that is made by the Lord is a day with a special purpose. We no longer languish without direction or meaning: Each day is a day to encounter the Risen Christ and to celebrate his victory over sin and death. Alleluia!

Acts 10:34a, 37–43
Psalm 118:1–2, 16–17, 22–23 (24)
Colossians 3:1–4 or 1 Corinthians 5:6b–8
John 20:1–9 or Mark 16:1–7 or, at an afternoon or evening Mass, Luke 24:13–35

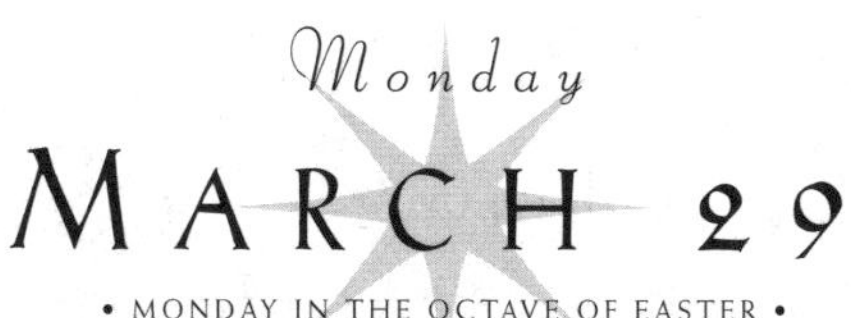

Monday MARCH 29

• MONDAY IN THE OCTAVE OF EASTER •

Mary Magdalene and the other Mary went away quickly from the tomb, fearful yet overjoyed, and ran to announce the news to his disciples.

—MATTHEW 28:8

We use the word *ambivalence* to describe the experience of feeling two conflicting emotions at the same time, such as the excitement and fear of riding a roller coaster. The result is that we scream out loud while smiling ear to ear. In today's Gospel, the women who came to the tomb and discovered it empty were overcome with ambivalence—they felt both overjoyed and fearful at the same time. When they encounter the Risen Christ, however, he quickly dispels their fear, telling them, "Do not be afraid." Fear is primarily a reaction to the unknown. Since the Lord is truly risen, there is no longer a reason to fear. During this Octave of Easter, may we fearlessly carry the joyful good news of our Risen Lord to all those we meet.

Acts 2:14, 22–33
Psalm 16:1–2a and 5, 7–8, 9–10, 11
Matthew 28:8–15

Tuesday MARCH 30

• TUESDAY IN THE OCTAVE OF EASTER •

Now when they heard this, they were cut to the heart,
and they asked Peter and the other Apostles, "What are we to do,
my brothers?"
—ACTS 2:37

It's not often that we are "cut to the heart." Generally, this occurs when our worldview collapses: The person we trusted implicitly betrays us; the job we were counting on for our future is eliminated; hopes and dreams disintegrate in the face of the diagnosis of a serious illness. In today's first reading, the crowds are cut to the heart by the words of St. Peter, which convict them of killing the Messiah who was to be the fulfillment of all the hopes and dreams of Israel. Conversion often involves being "cut to the heart" and results in questioning the next steps: "What are we to do, my brothers?" Peter's answer speaks to us today: We must stop denying reality and open our hearts to the Holy Spirit, who frees us from guilt and gives us new life.

Acts 2:36–41
Psalm 33:4–5, 18–19, 20 and 22
John 20:11–18

Wednesday

MARCH 31

• WEDNESDAY IN THE OCTAVE OF EASTER •

As they approached the village to which they were going, he gave the impression that he was going on farther. But they urged him, "Stay with us, for it is nearly evening and the day is almost over." So he went in to stay with them.

—LUKE 24:28–29

An often-overlooked component of the account of the two disciples on the road to Emmaus is that of hospitality. It is because of their hospitality, offered to a stranger (since they did not recognize the man walking with them) that the presence of the Risen Lord is revealed in the breaking of the bread. Hospitality is not simply creating some kind of touchy-feely, feel-good experience. Nor is it merely the frosting on the cake of discipleship. Rather, it is an essential ingredient that forms us into the Body of Christ and reveals his presence in our midst. May this Octave of Easter move us to grow in a spirit of hospitality.

Acts 3:1–10
Psalm 105:1–2, 3–4, 6–7, 8–9
Luke 24:13–35

Thursday APRIL 1

• THURSDAY IN THE OCTAVE OF EASTER •

The disciples of Jesus recounted what had taken place along the way, and how they had come to recognize him in the breaking of bread.
—LUKE 24:35

We don't know anything about the two disciples on the road to Emmaus except that one of them was named Cleopas. And yet, their account is one of the most famous narratives in the Gospels. That would not have happened unless Cleopas and his fellow traveler were invited to recount their experience—to tell their story—for the benefit of others, as today's Gospel reveals. As disciples of Christ, we must tell our stories. Where do we begin? Consider sharing stories of the following in your life: significant people, moments of joy (big or small), peak moments of grace, and milestones. Pray that, like the disciples on the road to Emmaus, our stories will outlive us and touch people's hearts and minds for years to come.

Acts 3:11–26
Psalm 8:2ab and 5, 6–7, 8–9
Luke 24:35–48

Friday

APRIL 2

• FRIDAY IN THE OCTAVE OF EASTER •

When they climbed out on shore, they saw a charcoal fire with fish on it and bread. Jesus said to them, "Bring some of the fish you just caught. . . . Come, have breakfast."
—JOHN 21:9–10,12

The imagery in today's Gospel is so rich and lush that you can smell it. You can taste it. A freshwater lake, the outdoors, seaweed, driftwood, a charcoal fire, grilled fish, bread—this Gospel is a feast for the senses and will no doubt make one hungry! And that is precisely the point: The Risen Christ invites us to a meal that satisfies all our hungers. Throughout the Gospels, meals play an important role in Jesus's ministry, and this is only heightened after his resurrection. Jesus invites you today: "Come, have breakfast." Bring your hungers and lay them before the Lord. Then, taste and see how good the Lord is!

Acts 4:1–12
Psalm 118:1–2 and 4, 22–24, 25–27a
John 21:1–14

Saturday APRIL 3

• SATURDAY IN THE OCTAVE OF EASTER •

Observing the boldness of Peter and John and perceiving them to be uneducated, ordinary men, the leaders, elders, and scribes were amazed, and they recognized them as the companions of Jesus.
—ACTS 4:13

Jesus's apostles were not trained in public speaking, yet they persuaded thousands of people to embrace the Risen Christ and be baptized. What was their key? Authenticity. The priests and elders were amazed that these ordinary, uneducated men were so bold and confident. Chris Anderson, the former head of the organization that sponsors TED talks, identifies four keys to successful persuasive speaking: Limit your talk to one major idea, give your listeners a reason to care, build your idea, and make your idea worth sharing. Peter and John and the other apostles mastered these keys. Today's Gospel reminds us that God relies on ordinary, authentic people to spread an idea: that following the Risen Christ is the key to understanding and navigating life.

Acts 4:13–21
Psalm 118:1 and 14–15ab, 16–18, 19–21
Mark 16:9–15

Sunday
APRIL 4

• SECOND SUNDAY OF EASTER (OR SUNDAY OF DIVINE MERCY) •

On the evening of that first day of the week, when the doors were locked, where the disciples were, for fear of the Jews, Jesus came and stood in their midst and said to them, "Peace be with you."
—JOHN 20:19

In most movies and adventure novels, when heroes return or bounce back from a humiliating defeat, they typically mete out revenge against their enemies. Jesus's suffering and death were by all counts a humiliating defeat. Many people betrayed, denied, and abandoned him, and those were among his friends. Then, of course, there were those who mocked, beat, and crucified him. And yet, upon his return following the Resurrection, Jesus's first words are "Peace be with you." Instead of revenge, Jesus brings mercy. On this Divine Mercy Sunday, rather than seeking revenge, may we find the grace we need to bring peace to our relationships and to our spheres of influence.

Acts 4:32–35
Psalm 118:2–4, 13–15, 22–24 (1)
1 John 5:1–6
John 20:19–31

Monday
APRIL 5

• THE ANNUNCIATION OF THE LORD •

And coming to her, he [the angel Gabriel] said, "Hail, full of grace! The Lord is with you." But she was greatly troubled at what was said and pondered what sort of greeting this might be.
—LUKE 1:28–29

The angel's greeting to Mary, "Hail, full of grace! The Lord is with you" seems pleasant enough. And yet, the Gospel account tells us that Mary was "deeply troubled" by these words that were associated with the heroes of Judaism who were called by God to undertake a crucial mission. Mary's fears are natural: It is common to react with hesitation when called to undertake a difficult challenge. How one responds to that fear is the key. Mary responded, not by doubting, but by inquiring more about God's will. On this Feast of the Annunciation, we look to Mary as the ultimate model of discernment and pray for the grace to know God's will for us.

Isaiah 7:10–14; 8:10
Psalm 40:7–8a, 8b–9, 10, 11 (8a, 9a)
Hebrews 10:4–10
Luke 1:26–38

The community of believers was of one heart and mind.
—ACTS 4:32

The description of the early church as being "of one heart and mind" sounds idyllic. This description, however, does not mean that there were no conflicts in the early church. Rather, it means that the community of believers had a shared purpose and a communal identity. This notion is at the heart of *synodality*—a way of being church together. Synodality is a commitment to being of one heart and one mind. Again, this does not mean that we agree on everything. But it does mean we have a way of being that emphasizes our unity and our shared mission. For ourselves, this means recognizing and being open to change, listening to others' voices, discerning the movement of the Holy Spirit, and being moved to action in a way that promotes unity, not just our own agenda.

Acts 4:32–37
Psalm 93:1ab, 1cd–2, 5
John 3:7b–15

Wednesday APRIL 7

• ST. JOHN BAPTIST DE LA SALLE, PRIEST •

God so loved the world that he gave his only-begotten Son, so that everyone who believes in him might not perish but might have eternal life.
—JOHN 3:16

Folks in the marketing world know how to condense a lot of information into sound bites, which is what you have to do when you're working with only thirty seconds of time or a few inches of text real estate to share your message. Today's Gospel includes one of the most famous sound bites from Scripture—John 3:16. This passage, taken to heart and memorized by countless Christians, is a succinct summary of the Good News. Such power-packed passages are known as the *kerygma*, a Greek word meaning "proclamation" of the core message of the gospel. Today, more than ever, followers of Jesus need to rely on the kerygma—power-packed sound bites—to proclaim the Good News of Jesus Christ to a world with a very short attention span.

Acts 5:17–26
Psalm 34:2–3, 4–5, 6–7, 8–9
John 3:16–21

Thursday APRIL 8

Peter and the Apostles said in reply,
"We must obey God rather than men."
—ACTS 5:29

Throughout the Easter season, the first reading at Mass, which is usually from the Old Testament, is instead from the Acts of the Apostles. These dramatic accounts tell us of the boldness of the apostles in proclaiming the gospel even in the face of great danger. The apostles had ringside seats during Jesus's last days before his crucifixion, and they saw him dragged before the authorities and interrogated. Now, filled with the Holy Spirit, the apostles ignore the warnings of the Sanhedrin and continue to teach "in that name" that the high priest cannot even bring himself to utter. These narratives of the apostles serve to inspire each of us to speak and act boldly and fearlessly about the teachings of Jesus, even in the face of opposition.

Acts 5:27–33
Psalm 34:2 and 9, 17–18, 19–20
John 3:31–36

Friday
April 9

So they collected them, and filled twelve wicker baskets with fragments from the five barley loaves that had been more than they could eat.
—John 6:13

When it came to serving meals for others, Jesus obviously believed in large portions. In today's Gospel, Jesus multiplies the five barley loaves and creates so much bread that the apostles collect twelve baskets of leftovers. Earlier in John's Gospel, at the wedding at Cana, Jesus produced dozens of gallons of wine from water. When Jesus offers nourishment, there is no shortage. While today all too many people go to bed physically hungry, many more of us go to bed spiritually hungry, wondering (perhaps unconsciously) what and who will sustain us in the coming day. Jesus's mighty deeds reveal that he alone is to be our source of sustenance—an abundant source that will never be depleted.

Acts 5:34–42
Psalm 27:1, 4, 13–14
John 6:1–15

Saturday

APRIL 10

When they had rowed about three or four miles, they saw Jesus walking on the sea and coming near the boat, and they began to be afraid. But he said to them, "It is I. Do not be afraid."
—JOHN 6:19–20

The disciples had much to fear: It was dark, the winds were strong, the sea was rough, and they had been separated from Jesus, who had promised to rendezvous with them but was seemingly delayed. As happens throughout Scripture, however, God remains true to his promise. The rough waters were no match for Jesus, who rose above the turbulence to reach his disciples and to calm their fears. At various moments in our lives, we experience fear of the darkness, strong winds, and rough waters that surround us and buffet us. We may feel separated from Jesus. Today's Gospel reminds us that nothing can separate us from the love of Christ, who comes to us through the turbulence and assures us of his presence.

Acts 6:1–7
Psalm 33:1–2, 4–5, 18–19
John 6:16–21

Sunday
APRIL 11

• THIRD SUNDAY OF EASTER •

[Jesus said] "Repentance, for the forgiveness of sins, would be preached in his name to all the nations, beginning from Jerusalem. You are witnesses of these things."
—LUKE 24:47–48

Catholics recognize repentance as part of the overall experience of the sacrament of reconciliation, also known as penance, or the making of amends for damages caused by our sins. These outward actions open us up to inward transformation, which is the heart of the gospel. The practice of penance is supported by Cognitive Behavioral Therapy, which emphasizes that outward actions (behaviors) can significantly impact our thoughts and emotions. One of the most powerful ways we can preach the gospel is by inviting people to help repair the damages caused by human sinfulness. Proclaiming the Good News is a call to action.

Acts 3:13–15, 17–19
Psalm 4:2, 4, 7–8, 9 (7a)
1 John 2:1–5a
Luke 24:35–48

Monday

APRIL 12

All those who sat in the Sanhedrin looked intently at him and saw that his face was like the face of an angel.
—ACTS 6:15

In today's first reading, we learn that Stephen left quite an impression on people, especially on the members of the Sanhedrin to whom his face "was like the face of an angel." This is not to be confused with our contemporary understanding of a baby with the face of an angel meaning sweet and innocent. In Scripture, angels are described as spiritual beings who stand in the presence of God and reflect his glory and presence. They are not docile but often provoke fear because they reveal God's power. May our faces seem "like the face of an angel" to those we encounter, not because we have a sweet baby face, but because God's powerful presence, wisdom, compassion, justice, and mercy are revealed through our words and actions—indeed, through our very lives.

Acts 6:8–15
Psalm 119:23–24, 26–27, 29–30
John 6:22–29

Tuesday APRIL 13

• ST. MARTIN I, POPE AND MARTYR •

Jesus said to them, "I am the bread of life; whoever comes to me will never hunger, and whoever believes in me will never thirst."
—JOHN 6:35

When we experience hunger, it is an indication that our body needs food and nutrients to restore our depleted energy so that we may function properly. In a comparable way, we become spiritually depleted as a result of the occurrences of everyday living that can drain us of energy. We develop hungry hearts, which we too often attempt to satisfy in all the wrong ways, the same way we too often turn to junk food to satisfy our physical hunger. In today's Gospel, Jesus tells us that he is the bread of life who alone can satisfy our spiritual hunger. We do well to feast on the bread of life that fortifies us with the nutrients of faith, hope, and love.

Acts 7:51—8:1a
Psalm 31:3cd–4, 6 and 7b and 8a, 17 and 21ab
John 6:30–35

Wednesday
APRIL 14

There was great joy in that city.
—ACTS 8:8

When a sports team ends a long drought and wins a championship, their long-suffering hometown fans let loose with joyful, wild, and loud celebrations, often rising to fever pitch. In today's first reading, we learn that "there was great joy" in the town of Samaria when Philip proclaimed the Messiah, healed the sick, and expelled demons. Like long-suffering sports fans, the people of Samaria felt like a forgotten people who had lost all hope. To have someone in their midst proclaiming good news and bringing hope to those who were suffering was a cause of great joy. They were invited to share in Christ's victory over sin and death. Like Philip, we are sent to bring the good news of Christ's victory to those in despair so that they may have great joy, even if only in the silence of their hearts.

Acts 8:1b–8
Psalm 66:1–3a, 4–5, 6–7a
John 6:35–40

Philip ran up and heard him reading Isaiah the prophet and said, "Do you understand what you are reading?" He replied, "How can I, unless someone instructs me?"

—ACTS 8:30–31

Thus began the first catechumenate session in church history as Philip engaged the Ethiopian seeker in a conversation that led him to a relationship with Christ. Since the early days of the church, seekers have been accompanied by disciples on their journey to the waters of baptism. Today's first reading reminds us that we do not come to the Lord on our own. We have been accompanied by others who have helped us to understand God's word and to deepen our relationship with Christ. For them, we give thanks. In turn, each of us is called to introduce others to Christ, often through simple encounters like the one between Philip and the Ethiopian man, using a Scripture passage (or any other available topic) as a starting point.

Acts 8:26–40
Psalm 66:8–9, 16–17, 20
John 6:44–51

Friday APRIL 16

Saul got up from the ground, but when he opened his eyes he could see nothing; so they led him by the hand and brought him to Damascus.
—ACTS 9:8

One of the frustrating moments we encounter during a conversion experience is confusion. Saul's confusion is symbolized by blindness. This period of darkness can be a moment of great temptation for us. Saul may have been tempted to continue his former mission of blindly attacking Christians at every stop. Or—like many of us at similar junctures—he may have looked for a quick fix or a way to anesthetize himself. But he didn't. Instead, he allowed himself to be led gently "by the hand." This is why it is so important for us disciples of Christ to be present to others who are experiencing their own moments of confusion: They may be on the threshold of either hope or despair. It is our job to ensure that hope prevails.

Acts 9:1–20
Psalm 117:1bc, 2
John 6:52–59

As a result of this, many of his disciples returned to their former way of life and no longer accompanied him. Jesus then said to the Twelve, "Do you also want to leave?" Simon Peter answered him, "Master, to whom shall we go? You have the words of eternal life."

—JOHN 6:66–68

Jesus never forces himself upon anyone; rather, he invites. In today's Gospel, we see that many found his teachings hard to endure or take seriously, and they left him. In our own times, many people have found the teachings of Jesus and his church hard to endure or take seriously. We pray for the grace that St. Peter found to hold fast to our commitment to Christ and to invite others to recognize that he alone has the words of eternal life so that they too may come to believe that Jesus is God's holy one.

Acts 9:31–42
Psalm 116:12–13, 14–15, 16–17
John 6:60–69

Sunday
APRIL 18

• FOURTH SUNDAY OF EASTER •

[Jesus said] "I am the good shepherd. A good shepherd lays down his life for the sheep."
—JOHN 10:11

Laying down one's life can mean to die physically, or to set aside self-fulfillment to tend to the needs of others. Parents and spouses do this each and every day, which is why marriage and parenthood can be two of the most significant conversion experiences in a person's life. But anyone who unselfishly and sincerely provides a service to others—teachers, first responders, customer service representatives, medical personnel, hairdressers, flight attendants—is participating in goodness. As disciples of the Good Shepherd, we are called to make a habit of keeping the best interests of others in mind.

Acts 4:8–12
Psalm 118:1, 8–9, 21–23, 26, 28, 29 (22)
1 John 3:1–2
John 10:11–18

[Jesus said] "When he has driven out all his own, he walks ahead of them, and the sheep follow him, because they recognize his voice."
—JOHN 10:4

Throughout our lives, we hear many voices—parents, siblings, elders, peers, teachers, celebrities, religious leaders, politicians—speaking to us about what is right and what is wrong; what is a priority and what is not. These voices are recorded in our hearts, minds, and consciences. It is our responsibility to discern which voices speak God's truth and which are to be avoided. In today's Gospel, Jesus uses the image of a shepherd leading his sheep who know his voice and follow. This reading invites us to pause and reflect on the voices that we are listening to, asking for the grace we need to discern whether these voices echo the voice of the Good Shepherd or some other ideology that in reality may be a wolf in sheep's clothing.

Acts 11:1–18
Psalm 42:2–3; 43:3, 4
John 10:1–10

[Jesus said] "I give them eternal life, and they shall never perish. No one can take them out of my hand."
—JOHN 10:28

For young children, security blankets and other comfort objects are healthy things. They are transitional objects to ease the trauma of recognizing that they are separate beings from their mothers. Unfortunately, as we grow older, we tend to become attached to more sophisticated "security blankets," not to ease the anxiety of separation from our mothers, but to ease what we perceive as our separation from God. In today's Gospel, Jesus reassures us that in his presence we are secure. He emphatically declares that no one can take us out of his hand, no more than the wolf can snatch sheep from the shepherd's hand. In Jesus's hands we are protected and cherished. Take a moment today to give thanks for the security we have in the strong hands of our Good Shepherd.

Acts 11:19–26
Psalm 87:1b–3, 4–5, 6–7 (117:1a)
John 10:22–30

Wednesday APRIL 21

• ST. ANSELM, BISHOP AND DOCTOR OF THE CHURCH •

While they were worshiping the Lord and fasting, the Holy Spirit said, "Set apart for me Barnabas and Saul for the work to which I have called them."

—ACTS 13:2

Hearing that the Holy Spirit spoke to them, many might assume that the members of the early church heard an incorporeal voice. This could leave us feeling frustrated that the Holy Spirit seems to have gone into hiding and no longer speaks to us this way. A closer read of this passage, however, tells us that the gathering in Antioch included "prophets and teachers" and that they were "worshiping the Lord." Undoubtedly this means that the Holy Spirit spoke through the prophets and teachers who were gathered to worship. Take some time to reflect on what the Holy Spirit may be saying through the prophets and teachers in your life, especially during experiences of worship.

Acts 12:24—13:5a
Psalm 67:2–3, 5, 6 and 8
John 12:44–50

[Jesus said] "Amen, amen, I say to you, whoever receives the one I send receives me, and whoever receives me receives the one who sent me."
—JOHN 13:20

Marketing experts tell us that in today's economy, while consumers are concerned about availability, quality, and cost, they primarily crave authenticity: someone or something they can identify with. Authenticity results when there is harmony between what one says and how one acts. As followers of Jesus, we have a "brand" that we are striving to promote: the Good News. We can learn a lesson from the world of marketing. People will not accept the word of Jesus if his followers are inauthentic. We evangelize most effectively not by debating people but by sharing words and deeds that authentically reflect the message of Jesus. When people accept our authenticity as followers of Jesus, there is a better chance they will accept the Lord himself.

Acts 13:13–25
Psalm 89:2–3, 21–22, 25 and 27
John 13:16–20

Friday APRIL 23

• ST. GEORGE, MARTYR • ST. ADALBERT, BISHOP AND MARTYR •

Thomas said to him, "Master, we do not know where you are going; how can we know the way?" Jesus said to him, "I am the way and the truth and the life. No one comes to the Father except through me."

—JOHN 14:5–6

These days it is hard to get lost when driving. More often than not, we can place our trust in our GPS to the extent that we no longer worry about the possibility of getting lost. In today's Gospel, Jesus begins by telling his disciples, "Do not let your hearts be troubled. You have faith in God; have faith also in me." Like Thomas, we may experience anxiety about which direction our life should take. Jesus assures us, however, that he is "the way." Today and every day, place your trust in Jesus, knowing that he will lead you on your spiritual journey.

Acts 13:26–33
Psalm 2:6–7, 8–9, 10–11ab
John 14:1–6

Saturday
APRIL 24

• ST. FIDELIS OF SIGMARINGEN, PRIEST AND MARTYR •

The disciples were filled with joy and the Holy Spirit.
—ACTS 13:52

Think of a time when you found yourself in a serious or solemn setting but saw, heard, or thought of something so funny that you couldn't stifle a laugh. As hard as you tried, you could not help but break out in a guffaw. In a similar way, Barnabas and Paul, although expelled from the Jewish territory and facing serious threats, "were filled with joy and the Holy Spirit." The power of the gospel is so powerful that it is unstoppable, even in the face of obstacles and challenges. Sometimes, however, we and others allow despair and anxiety to overwhelm us. At times like these, we need to recall the immense joy of knowing that the Holy Spirit is with us and allow that unstoppable joy to shine through.

Acts 13:44–52
Psalm 98:1, 2–3ab, 3cd–4
John 14:7–14

Sunday APRIL 25

• FIFTH SUNDAY OF EASTER •

[Jesus said] "I am the vine, you are the branches. Whoever remains in me and I in him will bear much fruit, because without me you can do nothing."
—JOHN 15:5

It is human nature to want to feel part of something bigger than ourselves since it promotes a sense of belonging, strength, and purpose. When we feel connected to something bigger than ourselves, we tend to be more productive. In today's Gospel, Jesus reminds us that we are connected to something bigger than ourselves, namely, to him. The image of the vine and the branches is an intimate one: We are not only loosely affiliated; we are grafted onto the vine. Knowing that we are part of this divine organism empowers us to draw strength, energy, and a sense of purpose for our everyday lives. May this knowledge help you today and every day to be productive and fruitful.

Acts 9:26–31
Psalm 22:26–27, 28, 30, 31–32 (26a)
1 John 3:18–24
John 15:1–8

[Jesus answered and said to him] "The Advocate, the Holy Spirit whom the Father will send in my name—he will teach you everything and remind you of all that I told you."
—JOHN 14:26

When I was serving as a catechist of eighth graders, a lesson called for us to focus on the Holy Spirit as our Advocate. Fortunately, I had the best example: My catechist aide was a nurse in the maternity ward at the local hospital. After she dramatically explained how she constantly advocates for her patients, making sure that they are getting the care they need, I told our young learners that this is a perfect example of who the Holy Spirit is and what the Spirit does for us. Throughout our lives, we can be sure that when we need assistance, we can call for our Advocate, the Holy Spirit, who intercedes for us and ensures that we have what we need.

Acts 14:5–18
Psalm 115:1–2, 3–4, 15–16
John 14:21–26

[Jesus answered and said to him] "Peace I leave with you; my peace I give to you. Not as the world gives do I give it to you."
—JOHN 14:27

Many people enjoy working on jigsaw puzzles, in which dozens if not hundreds of tiny pieces need to be fitted together to complete the image that the puzzle reveals. It can be frustrating when the pieces do not fit. At the same time, however, there is a feeling of great satisfaction when the pieces *do* fit! This feeling is a good metaphor for the gift of Jesus's peace that he offers to us. We experience the peace of Christ and extend Christ's peace to others when we pray for the grace to recognize how all of the pieces of our lives fit together to form an image of God's will for us.

Acts 14:19–28
Psalm 145:10–11, 12–13ab, 21
John 14:27–31a

Wednesday

APRIL 28

• ST. PETER CHANEL, PRIEST AND MARTYR *
ST. LOUIS MARY DE MONTFORT, PRIEST •

It was decided that Paul, Barnabas, and some of the others should go up to Jerusalem to the Apostles and presbyters about this question.

—ACTS 15:2

At times, it may seem that the experience of the early church, as described in the Acts of the Apostles, was quite utopian and that they never experienced any internal conflict. Acts 15 puts an end to any such illusion. The debate over whether Gentiles could be welcomed into the church without first undergoing circumcision threatened to disrupt the unity of the early church. Under the guidance of the Holy Spirit, however, the leaders of the church gathered in Jerusalem to prayerfully deal with the situation. It is this synodal spirit of the Council of Jerusalem that we continue to strive to practice today when we encounter conflict with our fellow disciples of Christ and together seek to discern God's will for his people.

Acts 15:1–6
Psalm 122:1–2, 3–4ab, 4cd–5
John 15:1–8

Thursday

APRIL 29

• ST. CATHERINE OF SIENA, VIRGIN AND DOCTOR OF THE CHURCH •

[Jesus said] "I have told you this so that my joy may be in you and your joy may be complete."
—JOHN 15:11

While joy is much more complex than just being happy, a big component of joy that is often overlooked is having fun. Too often, having fun is dismissed as frivolous child's play when, in reality, it is critical part of our overall health and is closely connected with joy. In her book *The Power of Fun: How to Feel Alive Again*, health and science journalist Catherine Price explains that true fun is characterized by three key ingredients: playfulness (a spirit of lightheartedness and freedom), connection (having a shared experience with someone), and flow (being fully engaged and focused). Jesus came that our joy—a fruit of the Holy Spirit—may be complete. On this day, may the Holy Spirit guide us to experience playfulness, connection, and flow so that our joy may be abundant and that we may share it with others.

Acts 15:7–21
Psalm 96:1–2a, 2b–3, 10
John 15:9–11

[Jesus said] "No one has greater love than this, to lay down one's life for one's friends."
—JOHN 15:13

Jesus laid down his life for us. Likewise, many martyrs, military personnel, and first responders have laid down their lives for their faith and for others. Is the greatest love out of reach, however, for the average person because we probably will not physically die because of our faith? Perhaps we have too narrowly defined what it means to lay down our life for others. It means to set our own needs aside at times to tend to the needs of others. You and I are called to do this every day at home and at work. May each of us be inspired to willingly pay attention to the needs of others. And in doing so, may we experience the greatest love imaginable.

Acts 15:22–31
Psalm 57:8–9, 10 and 12
John 15:12–17

When he had seen the vision, we sought passage to Macedonia at once, concluding that God had called us to proclaim the Good News to them.
—ACTS 16:10

Until this point in Acts, the author has written in the third person. Now, however, a switch is made to the first person as the author (thought by most scholars to be Luke) indicates personal involvement in the events being described. Even if the author was not historically present, he certainly identifies with the community, much as we might say, "We won today's game!" when speaking of our local sports team. This small grammatical shift can have profound implications on us as readers since we too are called to personal involvement in the ministry of proclaiming the Good News of Jesus to the world. This might inspire us to consider using phrases such as, "we believe" or "we teach" instead of the less personal "the church says" or "the church teaches."

Acts 16:1–10
Psalm 100:1b–2, 3, 5
John 15:18–21

In this is love: not that we have loved God, but that he loved us and sent his Son as expiation for our sins.
—1 JOHN 4:10

When you get a chance, take a look at an image of Michelangelo's fresco *The Creation of Adam*, which is on the ceiling of the Sistine Chapel. You will quickly notice which direction all of the energy is coming from: God is nearly falling out of heaven to reach out to Adam, who quite passively and perhaps even hesitantly positions his hand in God's general direction. The theology of this fresco is precisely on target: Our relationship with God—who is love—is God's initiative. In today's second reading, John reminds us of this dynamic. As we venture into this sixth week of Easter, take some time to reflect on and be thankful for all of the ways that God has shown love for you.

Acts 10:25–26, 34–35, 44–48
Psalm 98:1, 2–3, 3–4 (see 2b)
1 John 4:7–10
John 15:9–17

Monday MAY 3

• ST. PHILIP AND ST. JAMES, APOSTLES •

For I handed on to you as of first importance what I also received: that Christ died for our sins in accordance with the Scriptures.
—1 CORINTHIANS 15:3

From time to time, after I've given a presentation, someone will ask me if they can "steal" some of the concepts and approaches I included in my talk. I typically tell them that they will not be stealing anything since I'm simply handing on what I received from others. This is precisely what St. Paul is saying to the Corinthians in today's first reading; that he is passing along the Christian Creed that he himself received from the apostles. We do not own faith. We receive it and share it with others. As we celebrate the feast of Saints Philip and James today—two of the apostles—may we pause to remember and give thanks for those from whom we received our faith.

1 Corinthians 15:1–8
Psalm 19:2–3, 4–5
John 14:6–14

Tuesday MAY 4

About midnight, while Paul and Silas were praying and singing hymns to God as the prisoners listened, there was suddenly such a severe earthquake that the foundations of the jail shook.
—ACTS 16:25–26

I'm not sure which of the following is more awe-inspiring: that an earthquake shook the prison so hard that the doors flew open and chains were broken or that Paul and Silas, after being stripped, flogged, and chained in their prison cell, passed the time by praying and singing hymns! This account challenges us to consider how we ourselves respond to situations of despair and suffering. Many people who are incarcerated turn to prayer because they feel that they have exhausted all of their own resources and God is their only hope. We do well to embrace this realization any time we face hardship: It is God alone who sustains us. Such faith can rock the foundations of the despair that often imprisons us.

Acts 16:22–34
Psalm 138:1–2ab, 2cde–3, 7c–8
John 16:5–11

Wednesday MAY 5

Then Paul stood up in the Areopagus and said: "You Athenians, I see that in every respect you are very religious."
—ACTS 17:22

St. Pope John Paul II famously referred to social media as the "new Areopagus," referring to the cultural center or gathering place of the learned where St. Paul preached the gospel in Athens. In today's world, we are called to enter into the new Areopagus and use every tool at our fingertips to proclaim the Good News of Jesus effectively to the world. This can be done without being preachy. Consider how, on social media, you can simply post photos and or make references to grace-filled experiences you've had at home, work, or play; at your parish; or through inspirational resources such as books and videos. During this sixth week of Easter, may we take inspiration from St. Paul who courageously ventured into the cultural center of his world to proclaim the Good News to any who would listen.

Acts 17:15, 22—18:1
Psalm 148:1–2, 11–12, 13, 14
John 16:12–15

Thursday

MAY 6

• THE ASCENSION OF THE LORD •

While they were looking intently at the sky as he was going, suddenly two men dressed in white garments stood beside them. They said, "Men of Galilee, why are you standing there looking at the sky?"

—ACTS 1:10–11

A friend related how once, at a wedding reception, a helium balloon had drifted up to the ceiling, catching the attention of a crowd that soon gathered, looking up at the ceiling and strategizing how to retrieve it. He rightly noted that, with their attention fixed on the wayward balloon, they were distracted from the celebration taking place around them! Similarly, after Jesus ascended, two angels appeared and admonished the apostles for staring at the sky. Like them, we are not to stand around idly thinking of heaven lest we miss the celebration of the Holy Spirit in our midst, who invites us to roll up our sleeves and work together to renew the face of the earth.

Acts 1:1–11
Psalm 47:2–3, 6–7, 8–9 (6)
Ephesians 4:1–13 or 4:1–7, 11–13 or 1:17–23
Mark 16:15–20

Friday MAY 7

When a woman is in labor, she is in anguish because her hour has arrived; but when she has given birth to a child, she no longer remembers the pain because of her joy that a child has been born into the world.

—JOHN 16:21

To me, the greatest proof of the existence of God is the fact that women, after enduring hours of painful labor while giving birth, are willing to repeat the experience! As described in today's Gospel, somehow women no longer remember the pain because of the joy of new life. Jesus uses this image to reassure us at those times when find ourselves weeping and mourning at injustices while the rest of the world seems to be obliviously rejoicing. Jesus assures us that our sorrow will be turned to joy. May this Easter season strengthen our resolve to look beyond the pain of our struggles and continue to work against injustice and oppression.

Acts 18:9–18
Psalm 47:2–3, 4–5, 6–7
John 16:20–23

Saturday MAY 8

He [Apollos] began to speak boldly in the synagogue; but when Priscilla and Aquila heard him, they took him aside and explained to him the Way of God more accurately.
—ACTS 18:26

Today, because of social media, it is quite common to see people (including Christians) publicly and even uncivilly disagreeing with one another on a wide range of topics. It would seem that, to a great extent, the art of disagreeing discreetly has been lost. In today's first reading, we see a good example of discretion by Priscilla and Aquila who, we are told, corrected Apollos by taking him aside and providing him a more accurate understanding of the Way of God than the one he had been preaching. Their discretion can serve as a model for each of us to settle disagreements and correct others outside of the limelight, avoiding the temptation to publicly shame others or to pridefully display our own perceived superiority.

Acts 18:23–28
Psalm 47:2–3, 8–9, 10
John 16:23b–28

[Jesus said] "I do not ask that you take them out of the world but that you keep them from the evil one. They do not belong to the world any more than I belong to the world."
—JOHN 17:15–16

The world can sometimes be so frightening and confusing that we can be tempted to withdraw from it. And while retreating a safe distance in order to maintain our sanity and perspective is a good thing, we are not called to withdraw from the world. Rather, Jesus sends us out into the world, reminding us that we do not belong to it. In other words, as followers of Jesus, we are called to avoid conforming to worldly values. Dr. Martin Luther King Jr. went as far as to say that we are called to be maladjusted to anything that Jesus would oppose. Pray today for the grace to be maladjusted to anything that is contrary to the Good News of Jesus.

Acts 1:15–17, 20a, 20c–26
Psalm 103:1–2, 11–12, 19–20 (19a)
1 John 4:11–16
John 17:11b–19

Monday

May 10

• St. Damien Joseph de Veuster of Moloka'i, Priest •

And when Paul laid his hands on them,
the Holy Spirit came upon them.
—Acts 19:6

Children innately understand that certain realities or qualities can be transferred by touch, which is why they play games such as It or Tag. Throughout Scripture, touch is used to transfer power and authority from one person to another, such as in today's first reading when Paul laid hands on people to transfer the power of the Holy Spirit. While the sacramental action of laying on of hands is reserved for ordained ministers, it can serve as a reminder to all of us that the Holy Spirit who dwells within us can and should be transferred to all those whom we bump into in our daily lives. Ask the Holy Spirit for the grace you need this day to touch people's hearts and minds with the transforming love of Christ so that it rubs off on them.

Acts 19:1–8
Psalm 68:2–3ab, 4–5acd, 6–7ab
John 16:29–33

Tuesday

May 11

[Jesus said] "Now this is eternal life, that they should know you, the only true God, and the one whom you sent, Jesus Christ."
—JOHN 17:3

The concept of eternal life often seems beyond our ability to grasp. And yet, in today's Gospel, Jesus offers us a simple description of eternal life: to know God and to know Jesus. It helps us to remember that in Hebrew, to know someone was to have a deep, personal, and even intimate relationship with them. When we reach intimacy with another person, it can be as if time stands still. To truly know God is to enter into *Kairos*, or God's time, which is eternal. We come to know God not by memorizing facts about God but through prayer, discernment of God's will, the sacraments (especially the Eucharist), and love of neighbor. May you taste eternal life today and every day of your life.

Acts 20:17–27
Psalm 68:10–11, 20–21
John 17:1–11a

Wednesday MAY 12

• ST. NEREUS AND ST. ACHILLEUS, MARTYRS * ST. PANCRAS, MARTYR •

Keep in mind the words of the Lord Jesus who himself said, "It is more blessed to give than to receive."
—ACTS 20:35

These words of Jesus are some of his only words that do not appear in any of the four Gospels, and yet we can trust that they were from the lips of Jesus because of the source: St. Paul. Paul spent years learning from the other apostles about the teachings and actions of Jesus, and he no doubt was taught this phrase—that giving is more blessed than receiving—by someone who walked with Jesus. This phrase epitomizes Jesus's philosophy of life, which was driven by selfless love. As you proceed through your day today, you will be asked to give of yourself to many people in many ways. Rather than resenting these requests, be sure to thank God for the blessing of the opportunity to give rather than receive.

Acts 20:28–38
Psalm 68:29–30, 33–35a, 35bc–36ab
John 17:11b–19

• OUR LADY OF FATIMA •

Keep me, O God, for in you I take refuge;
I say to the LORD, "My Lord are you."
O LORD, my allotted portion and my cup,
you it is who hold fast my lot.
—PSALM 16:1–2A AND 5

In a popular TED talk, "Why Good Leaders Make You Feel Safe," management theorist Simon Sinek emphasizes that when people feel secure and within a circle of trust, remarkable things can happen. In today's responsorial, we proclaim that God is our refuge who keeps us safe from the dangers of sin, despair, anxiety, hatred, and fear. How appropriate to pray these words on this Feast of Our Lady of Fatima, who promised Lucia, "My Immaculate Heart will be your refuge and the way that will lead you to God." Today, like any other day, you will face challenges. How wonderful to know that you can take refuge—find safety—in our loving God!

Acts 22:30; 23:6–11
Psalm 16:1–2a and 5, 7–8, 9–10, 11
John 17:20–26

Friday MAY 14

• ST. MATTHIAS, APOSTLE •

So they proposed two, Joseph called Barsabbas, who was also known as Justus, and Matthias. . . . Then they gave lots to them, and the lot fell upon Matthias, and he was counted with the Eleven Apostles.

—ACTS 1:23, 26

When the apostles gathered to select a replacement for Judas, they seemingly left this major decision to chance by casting lots between two qualified candidates. In reality, this was a sign of complete trust in the Holy Spirit and an example of decision-making by consensus. In a majority vote, there are winners and losers. In consensus, the final decision is one that everybody can live with. Clearly there are times when we feel compelled to take sides on an issue. Striving for consensus, however, requires active listening to different perspectives, searching for common ground, and fostering collaboration. Let us pray for the grace we need to build consensus in our homes, communities, and workplaces.

Acts 1:15–17, 20–26
Psalm 113:1–2, 3–4, 5–6, 7–8
John 15:9–17

There are also many other things that Jesus did, but if these were to be described individually, I do not think the whole world would contain the books that would be written.
—JOHN 21:25

John's Gospel ends with this peculiar disclaimer that the story of Jesus does not really end here at all but rather continues on. The glorious thing about Jesus is that he cannot be contained within the parameters of a book, or within the parameters of anything, for that matter! Jesus Christ transcends all of reality, which, rather than confounding us, should reassure us that no matter where we go or what we experience, we will encounter the Risen Christ there. No book can contain all that Jesus did because he has done and continues to do wonderful things for his people throughout the ages. Keep your eyes open for the great things that Jesus is doing and will do for you today!

Acts 28:16–20, 30–31
Psalm 11:4, 5 and 7
John 21:20–25

Sunday

MAY 16

• PENTECOST SUNDAY •

And they were all filled with the Holy Spirit and began to speak in different tongues, as the Spirit enabled them to proclaim.
—ACTS 2:4

Why have TED talks been so successful? In short, it's because they connect with people. The inclusion of stories, a conversational approach, the credibility of the speaker, the building of rapport, and the authenticity and relatability of the content all serve to enhance the connection between speaker and audience. Pentecost is about connectivity—something that is desperately needed in a polarized world. To be Spirit-filled is not to be right or correct but rather to be connected to God and to others. May the Spirit enable each one of us to express ourselves in ways that connect with others and build bridges so that the fruit of the Holy Spirit will set the world on fire.

VIGIL:
Genesis 11:1–9 or Exodus 19:3–8a, 16–20b
or Ezekiel 37:1–4 or Joel 3:1–5
Psalm 104:1–2, 24, 35, 27–28, 29, 30
Romans 8:22–27
John 7:37–39

DAY:
Acts 2:1–11
Psalm 104:1, 24, 29–30, 31, 34
1 Corinthians 12:3b–7, 12–13 or Galatians 5:16–25
John 20:19–23 or 15:26–27; 16:12–15

Monday
MAY 17

• MEMORIAL OF THE BLESSED VIRGIN MARY, MOTHER OF THE CHURCH •

All these devoted themselves with one accord to prayer,
together with some women,
and Mary the mother of Jesus, and his brothers.
—ACTS 1:14

After Jesus departed from their sight, the disciples gathered together in prayer. Among them was Mary, quietly present in the heart of the community, steady in faith and attentive to the movement of the Holy Spirit. In the uncertainty of those days, her presence must have been a comfort to the disciples. As Mother of the Church, Mary continues to walk with us in much the same way, accompanying us with gentle care as we seek to follow Christ in our own lives. There are moments when, like the early disciples, we find ourselves waiting for clarity, healing, direction, peace. We may not always know what comes next but we can remain rooted in prayer and open to God's grace. Today, ask Mary to intercede for the Church and for your own heart, that you may grow in patience, trust, and courage.

Genesis 3:9–15, 20 or Acts 1:12–14
Psalm 87:1–2, 3 and 5, 6–7
John 19:25–34

Tuesday MAY 18

• ST. JOHN I, POPE AND MARTYR •

But they remained silent. They had been discussing among themselves on the way who was the greatest.
—MARK 9:34

Tooting your own horn used to be frowned upon. In ancient Greece, it was the job of the mythological goddess Nemesis to dole out retribution to humans who got a bit too arrogant before the gods. In many cultures, initiation rites are used to socialize the individual and lead him or her to take on a collective identity rather than an individual one. In today's Gospel, Jesus reminds the apostles and us that in his kingdom, self-promotion is frowned upon! Humility, on the other hand, is liberating: It enables us to create space for others—and God. Gratitude is the first step to creating this space since it compels us to recognize that God, not ourselves, is the source of all of the blessings in our lives. Let us give thanks to the Lord our God!

Sirach 2:1–11
Psalm 37:3–4, 18–19, 27–28, 39–40
Mark 9:30–37

Wednesday
MAY 19

Wisdom breathes life into her children
and admonishes those who seek her.
He who loves her loves life;
those who seek her will be embraced by the Lord.
—SIRACH 4:11–12

Wisdom is the ability to see life from God's perspective. We all know wise people who lead us to feel that talking with and listening to them is like spending some time with God. It's not that they have all the answers and solutions to life's problems, but that they seem to know how to approach them in a healthier, more positive manner. How does one get that way? Well, it makes sense that if we want to think and see as God does, we read Scripture and spend time in prayer. On this Wednesday of the seventh week in Ordinary Time, pray for the grace to see life from God's perspective and strive to share your wisdom, especially with those whose perspective has been damaged by loss, fear, anxiety, or despair.

Sirach 4:11–19
Psalm 119:165, 168, 171, 172, 174, 175
Mark 9:38–40

Thursday MAY 20

• ST. BERNARDINE OF SIENA, PRIEST •

[Jesus replied] "Salt is good, but if salt becomes insipid, with what will you restore its flavor?"
—MARK 9:50

I'm stating the obvious here, but it's important to note that saltiness is salt's defining characteristic and is crucial to its identity. If salt cannot add saltiness to a dish, it is useless. Similarly, as followers of Christ, we are called to have a distinct identity—a *flavor*, so to speak. We are called to add the flavors of hope, joy, compassion, and justice to the world. These and other defining characteristics of followers of Christ provide us with a distinct identity. Each and every day, we are called to add gospel flavors to our encounters with others and to the world in general. Salt and other minerals and spices enhance and bring to life otherwise bland foods. Who is salt in your life? How can you be salt for others today?

Sirach 5:1–8
Psalm 1:1–2, 3, 4 and 6
Mark 9:41–50

Friday
MAY 21

• ST. CHRISTOPHER MAGALLANES, PRIEST, AND COMPANIONS, MARTYRS •

A faithful friend is a sturdy shelter;
he who finds one finds a treasure.
A faithful friend is beyond price,
no sum can balance his worth.
A faithful friend is a life-saving remedy.
—SIRACH 6:14–16

Of the many features that Facebook offers, one is a notification of your "friendiversary," a message that reminds you of the date that you and someone else became Facebook friends so you can celebrate the relationship. One of the best ways to keep a relationship healthy is to celebrate it. A good way to do this is to establish relationship rituals, which are recurring, intentional shared actions and experiences that friends perform to strengthen their bond, foster a deeper connection, and reinforce positive emotions. Which of your friends do you consider a *treasure* or a *remedy*? Cherish and celebrate those friendships and strive to be a treasure and a remedy for others.

Sirach 6:5–17
Psalm 119:12, 16, 18, 27, 34, 35
Mark 10:1–12

Saturday MAY 22

• ST. RITA OF CASCIA, RELIGIOUS •

When Jesus saw this he became indignant and said to them, "Let the children come to me; do not prevent them, for the Kingdom of God belongs to such as these. Amen, I say to you, whoever does not accept the Kingdom of God like a child will not enter it."
—MARK 10:14–15

One of the most obvious characteristics of children is their dependency on others. For as much as children exert their autonomy, they ultimately rely on adults—parents, teachers, coaches, authority figures—to help them navigate through life as they grow. When Jesus teaches us to be childlike, he is helping us remember that we are not self-sufficient. We are not lords of our own kingdom. Rather, we are fully dependent on God, who reigns over his kingdom with love, compassion, mercy, and forgiveness. What a gift it is to know that we are not left alone to navigate through this world. Today and every day, depend on God as a child depends on a loving parent.

Sirach 17:1–15
Psalm 103:13–14, 15–16, 17–18
Mark 10:13–16

Sunday MAY 23

• THE MOST HOLY TRINITY •

Then Jesus approached and said to them, . . . "Go, therefore, and make disciples of all nations, baptizing them in the name of the Father, and of the Son, and of the Holy Spirit."
—MATTHEW 28:19

Each of us is made in the image and likeness of God, and God has revealed himself to us as Father, Son, and Holy Spirit. This means that we are made in the image of a Trinitarian God—a community of Persons whose love is so intimate that they are One. God's essence, then, is relational. Today's celebration of the Most Holy Trinity is not a day to try to solve the mystery of the Trinity, but rather a day to remember that we are called to live and love in relationship with others. We most resemble God when we live in good relationship with our neighbor. Today is a day to celebrate your relationships, to build new ones, and to repair broken ones.

Deuteronomy 4:32–34, 39–40
Psalm 33:4–5, 6, 9, 18–19, 20, 22 (12b)
Romans 8:14–17
Matthew 28:16–20

Monday MAY 24

Jesus looked around and said to his disciples, "How hard it is for those who have wealth to enter the Kingdom of God!"
—MARK 10:23

Jesus never said that wealth is evil. He did, however, warn that it is dangerous. The danger of wealth is that it is a mirage that fools us into thinking we are capable of sustaining ourselves at our deepest level. We are not. We need God to sustain us. Unfortunately, we are too often incapable of recognizing the difference between the mirage of wealth and the sustaining grace of God. It's okay to have wealth, but when we convince ourselves that our wealth, possessions, and status define and sustain us, we are essentially drinking the sand, mistaking it for living waters. Whatever your economic status, commit to sharing generously with others, recognizing that all of us are simply stewards of the treasures that have come our way.

Sirach 17:20–24
Psalm 32:1–2, 5, 6, 7
Mark 10:17–27

Tuesday MAY 25

• ST. BEDE THE VENERABLE, PRIEST AND DOCTOR OF THE CHURCH • ST. GREGORY VII, POPE • ST. MARY MAGDALENE DE' PAZZI, VIRGIN •

With each contribution show a cheerful countenance,
and pay your tithes in a spirit of joy.
Give to the Most High as he has given to you,
generously, according to your means.
—SIRACH 35:11–12

We tend to think of generosity as an occasional act of kindness expressed monetarily: We send a check to a charity, drop an envelope in the church basket, purchase Girl Scout cookies, put some money in the Salvation Army kettle, and so on. These are generous acts that tend to make us feel better about ourselves. Generosity, however, is much more than an action, and it does not always involve money. It is not a feeling that comes and goes. True generosity is a permanent disposition: an attitude and a way of proceeding. Generosity is one of God's primary attributes. As people made in God's image and likeness, we resemble God when we practice a generous spirit.

Sirach 35:1–12
Psalm 50:5–6, 7–8, 14 and 23
Mark 10:28–31

Wednesday MAY 26

• ST. PHILIP NERI, PRIEST •

[Jesus said] "Whoever wishes to be great among you will be your servant; whoever wishes to be first among you will be the slave of all."
—MARK 10:43–44

People's accents give them away. Quite often we can tell what part of town, what part of the country, or what part of the world someone is from because of the way they talk. Similarly, people should be able to identify those who reside in the kingdom of God, not so much by the way they talk, but by their actions. Citizens of God's kingdom have unusual habits that go against the norm. In today's Gospel, Jesus teaches us one of those habits: serving others in order to achieve greatness. To serve the needs of others is to put their needs before our own. We don't normally think of that as greatness, yet this selfless love is what Jesus calls us to strive for.

Sirach 36:1, 4–5a, 10–17
Psalm 79:8, 9, 11 and 13
Mark 10:32–45

Thursday MAY 27

• ST. AUGUSTINE OF CANTERBURY •

On hearing that it was Jesus of Nazareth, he began to cry out and say, "Jesus, son of David, have pity on me!"
—MARK 10:47

Author Anne Lamott suggests that the following three words are the basis of a healthy prayer life: *help*, *thanks*, and *wow*. Today's Gospel is an example of the power of asking for *help*. To pray for help from our Lord is to acknowledge that we ourselves are powerless and that we are dependent on God's grace to sustain and heal us. Such a prayer opens us up to God's amazing grace. Too often we think that our prayers must sound like poetry when, in truth, asking God for help is one of the most powerful prayers available to us. It may not be fancy, but it's honest and authentic. As we call to God for help, let us remember that even our plea for help is a response to God's invitation to draw near to him.

Sirach 42:15–25
Psalm 33:2–3, 4–5, 6–7, 8–9
Mark 10:46–52

They came to Jerusalem, and on entering the temple area he began to drive out those selling and buying there. He overturned the tables of the money changers and the seats of those who were selling doves.

—MARK 11:15

The account of Jesus cleansing the temple is not about Jesus's anger over greedy and unscrupulous merchants. These merchants were performing a necessary service for temple worship: providing animals for sacrificial worship. Jesus was not angry over excessive fees or dishonest practices. He was demonstrating the end of an entire form of worship that involved animal sacrifice and replacing it with the sacrifice of his own body and blood on the cross. Today's Gospel invites us to reflect on genuine worship as a call to holiness that is not achieved by sacrificing animals but by uniting the sacrifice of our lives to the sacrifice of Jesus on the cross.

Sirach 44:1, 9–13
Psalm 149:1b–2, 3–4, 5–6a and 9b
Mark 11:11–26

As he was walking in the temple area, the chief priests, the scribes, and the elders approached him and said to him, "By what authority are you doing these things?"
—MARK 11:27–28

It's not uncommon to hear one angry child say, "Oh yeah, says who?" when arguing with another child. Even from a young age, we question the authority of others, especially when we think the other person is our equal and is undeserving of claiming superiority. In today's Gospel, we encounter such a playground scuffle as the chief priests, scribes, and elders question Jesus's authority. Throughout Mark's Gospel, people have been asking about Jesus's identity and his source of power and authority. To those questions, we proudly profess in the Creed that Jesus is "God from God, Light from Light, true God from true God!" How wonderful it is for us to know that Jesus is no ordinary man but is truly God with us.

Sirach 51:12cd–20
Psalm 19:8, 9, 10, 11
Mark 11:27–33

Sunday MAY 30

• THE MOST HOLY BODY AND BLOOD OF CHRIST (CORPUS CHRISTI) •

Then he took a cup, gave thanks, and gave it to them,
and they all drank from it.
He said to them,
"This is the blood of my covenant,
which will be shed for many."
—MARK 14:23–24

For the Hebrew people, to share a cup was a sign of commitment and acceptance of a way of life. In the Seder meal, to drink from the four cups of wine is to proclaim that God alone saves us. On this Feast of the Most Holy Body and Blood of Christ, we embrace and partake of the *cup of salvation* that Jesus instituted at the Last Supper. To receive the Eucharist is not only the reception of salvation but is also a powerful expression of our commitment to God's saving plan for the world and our proclamation that, in and through Jesus Christ, we are saved.

Exodus 24:3–8
Psalm 116:12–13, 15–16, 17–18 (13)
Hebrews 9:11–15
Mark 14:12–16, 22–26

Monday MAY 31

• THE VISITATION OF THE BLESSED VIRGIN MARY •

[Elizabeth said] "For at the moment the sound of your greeting reached my ears, the infant in my womb leaped for joy."
—LUKE 1:44

When certain people enter a room or gathering, our reactions vary from "Oh good, so-and-so is here!" to "Oh no, so-and-so is here!" How about when we enter a room? Are people happy that we've arrived or dreading our appearance? We cannot control how people react to us; however, our goal should always be to imitate Mary, who carried the Divine Presence within herself and drew from that life to stir the life within the womb of her cousin Elizabeth. Mary's display of eagerness to be with her cousin during her time of need brought great joy to Elizabeth. May we do our best to let others know that we are eager to be with them, and may our presence, our words, and our actions stir life within those we encounter.

Zephaniah 3:14–18a or Romans 12:9–16
Isaiah 12:2–3, 4bcd, 5–6
Luke 1:39–56

Tuesday JUNE 1

• ST. JUSTIN, MARTYR •

So Jesus said to them, "Repay to Caesar what belongs to Caesar and to God what belongs to God."
—MARK 12:17

Jesus asked the Pharisees and Herodians to produce a coin and drew their attention to the *image* on it, no doubt alluding to Scripture's assertion that human beings are made in the image and likeness of God (Genesis 1:26–27). We are not made in the image of an emperor or earthly leader. We are made in the *Imago Dei*—the image of God. To the emperor, we owe taxes. To God, we owe our lives. The former we typically pay grudgingly. The latter, we respond to with gratitude. Jesus teaches us not to confuse the will of the state with the will of God. Reflect this day on what it means to give to God what is God's and how you can reflect the *Imago Dei* to those you encounter, especially to those in need.

Tobit 2:9–14
Psalm 112:1–2, 7–8, 9
Mark 12:13–17

Wednesday JUNE 2

• ST. MARCELLINUS AND ST. PETER, MARTYRS •

Your ways, O LORD, make known to me;
teach me your paths,
Guide me in your truth and teach me,
for you are God my savior.
—PSALM 25:4–5AB

The spirit of this psalm verse was captured poignantly in the movie *It's a Wonderful Life*, when George Bailey (played by Jimmy Stewart) prayed to God in desperation: "Show me the way!" At various times in our lives, we find ourselves at a crossroads, not knowing which way is the best for us to follow. At times like this, we pray to God to make his ways known to us. In addition to those moments of desperation, however, we can pray these words to God each day, asking him to show us the way, to guide us, and to teach us. And then, we need to listen and watch closely for the subtle but very real ways that God makes his will known to us.

Tobit 3:1–11a, 16–17a
Psalm 25:2–3, 4–5ab, 6 and 7bc, 8–9
Mark 12:18–27

Thursday

JUNE 3

• ST. CHARLES LWANGA AND COMPANIONS, MARTYRS •

One of the scribes came to Jesus and asked him,
"Which is the first of all the commandments?"
Jesus replied, "The first is this:
'Hear, O Israel!
The Lord our God is Lord alone!
You shall love the Lord your God with all your heart,
with all your soul,
with all your mind,
and with all your strength.
—MARK 12:28–31

While John's Gospel often portrays Jesus as quite verbose, the Gospel of Mark presents Jesus as very concise. Today's Gospel is a perfect example. In about fifty words, Jesus summarizes the Law and reveals to us that love of God and love of neighbor are inseparable. He also beautifully describes how we are to love God: with our whole heart, soul, mind, and strength. Ask God for the grace to love him fully and to express this through love of neighbor.

Tobit 6:10–11; 7:1bcde, 9–17; 8:4–9a
Psalm 128:1–2, 3, 4–5
Mark 12:28–34

Friday JUNE 4

• SOLEMNITY OF THE MOST SACRED HEART OF JESUS •

But when they came to Jesus and saw that he was already dead, they did not break his legs, but one soldier thrust his lance into his side, and immediately blood and water flowed out.
—JOHN 19:33–34

A well-known TV commercial asks, "What's in your wallet?" In a life of faith, we ask a different question: "What's in your heart?" We may not fully know what's in a person's heart, but it is revealed through their words and actions. Through his teachings, his miracles, his interactions with others, and especially through his suffering and death on the cross, Jesus reveals his heart to be filled with a selfless love. For this reason, we refer to Jesus's heart as Sacred. On this Feast of the Most Sacred Heart, may we be filled with this selfless love and reveal Jesus's Sacred Heart to those most in need of mercy and compassion.

Hosea 11:1, 3–4, 8c–9
Isaiah 12:2–3, 4, 5–6 (3)
Ephesians 3:8–12, 14–19
John 19:31–37

Saturday JUNE 5

• THE IMMACULATE HEART OF THE BLESSED VIRGIN MARY •

He went down with them and came to Nazareth, and was obedient to them; and his mother kept all these things in her heart.
—LUKE 2:51

To keep something in your heart is to hold onto something of deep significance, to cherish it, reflect upon it, and to allow it to be woven into your very being. Scripture tells us on several occasions that Mary kept experiences related to her son, Jesus, in her heart and that she pondered them. Today's Feast of the Immaculate Heart of Mary reminds us of the importance of interiority in the spiritual life. Like Mary, we need to ponder the mysteries of life, both joyful and sorrowful. As you go through this day, search your heart to see what you hold there and look to Mary as a model for trusting God to lead you through life's trials and challenges while celebrating life's joys.

Tobit 12:1, 5–15, 20
Tobit 13:2, 6efgh, 7, 8
Luke 2:41–51

Sunday JUNE 6

• TENTH SUNDAY IN ORDINARY TIME •

We look not to what is seen but to what is unseen; for what is seen is transitory, but what is unseen is eternal.
—2 CORINTHIANS 4:18

Each time we proclaim the Nicene Creed, we state our belief in invisible realities. We proclaim that God the Father is Creator of all things "visible and invisible." By shifting our attention from seen realities that are fleeting to unseen realities that are eternal, we become capable of living for a higher purpose and remaining resilient in the face of hardships. While it is good to live in the present moment, some of what we see can bring despair. And while we cannot see the future, we live in the confident hope that God's abundant and saving grace awaits us at every turn, not only in heaven but also in this life where God's kingdom is present with us, though not in its fullness.

Genesis 3:9–15
Psalm 130:1–2, 3–4, 5–6, 7–8 (7bc)
2 Corinthians 4:13—5:1
Mark 3:20–35

Monday

JUNE 7

Who encourages us in our every affliction, so that we may be able to encourage those who are in any affliction with the encouragement with which we ourselves are encouraged by God.
—2 CORINTHIANS 1:4

In today's first reading, St. Paul encourages the practice of *paying it forward*—the act of responding to one person's generosity, kindness, or largesse by treating another person in the same way. This makes perfect sense since we cannot possibly repay God, who is not in need. Instead, we show our love and gratitude to God by sharing love, compassion, and mercy with others. In this brief verse, St. Paul beautifully sums up the Law: Love God and love your neighbor, which, said another way, means that we show love for God by showing love for our neighbor. In gratitude for God's abundant graces, be sure today to pay it forward to those who need it most.

2 Corinthians 1:1–7
Psalm 34:2–3, 4–5, 6–7, 8–9
Matthew 5:1–12

Tuesday JUNE 8

For however many are the promises of God, their Yes is in him [Jesus]; therefore, the Amen from us also goes through him to God for glory.

—2 CORINTHIANS 1:20

One of the most effective ways of establishing trust is to keep one's promises. A broken promise results in broken trust. Our story of salvation history is replete with promises made by God to rescue and restore his people and to reassure them of his steadfast love. Thankfully, God kept his promise and sent his only Son, Jesus Christ, to save us from sin and to remain with us forever through the Holy Spirit and the sacraments of the church, especially the Eucharist. St Paul reminds the Corinthians, and us, that Jesus is the fulfillment of God's promises. We place our trust in God, knowing that through his Son we are rescued, restored, and reassured.

2 Corinthians 1:18–22
Psalm 119:129, 130, 131, 132, 133, 135
Matthew 5:13–16

Wednesday
JUNE 9

• ST. EPHREM DEACON AND DOCTOR OF THE CHURCH •

[Jesus said] "Do not think that I have come to abolish the law or the prophets. I have come not to abolish but to fulfill."
—MATTHEW 5:17

There is a tendency among some Christians to view the Old Testament as obsolete, as if it has been replaced by something and someone completely disconnected with the law and the prophets. In today's Gospel, Jesus makes it quite clear that he did not come to abolish the law and prophets, but rather to fulfill them. Throughout all of Scripture, the message remains the same: Love God with all your heart, soul, mind, and strength, and love your neighbor as yourself. What's *new* is that Jesus himself, through his death and resurrection, is the fulfillment of the law and the prophets. We live according to God's law when we love as Jesus loved: selflessly, generously, and indiscriminately.

2 Corinthians 3:4–11
Psalm 99:5, 6, 7, 8, 9
Matthew 5:17–19

Thursday
JUNE 10

For God who said, "Let light shine out of darkness," has shone in our hearts to bring to light the knowledge of the glory of God on the face of Jesus Christ.
—2 CORINTHIANS 4:6

The Jesuits are known for their motto *Ad Majorem Dei Gloriam* (often shortened to the acronym AMDG), which means "For the Greater Glory of God." This motto is a reminder that in all that we do and say, our goal is to bring glory not to ourselves but to God. One of the best examples of this was Mary, the Mother of God, who, though worthy of praise for her acceptance of God's will, chose not to call attention to herself, but rather to her son, Jesus. St. Paul reminds us today to reflect the light that God has shone in our hearts so that others may come to know his Son, Jesus, who is the Light of the world.

2 Corinthians 3:15—4:1, 3–6
Psalm 85:9ab and 10, 11–12, 13–14
Matthew 5:20–26

In those days a great number who believed turned toward the Lord.
The news about them reached the ears
of the Church in Jerusalem,
and they sent Barnabus to go to Antioch.
When he arrived and saw the grace of God,
he rejoiced and encouraged them all
to remain faithful to the Lord in firmness of heart.
—ACTS 11:22–23

Today, as we celebrate the Feast of St. Barnabas, we are told that he rejoiced to see evidence in Antioch of God's grace, no doubt in the form of mercy, compassion, forgiveness, justice, and charity. Marketing experts tell us that consumers need evidence that a product can deliver what it claims to offer. In the same way, people need evidence that a life of discipleship is a graced way to live. What evidence are you providing this day that God's grace is a blessing in your life?

Acts 11:21b–26; 13:1–3
Psalm 98:1, 2–3ab, 3cd–4, 5–6
Matthew 10:7–13

So we are ambassadors for Christ, as if
God were appealing through us. We implore you on behalf of
Christ, be reconciled to God.
—2 CORINTHIANS 5:20

To be an ambassador is to serve as a representative of a country or sovereign. Someone who sends an ambassador needs to be sure that this person will represent them faithfully. Most importantly, ambassadors are responsible for establishing relationships with other groups of people, often with adversaries. St. Paul reminds us that we are ambassadors for Christ! What a privilege, but also, what a responsibility! The first step, according to Paul, is to be reconciled with God, which means to be in a healthy relationship with him so that we can represent him well and build loving relationships with those we encounter—even with adversaries. Ask God for the grace you need to represent him well to all those you meet this day.

2 Corinthians 5:14–21
Psalm 103:1–2, 3–4, 9–10, 11–12
Matthew 5:33–37

Sunday

JUNE 13

• ELEVENTH SUNDAY IN ORDINARY TIME •

[Jesus said] "This is how it is with the kingdom of God; it is as if a man were to scatter seed on the land and would sleep and rise night and day and through it all the seed would sprout and grow, he knows not how."

—MARK 4:26–27

The first stages of plant life take place beneath the soil where we cannot see. In today's Gospel, Jesus tells us that this is how it is with the reign of God. Indeed, we often do not recognize God's handiwork within us until something new sprouts. The seeds of transformation that God plants within us often take root and begin to grow without our awareness. God is working quietly within you right now to bring about new life. What do you hope to see sprout as a result of God's movement within you? Pray for the grace to nurture this new life.

Ezekiel 17:22–24
Psalm 92:2–3, 13–14, 15–16
2 Corinthians 5:6–10
Mark 4:26–34

Monday
JUNE 14

[Jesus said] "But I say to you, offer no resistance to one who is evil. When someone strikes you on your right cheek, turn the other one to him as well."
—MATTHEW 5:39

Popular author and podcaster Mel Robbins recommends not letting others get inside your head lest the prolonged resentment and conflict take a toll on you. This is what Jesus is after when he talks about turning the other cheek. It is not about letting others walk all over you but about refusing to engage in their destructive activity. In other words, not every conflict requires a response from us. To turn the other cheek is in essence to refuse to engage on their terms. The bottom line is, we spend way too much energy trying to change others when we can only control our own thoughts, words, and actions. Ask God for the grace to *rise above it*.

2 Corinthians 6:1–10
Psalm 98:1, 2b, 3ab, 3cd–4
Matthew 5:38–42

Tuesday

JUNE 15

[Jesus said] "But I say to you, love your enemies, and pray for those who persecute you, that you may be children of your heavenly Father, for he makes his sun rise on the bad and the good, and causes rain to fall on the just and the unjust."
—MATTHEW 5:44–45

Oh, how we long for the sun to rise only on the good! We would like to see bad things happen to bad people. But that's not the way it works. In today's Gospel, Jesus reminds us that there are rarely clear-cut lines between the *good* and the *bad* and that our God is God of all. Perhaps if we looked at our enemies and persecutors through God's eyes, we would see differently and learn to love even those who are most difficult to love. Pray today for the grace to see others as God sees them.

2 Corinthians 8:1–9
Psalm 146:2, 5–6ab, 6c–7, 8–9a
Matthew 5:43–48

Wednesday

JUNE 16

Whoever sows sparingly will also reap sparingly, and whoever sows bountifully will also reap bountifully. Each must do as already determined, without sadness or compulsion, for God loves a cheerful giver.

—2 CORINTHIANS 9:6–7

Almost all of the quotes that are attributed to Jesus come from the Gospels. One quote, however, appears only in the Acts of the Apostles (20:35). There, St. Paul attributes the following phrase to Jesus: "It is more blessed to give than to receive." Paul must have had this teaching of Jesus in mind when he wrote to the Corinthians and encouraged them to give *cheerfully*. Every day is an opportunity for us to be cheerful givers. As your day unfolds, reflect on how you can cheerfully give of your time, your talents, and your treasures, especially to those in need. And give thanks for those who cheerfully give of themselves to you!

2 Corinthians 9:6–11
Psalm 112:1bc–2, 3–4, 9
Matthew 6:1–6, 16–18

Thursday

JUNE 17

[Jesus said] "In praying, do not babble like the pagans, who think that they will be heard because of their many words. Do not be like them. Your Father knows what you need before you ask him."
—MATTHEW 6:7

A dad once listened as his daughter said her bedtime prayers. He heard her reciting the alphabet and asked, "Honey, why are you saying your ABC's instead of your prayers?" The daughter responded, "I couldn't think of the words to pray with, and since God knows what's in my heart, I just gave him the letters so he could arrange them into words." Forming words for prayer is for our own benefit since it helps us to clarify our thoughts and feelings. But don't get too hung up on words. God knows what you need. The important thing is to bring your heart and mind to God.

2 Corinthians 11:1–11
Psalm 111:1b–2, 3–4, 7–8
Matthew 6:7–15

Friday
JUNE 18

[Jesus said] "Do not store up for yourselves treasures on earth, where moth and decay destroy, and thieves break in and steal. But store up treasures in heaven, where neither moth nor decay destroys, nor thieves break in and steal."
—MATTHEW 6:19–20

To *treasure* something is to attach great value to it and make it a priority in our lives. In a sense, to treasure something is to give our heart to it. Jesus warns us today about treasuring or giving our heart to that which has little lasting value and instead to find value in *heavenly treasures* such as love, charity, compassion, mercy, friendship, hope, faith, and joy. Each day, upon awakening, ask God to detach your heart from fleeting earthly treasures and instead attach it to heavenly treasures that will last an eternity.

2 Corinthians 11:18, 21–30
Psalm 34:2–3, 4–5, 6–7
Matthew 6:19–23

Saturday
JUNE 19

• ST. ROMUALD, ABBOT •

Three times I begged the Lord about this, that it might leave me, but he said to me, "My grace is sufficient for you, for power is made perfect in weakness."
—2 CORINTHIANS 12:8–9

People who lose their homes and possessions as a result of fire, tornado, hurricane, or flood often express a deep-down gladness just to be alive. This is a recognition of God's grace, which alone truly sustains us. St. Paul came to this realization in the midst of many sufferings and hardships that led him to recognize that the only thing that really sustained him was the grace of God and that it is through weakness, loss, and brokenness that we come to find this strength. St. Ignatius of Loyola expressed this same sentiment in his *Suscipe* prayer that ends with the words, "Give me only your love and your grace, that is enough for me." May this be your prayer today and every day.

2 Corinthians 12:1–10
Psalm 34:8–9, 10–11, 12–13
Matthew 6:24–34

Sunday JUNE 20

• TWELFTH SUNDAY IN ORDINARY TIME •

So whoever is in Christ is a new creation: the old things have passed away; behold, new things have come.
—2 CORINTHIANS 5:17

One of the simple pleasures of life is hopping into a newly purchased automobile and taking in the *new car smell*—an aromatic reminder of newness that replaces the stale smell of an old car. Newness is refreshing. It speaks of beginnings and possibilities. Newness is filled with hope. Newness is at the heart of Christianity because of the Resurrection: Jesus himself is filled with new life after experiencing death. When we encounter Christ and enter into his Paschal mystery through baptism, we experience that newness and the hope and possibilities that come with new life. Each day is an opportunity to renew our baptism and to let go of what is old and stale and replace it with a newness that never grows old.

Job 38:1, 8–11
Psalm 107:23–24, 25–26, 28–29, 30–31 (1b)
2 Corinthians 5:14–17
Mark 4:35–41

Monday

JUNE 21

• ST. ALOYSIUS GONZAGA, RELIGIOUS •

[Jesus said] "You hypocrite, remove the wooden beam from your eye first; then you will see clearly to remove the splinter from your brother's eye."
—MATTHEW 7:5

We waste too much time and energy being concerned with other people whom we cannot change instead of focusing on the only person we can change: ourselves. It is easy to go about criticizing others, and it can even make us feel good to tear them down. Jesus, however, reminds us that we should be less concerned with the faults of others and more concerned with our own faults. The Daily Examen taught by St. Ignatius of Loyola is an excellent tool to help us review our day to see our own shortcomings more clearly. Take fifteen minutes at the end of your day to review your own thoughts, words, and actions, and devote your time and energy to working on what you can change: yourself.

Genesis 12:1–9
Psalm 33:12–13, 18–19, 20 and 22
Matthew 7:1–5

Tuesday
JUNE 22

• ST. PAULINUS OF NOLA, BISHOP * ST. JOHN FISHER, BISHOP AND MARTYR, AND ST. THOMAS MORE, MARTYR •

[Jesus said] "Do to others whatever you would have them do to you. This is the Law and the Prophets."
—MATTHEW 7:12

If you're like most people, you want to be treated fairly. You want others to think well of you, to respect you, to treat you in a dignified manner. You want others to be friendly toward you and to give you the time of day. You want others to avoid cruelty and impatience in their dealings with you. The list goes on. The bottom line is, Jesus wants you to think of others as *another you*—an extension of yourself. If we approach others as completely other, we can too easily treat them differently than we ourselves wish to be treated. Instead, we are called to live in solidarity with others, knowing that we share a common bond as children of God created in his image and likeness.

Genesis 13:2, 5–18
Psalm 15:2–3a, 3bc–4ab, 5
Matthew 7:6, 12–14

Wednesday

JUNE 23

[Jesus said] "A good tree cannot bear bad fruit, nor can a rotten tree bear good fruit. Every tree that does not bear good fruit will be cut down and thrown into the fire. So by their fruits you will know them."

—MATTHEW 7:18–20

Each day, we have an opportunity to *bear fruit*: to let others know who we are and what we believe in through our words and actions. Jesus speaks of this as bearing good fruit. Our Christian tradition speaks of the fruit of the Holy Spirit: "love, joy, peace, patience, kindness, generosity, faithfulness, gentleness, self-control" (Galatians 5:22–23). Throughout our day, we have the opportunity to bear fruit so that each person we encounter might come to recognize the presence of the Holy Spirit within us and seek the Spirit's inspiration in their own life. We do well to remind ourselves that faith is *caught* rather than *taught*.

Genesis 15:1–12, 17–18
Psalm 105:1–2, 3–4, 6–7, 8–9
Matthew 7:15–20

Thursday

JUNE 24

• THE NATIVITY OF ST. JOHN THE BAPTIST •

[The angel of the Lord said] "He will go before him in the spirit and power of Elijah to turn the hearts of fathers toward children and the disobedient to the understanding of the righteous, to prepare a people fit for the Lord."

—LUKE 1:16–17

Farmers and gardeners know that in order for seeds to grow, the soil must be prepared. Tilling the soil predisposes it to accept the seed so that it can be nurtured and grow to maturity. Each of us, likewise, must be predisposed to hear and embrace the Word of God. John the Baptist did just this, preparing people to receive the Good News of Jesus. Just as soil needs to be tilled every spring, we too need to be predisposed repeatedly throughout life lest our hearts become hardened. Today is another opportunity to open yourself up to the Lord. May we each do all we can to be predisposed to embracing the gospel.

VIGIL:
Jeremiah 1:4–10
Psalm 71:1–2, 3–4a, 5–6ab, 15ab and 17
1 Peter 1:8–12
Luke 1:5–17

DAY:
Isaiah 49:1–6
Psalm 139:1b–3, 13–14ab, 14c–15
Acts 13:22–26
Luke 1:57–66, 80

Friday

JUNE 25

And then a leper approached, did him homage, and said, "Lord, if you wish, you can make me clean." He stretched out his hand, touched him, and said, "I will do it. Be made clean."
—MATTHEW 8:2–3

In the Lord's Prayer, we pray the words, "Thy will be done." These are beautiful words; however, how do we know what God's will is? It is important to remind ourselves that God never wills for us to experience evil for the purpose of having something good come out of it. God's will is always for us to prosper. The reality of sin that allowed evil to enter our world often hinders us from realizing God's plan. Like the man in today's Gospel suffering from leprosy, we approach God knowing that God's will is for our betterment, whether physically, spiritually, or both, and that he will indeed stretch out his hand to bring healing to our lives.

Genesis 17:1, 9–10, 15–22
Psalm 128:1–2, 3, 4–5
Matthew 8:1–4

The centurion said in reply, "Lord, I am not worthy to have you enter under my roof; only say the word and my servant will be healed."
—MATTHEW 8:8

When was the last time you heard anyone say, in all sincerity, "I am not worthy?" It's not in vogue to show such humility. On the contrary, it is more common to claim that we are quite worthy, thank you! We tend to think of humility as a sign of weakness in a world that adores strength. In today's Gospel, the centurion shows great humility in telling Jesus that he is unworthy for Jesus to even enter under his roof. His deep humility and trust in Jesus open the floodgates for Jesus's healing mercy. May the centurion's words, which we paraphrase before coming forward for Holy Communion at Mass, be always in our hearts and on our lips.

Genesis 18:1–15
Luke 1:46–47, 48–49, 50 and 53, 54–55
Matthew 8:5–17

Sunday
JUNE 27

• THIRTEENTH SUNDAY IN ORDINARY TIME •

He took the child by the hand and said to her, "Talitha koum," *which means, "Little girl, I say to you, arise!" The girl, a child of twelve, arose immediately and walked around.*

—MARK 5:41–42

Jesus was not a show-off. He did not perform miracles to draw attention to himself but rather to reveal God's saving and healing power. Among Jesus's most impressive miracles are the times that he raised people from the dead. God alone possesses the power of life. Jesus not only reveals God's power, but he also reveals God's love and affection as he addresses the young lady as *Talitha*—a term of endearment that a parent would use for their little girl. As you approach Jesus in prayer this day and every day, know that he approaches you with deep affection and with the power to restore you to life when the effects of sin have drained life from within you.

Wisdom 1:13–15; 2:23–24
Psalm 30:2, 4, 5–6, 11, 12, 13 (2a)
2 Corinthians 8:7, 9, 13–15
Mark 5:21–43 or, for shorter form, Mark 5:21–24, 35b–43

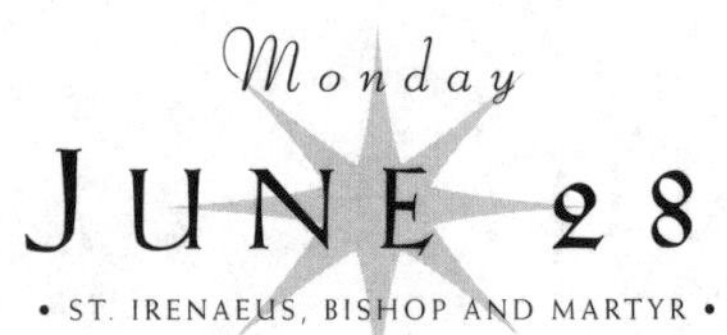

Monday

JUNE 28

• ST. IRENAEUS, BISHOP AND MARTYR •

Merciful and gracious is the LORD,
slow to anger and abounding in kindness.
—PSALM 103:8

It is not uncommon for people to think that God acted differently in the Old Testament than he did in the New Testament. In fact, sometimes people refer to the *God of the Old Testament* as an angry deity and the *God of the New Testament* as a loving and compassionate deity, as if there were two separate gods. While it's true that God's wrath is revealed in the Old Testament, it is never meted out randomly or impulsively but rather as the consequence of rejecting God's loving will. It makes sense, then, to turn to God's own children, the Jewish people, for their impression of the Father. Today's responsorial reveals that, without hesitation, God's children viewed their Father as slow to anger and abounding in kindness. We can approach our God without fear, knowing that he is merciful and gracious.

Genesis 18:16–33
Psalm 103:1b–2, 3–4, 8–9, 10–11
Matthew 8:18–22

Tuesday JUNE 29

• SAINS PETER AND PAUL, APOSTLES •

He said to them, "But who do you say that I am?" Simon Peter said in reply, "You are the Christ, the Son of the living God." Jesus said to him in reply, "Blessed are you, Simon son of Jonah."

—MATTHEW 16:15–17

In the Gospels, when Peter opens his mouth, there seems to be a fifty-fifty chance that he will either insert his foot or say the most amazing thing. The same Peter who would tell Jesus not to go to Jerusalem, protest Jesus washing his feet, and later deny him three times, proclaims, in today's Gospel, that Jesus is the Son of the living God. This should serve as inspiration for all of us who have clay feet! Peter was not perfect. Nor was Paul. And yet, today we celebrate the feast of two of the greatest apostles who were responsible for establishing and spreading the church throughout the world. Through their intercession, may we also boldly proclaim the Good News through our words and actions.

VIGIL:
Acts 3:1–10
Psalm 19:2–3, 4–5
Galatians 1:11–20
John 21:15–19

DAY:
Acts 12:1–11
Psalm 34:2–3, 4–5, 6–7, 8–9
2 Timothy 4:6–8, 17–18
Matthew 16:13–19

Wednesday JUNE 30

• THE FIRST HOLY MARTYRS OF THE HOLY ROMAN CHURCH •

The demons pleaded with him, "If you drive us out, send us into the herd of swine." And he said to them, "Go then!"
—MATTHEW 8:31–32

Jesus has no patience for demons—those spirits that are contrary to God's will. In today's Gospel, Jesus commands the demons, "Go then!" and sends them to their demise. The message is clear: There is no room for those who actively work against God's compassion, mercy, forgiveness, justice, and life-giving grace. Throughout our day, we may be bothered by demons who seek to drain us of divine life by sowing fear, anxiety, temptation, sloth, or even hatred. Like Jesus, our response should be "Go!" In doing so, we leave room only for God's abundant and life-giving grace that nourishes and strengthens us to go forth and share abundant life with others, especially those in need who are vulnerable to the demon of despair.

Genesis 21:5, 8–20a
Psalm 34:7–8, 10–11, 12–13
Matthew 8:28–34

Isaac continued, "Here are the fire and the wood, but where is the sheep for the burnt offering?"
"Son," Abraham answered, "God himself will provide the sheep for the burnt offering."
—GENESIS 22:7–8

The phrase "truer words were never spoken" describes something that is incontrovertible, meaning that its veracity cannot be disputed. This phrase can certainly be applied to Abraham's response to his son, telling him that God would provide the sheep for the sacrifice. In hindsight, we know that God provided his own Son, Jesus Christ—the Lamb of God—who laid down his life to save us all. As followers of Jesus, we are called to lay down our lives each day to care for the needs of others. It is this selfless love that is at the heart of the gospel. May God give us the grace to practice such love today and every day.

Genesis 22:1b–19
Psalm 115:1–2, 3–4, 5–6, 8–9
Matthew 9:1–8

Friday July 2

The Pharisees saw this and said to his disciples, "Why does your teacher eat with tax collectors and sinners?" He heard this and said, "Those who are well do not need a physician, but the sick do."

—MATTHEW 9:10–12

When Jesus referred to those who are well and those who are sick, he was no doubt speaking tongue-in-cheek since, in truth, none of us are well. Jesus was implying that the Pharisees saw themselves as *well* and not in need of the Divine Physician. The key to opening up to transformative grace is the admission of brokenness. This wisdom is at the heart of twelve-step programs that hold that healing cannot occur until we admit our powerlessness. Catholics begin each Mass with a Penitential Act in which we admit our sinfulness. This is not wallowing in sin, but an admission that gloriously opens us up to the healing grace of God.

Genesis 23:1–4, 19; 24:1–8, 62–67
Psalm 106:1b–2, 3–4a, 4b–5
Matthew 9:9–13

Thomas answered and said to him, "My Lord and my God!"
—JOHN 20:28

How unfair that Thomas has been named "Doubting Thomas" throughout history when his fellow apostle Peter escaped the tag "Denying Peter"! After all, Peter's transgression of denying even knowing the Lord would seem to be more serious than Thomas's moment of doubt. Thomas immediately redeems himself by proclaiming the words *my Lord and my God,* which are the words Catholics are taught to pray silently at Mass when the priest holds up the consecrated bread (Body of Christ) and wine (Precious Blood). It is human nature to doubt. In fact, doubt has been referred to as a *first cousin* of faith, meaning that faith is not the absence of doubt but a deep trust in spite of our doubts. Today, we look to Thomas for inspiration as we grapple with our own doubts and pray for the grace to trust and proclaim, *my Lord and my God!*

Ephesians 2:19–22
Psalm 117:1bc, 2
John 20:24–29

Sunday JULY 4

• FOURTEENTH SUNDAY IN ORDINARY TIME • INDEPENDENCE DAY •

They said, "Where did this man get all this? What kind of wisdom has been given him? What mighty deeds are wrought by his hands! Is he not the carpenter, the son of Mary, and the brother of James and Joses and Judas and Simon?"
—MARK 6:2–3

Tearing other people down is nothing new. Today's Gospel reveals to us that the people who first encountered Jesus couldn't accept what they were seeing and hearing. Jesus, however, forged ahead, remaining true to himself and to his mission, knowing that "haters will always hate." As we go forth as followers of Jesus bringing his mission to the world, we will encounter similar attitudes. Like Jesus, we must remain focused and forge ahead, asking God for the grace we need to be true ambassadors for Christ.

Ezekiel 2:2–5
Psalm 123:1–2, 2, 3–4
2 Corinthians 12:7–10
Mark 6:1–6

Monday JULY 5

• ST. ELIZABETH OF PORTUGAL • ST. ANTHONY MARY ZACCARIA, PRIEST •

When Jacob awoke from his sleep, he exclaimed, "Truly, the LORD is in this spot, although I did not know it!"
—GENESIS 28:16

In her book *Braving the Thin Places*, Julianne Stanz speaks of thin places as those locations or moments when it seems like the veil between heaven and earth is quite thin and God's presence is more palpable than usual. In today's first reading, Jacob recognizes a thin place in his life where he has encountered God and joyfully proclaims God's presence. Such thin places are not to be seen as locations where we have confined God. Rather, they are portals that give us a glimpse of the omnipresent God. Take some time today to reflect on some of the thin places in your life—locations or moments when you felt without a doubt that "truly, the Lord is in this spot!" Each day, keep your eyes peeled for the thin places that pop up all around you.

Genesis 28:10–22a
Psalm 91:1–2, 3–4, 14–15ab
Matthew 9:18–26

Tuesday

JULY 6

• ST. MARIA GORETTI, VIRGIN AND MARTYR •

At the sight of the crowds, his heart was moved with pity for them because they were troubled and abandoned, like sheep without a shepherd.
—MATTHEW 9:36

Throughout the four Gospels, we encounter a Christ who is driven by compassion as he reaches out to the most vulnerable: those who are sick, poor, mourning, widowed, and so on. Today's Gospel is a good example as we are told that Jesus's heart was moved with pity at the sight of the crowds. Jesus reveals that compassion is not just some warm and fuzzy feeling that God gets every so often but that it is a divine attribute. When it comes to discipleship, compassion is nonnegotiable: We are obligated to cultivate a compassionate approach to life. Each of us will become more recognizable as a child of God, made in God's image and likeness, if we show compassion to others. How can you reach out to someone today with compassion?

Genesis 32:23–33
Psalm 17:1b, 2–3, 6–7ab, 8b and 15
Matthew 9:32–38

Wednesday JULY 7

[Jesus said] "As you go, make this proclamation: 'The Kingdom of heaven is at hand.'"
—MATTHEW 10:7

When something is "at hand," that means it is nearby. When Jesus said this, it was to reveal that the kingdom—God's will being done on earth as it is in heaven—was present through him. What does this mean for us? As followers of Jesus, we are sent to proclaim that the kingdom of heaven is at hand. This is not a proclamation of the end of the world. It is a bold proclamation of the nearness of God. In a world that often seems to suggest that God is absent, the message of the gospel—through words and/or actions—reassures people that they are not alone and that God's compassion, mercy, justice, and love are all accessible to them. As you go your way today, find ways to proclaim the nearness of God to those you encounter.

Genesis 41:55–57; 42:5–7a, 17–24a
Psalm 33:2–3, 10–11, 18–19
Matthew 10:1–7

Thursday JULY 8

[Joseph said] "I am your brother Joseph, whom you sold into Egypt. But now do not be distressed, and do not be angry with yourselves for having sold me here. It was really for the sake of saving lives that God sent me here ahead of you."

—GENESIS 45:5

Forgiving those who have wronged us is not easy. In today's first reading, Joseph, who had been sold into slavery by his own brothers, encounters them years later when he has risen to a prominent role in Egypt. Instead of seeking revenge against his brothers, who had come to him for help during a famine, Joseph forgives them and explains that something good came out of a bad experience. Rather than letting the hurt and anger possess and paralyze him, Joseph chose to move on. Pray today for the grace that God gave to Joseph so you might also be freed from any anger and hurt you are carrying.

Genesis 44:18–21, 23b–29; 45:1–5
Psalm 105:16–17, 18–19, 20–21
Matthew 10:7–15

Friday JULY 9

• ST. AUGUSTINE ZHAO RONG, PRIEST, AND COMPANIONS, MARTYRS •

Jesus said to his Apostles: "Behold, I am sending you like sheep in the midst of wolves; so be shrewd as serpents and simple as doves."
—MATTHEW 10:16

At times, it can indeed feel as though we are sheep surrounded by wolves! It is reassuring, however, that Jesus recognized and warned us about this reality. In the same sentence, he equips us with the strategy we need to rise to the challenge: "Be shrewd as serpents and simple as doves." This shrewdness is not to be interpreted as dishonesty. Likewise, this simplicity is not to be interpreted as gullibility. Like a serpent, our shrewdness includes anticipating danger and protecting ourselves while observing and choosing the best moment to act. Like a dove, that action should be peaceful and nonaggressive. We are to be wise realists without losing our childlike trust in God's transforming grace. May you face today's challenges with shrewdness and simplicity.

Genesis 46:1–7, 28–30
Psalm 37:3–4, 18–19, 27–28, 39–40
Matthew 10:16–23

Saturday

JULY 10

[Jesus said] "Nothing is concealed that will not be revealed, nor secret that will not be known. What I say to you in the darkness, speak in the light; what you hear whispered, proclaim on the housetops."
—MATTHEW 10:26–27

Sometimes our spiritual experiences can seem very private, and indeed, they can be. However, our encounters with God are always intended to lead us outward to others. Faith is not so much a *me and God* experience as it is a *we and God* experience. In today's Gospel, Jesus reminds us that what he has whispered to us in the darkness of our private encounters with him is intended to be shared with others through our words and actions. Take a moment today to reflect on what God has whispered to you in the darkness or privacy of your own prayer life and how you can proclaim it *in the light* through your words and actions.

Genesis 49:29–32; 50:15–26a
Psalm 105:1–2, 3–4, 6–7
Matthew 10:24–33

Sunday JULY 11

• FIFTEENTH SUNDAY IN ORDINARY TIME •

In him you also, who have heard the word of truth,
the gospel of your salvation, and have believed in him, were sealed
with the promised Holy Spirit, which is the first installment of
our inheritance toward redemption as God's possession,
to the praise of his glory.
—EPHESIANS 1:13–14

The Good News of Jesus Christ is that we are heirs to the abundant riches (graces) of God's kingdom and are called to begin sharing in this inheritance *now*. This is what St. Paul tells us in his Letter to the Ephesians when he says that we have received the first installment of our inheritance toward redemption. We are called to start a new life filled with an abundance of riches that we have inherited. This is the essence of discipleship: to live as an heir of God's kingdom and to invite others to share in its abundant riches.

Amos 7:12–15
Psalm 85:9–10, 11–12, 13–14 (8)
Ephesians 1:3–14
Mark 6:7–13

Monday

JULY 12

[Jesus said] "And whoever gives only a cup of cold water to one of these little ones to drink because he is a disciple—amen, I say to you, he will surely not lose his reward."
—MATTHEW 10:42

Jesus reminds us today of the importance of charity, especially toward those who are vulnerable ("these little ones") and in need. In his Apostolic Exhortation *Dilexi Te*, Pope Leo XIV made it abundantly clear that charity is not simply a matter of being kind but is actually one of the most powerful ways that God's merciful presence is revealed and "is a fundamental way of encountering the Lord of history" (*DT*, 5). As you proceed through your day today, consider all of the opportunities you have to perform works of mercy—small or large—that reveal God's loving presence to the world.

Exodus 1:8–14, 22
Psalm 124:1b–3, 4–6, 7–8
Matthew 10:34—11:1

When the child grew, she brought him to Pharaoh's daughter,
who adopted him as her son and called him Moses;
for she said, "I drew him out of the water."
—EXODUS 2:10

On the surface, the narrative of Moses in the reeds might seem like simply a children's story. It is, however, filled with deep meaning. The experience of baby Moses echoes that of Noah: Both enter waters that killed others of their generation; both are protected from danger by an ark; both pass from danger to freedom; both become leaders of God's people; and both take on a new identity—Noah as the new Adam and the baby being given the name Moses. Both narratives prefigure baptism, through which each of us pass from the danger of sin to freedom in Christ and take on a new identity. Take a moment today to thank God for the gift of your baptism.

Exodus 2:1–15a
Psalm 69:3, 14, 30–31, 33–34
Matthew 11:20–24

Wednesday JULY 14

• ST. KATERI TEKAKWITHA, VIRGIN •

As he looked on, he was surprised to see that the bush, though on fire, was not consumed. So Moses decided, "I must go over to look at this remarkable sight, and see why the bush is not burned."
—EXODUS 3:2–4

Moses encountered God's mysterious presence through a burning bush that was not being consumed. Like most human beings, Moses is drawn to mystery. This is how God invites us: through moments of encounter with divine mystery that compel us to explore more deeply. God reveals his mysterious presence to us in the world around us. A burning bush was no big deal in a desert region. However, a closer look revealed something deeper occurring. In our own lives, we too must look more deeply at the ordinary so that the extraordinary may be revealed. Keep your eyes open today to see how God's mysterious presence is being revealed to you.

Exodus 3:1–6, 9–12
Psalm 103:1b–2, 3–4, 6–7
Matthew 11:25–27

Thursday JULY 15

• ST. BONAVENTURE, BISHOP AND DOCTOR OF THE CHURCH •

[Jesus said]"Come to me, all you who labor and are burdened, and I will give you rest."
—MATTHEW 11:28

What a welcome relief it is when, in the midst of a laborious task, someone tells us to take a break. Without a break, we can become overfatigued and unable to continue on. Jesus is well aware of the reality of life's overwhelming and burdensome struggles. Thankfully, Jesus calls us to rest in him when we are weary. To rest in Jesus is to allow him to refresh and renew us in body, mind, and spirit. The main vehicle for this rest is prayer—those times when we pause from *doing* and pay attention to our *being*. Take some time today to assess your own spiritual wellness: Are you burdened? Weary? Depleted? Overwhelmed? If so, turn to the Lord in prayer and open yourself up to his renewing spirit.

Exodus 3:13–20
Psalm 105:1 and 5, 8–9, 24–25, 26–27
Matthew 11:28–30

Friday JULY 16

• OUR LADY OF MOUNT CARMEL •

[Jesus said] "If you knew what this meant, 'I desire mercy, not sacrifice,' you would not have condemned these innocent men. For the Son of Man is Lord of the sabbath."
—MATTHEW 12:7–8

Religious rituals and rubrics are important and helpful for us in our worship. However, it is possible to become obsessive and overly pious about external expressions at the expense of internal transformation. In today's Gospel, Jesus confronts some overly pious Pharisees who are obsessing over externals. Jesus reminds them that long ago, God told his people Israel that he desires mercy, not sacrifice. Mercy is something that comes from deep within us, while sacrifice can too often be merely an outward expression devoid of any internal transformation. In your own life of prayer and worship, ask God for the grace that enables your outward expressions of faith to be intimately tied to your own internal change of heart.

Exodus 11:10—12:14
Psalm 116:12–13, 15 and 16bc, 17–18
Matthew 12:1–8

And in his name the Gentiles will hope.
—MATTHEW 12:21

For many sports fans, the mention of a star player's name can bring hope in the midst of what appears to be a lost cause. Just the thought that this player might come to bat, take the mound, steal the puck, take over as quarterback, or line up a three-point shot at the buzzer can make hope leap to the surface. In today's Gospel, Jesus reminds us that, as Isaiah promised, the very mention of God's name will bring hope to the Gentiles, which means to the whole world. As followers of Jesus, we are responsible for bringing this hope to our part of the world through our words and actions. We can bring hope to others by alleviating suffering, listening to others, assisting someone in need, or offering encouragement.

Exodus 12:37–42
Psalm 136:1 and 23–24, 10–12, 13–15
Matthew 12:14–21

Sunday JULY 18

• SIXTEENTH SUNDAY IN ORDINARY TIME •

This is the name they give him:
"The LORD our justice."
—JEREMIAH 23:6

Too often, justice is thought of in legal terms and is equated with punishment or even vengeance. However, justice is a positive thing and refers to holding up our end of the bargain. When we enter into a formal relationship, such as a contract or a covenant, each party owes something to the other party for the agreement to flourish. To live justly is to make sure that we give others what we owe them so we live in right relationship with one another. God's justice is God's way of holding up his end of the covenant he has established with his people. That same covenant calls us to live in right relationship with one another. Today, seek to live justly, holding up your end of the bargain to love God by loving others.

Jeremiah 23:1–6
Psalm 23:1–3, 3–4, 5, 6 (1)
Ephesians 2:13–18
Mark 6:30–34

Monday

JULY 19

But Moses answered the people, "Fear not! Stand your ground and see the victory the LORD will win for you today."
—EXODUS 14:13

It would seem that the people of Israel, in the midst of being led to freedom by Moses, experienced a type of *buyer's remorse*—that sense of regret people often feel after acquiring something they greatly desired. The people of Israel actually complained to Moses that they were better off in Egypt as slaves! Moses, however, stops them in their tracks and reassures them that the best is yet to come. As you move forward on your spiritual journey, you may be experiencing buyer's remorse about some choices you have made about your future. In the words of Moses, "Fear not!" Even as you journey through parched lands, place your trust in the Lord, knowing that he will not lead you astray.

Exodus 14:5–18
Exodus 15:1bc–2, 3–4, 5–6
Matthew 12:38–42

Tuesday JULY 20

• ST. APOLLINARIUS, BISHOP AND MARTYR •

When the water was thus divided,
the children of Israel marched into the midst
of the sea on dry land,
with the water like a wall to their right and to their left.
—EXODUS 14:21–22

Water has so many qualities and uses: It cleans, refreshes, restores, quenches, and sustains. By the same token, however, water can be dangerous: Human beings cannot breathe under water. Today's first reading tells of the miraculous parting of the Red Sea that enabled the people of Israel to pass from slavery to freedom. This is why water is used in baptism: When we are plunged into the water, we *die* to sin and then burst forth with new life. As you encounter water today in myriad ways, remind yourself how Jesus, the Living Water, cleans, refreshes, restores, quenches, and sustains you, but most importantly, how he leads you through death into new life.

Exodus 14:21—15:1
Exodus 15:8–9, 10 and 12, 17
Matthew 12:46–50

Wednesday JULY 21

• ST. LAWRENCE OF BRINDISI, PRIEST AND DOCTOR OF THE CHURCH •

But some seed fell on rich soil, and produced fruit, a hundred or sixty or thirtyfold.
—MATTHEW 13:8

In my book *Preparing Hearts and Minds*, I say, "The New Evangelization will not be powered by TV ads, print ads, billboards, or social media advertising. It will be accomplished by ordinary, everyday people who are not afraid of getting their fingernails dirty by tilling the soil and planting seeds—by sharing their stories of how living as disciples of Jesus Christ has transformed their lives and enabled them to live a better way." God uses us to spread the seed as one uses a spreader to scatter grass seed on a lawn. Each day, we have opportunities to find good soil where the seed of God's word can be sown and multiply. Seize these opportunities to share your stories of how the Lord has transformed your life and enabled you to live a fuller life.

Exodus 16:1–5, 9–15
Psalm 78:18–19, 23–24, 25–26, 27–28
Matthew 13:1–9

Thursday JULY 22

• ST. MARY MAGDALENE •

Mary Magdalene went and announced to the disciples,
"I have seen the Lord,"
and then reported what he told her.
—JOHN 20:18

With the advent of social media, each of us now has the opportunity to be the herald of news, good or bad. And with that, of course, comes the desire to "break the story" and scoop everyone else. If there were a patron saint for this, it would be St. Mary Magdalene, the first to announce the resurrection of Jesus to others! Today, we celebrate the Feast of St. Mary Magdalene and recall how this great saint inspires each of us to announce the Good News to others, even those who, like the apostles, may not initially be receptive to our message. We pray also for the grace to stand with others who are suffering, just as Mary Magdalene stood at the foot of the cross as Jesus suffered and died.

Song of Songs 3:1–4b or 2 Corinthians 5:14–17
Psalm 63:2, 3–4, 5–6, 8–9
John 20:1–2, 11–18

• ST. BRIDGET OF SWEDEN, RELIGIOUS •

I, the LORD, *am your God,*
who brought you out of the land of Egypt, that place of slavery.
You shall not have other gods besides me.
—EXODUS 20:2

Sometimes we need to be reminded of who loves us most. Throughout Scripture, God reminds his people of his great love for them. A closer look at the first commandment illustrates how God does this as he reminds his children of what he has done for them in the past. In fact, if you wanted to paraphrase the first commandment, the question, "Who loves you most?" would suffice. The answer is unequivocally "God!" As followers of Jesus Christ, we are called to bring the steadfast love and goodness of God to others—always having their best interest in mind—so that they know they are loved and may be led to respond by placing God at the center of their lives.

Exodus 20:1–17
Psalm 19:8, 9, 10, 11
Matthew 13:18–23

Saturday JULY 24

• ST. SHARBEL MAKHLUF, PRIEST •

Let them grow together until harvest; then at harvest time I will say to the harvesters, "First collect the weeds and tie them in bundles for burning; but gather the wheat into my barn."
—MATTHEW 13:30

Perhaps the two most important words in today's Gospel are "let them." It is not easy to refrain from interjecting our opinion when we encounter someone doing or saying something we find disagreeable. And yet, sometimes we must *let them*. In her book *Let Them*, author Mel Robbins proposes a strategy for accepting what we cannot change in others by saying "let them." This strategy echoes the Serenity Prayer, in which we ask God for serenity to accept things we cannot change, and courage and wisdom to change the things we can. Jesus's parable of the weeds and wheat teaches us that this is the way of God's kingdom.

Strive today to say, "let them."

Exodus 24:3–8
Psalm 50:1b–2, 5–6, 14–15
Matthew 13:24–30

Sunday JULY 25

• SEVENTEENTH SUNDAY IN ORDINARY TIME •

So they collected them, and filled twelve wicker baskets with fragments from the five barley loaves that had been more than they could eat.
—JOHN 6:13

In many cultures it is customary to keep an abundance of food in the refrigerator and pantry even after the children have grown up and moved away. Mothers especially would be mortified if someone dropped in and there was no food to serve! Jesus seemed to follow in this tradition. In today's Gospel, Jesus not only feeds the huge crowd but ensures that there are abundant leftovers: twelve baskets full! This echoes his first miracle at Cana, when he turned six huge jars of water into wine so the celebration could continue. The message is clear: God's grace is overflowing. We can show our appreciation for God's abundant grace by generously sharing our time, talent, and treasure with others, knowing that God's grace will never be depleted.

2 Kings 4:42–44
Psalm 145:10–11, 15–16, 17–18
Ephesians 4:1–6
John 6:1–15

Monday
JULY 26

• ST. JOACHIM AND ST. ANNE, PARENTS OF THE BLESSED VIRGIN MARY •

They said to me, 'Make us a god to be our leader;
as for the man Moses who brought us out of the land of Egypt,
we do not know what has happened to him.'
—EXODUS 32:23

In today's first reading, we see how the people of Israel had grown impatient not only with Moses, but with God—who had just miraculously led them out of slavery into freedom. Like the people of Israel, we can find ourselves cynically asking God, "What have you done for me lately?" Perhaps asking that question is not such a bad idea if we acknowledge that God is sustaining us each moment of each day. In fact, asking God, "What have you done for me lately?" is the essence of the Daily Examen prayer that invites us to reflect in gratitude on the many things God has done for us lately! Go ahead and ask!

Exodus 32:15–24, 30–34
Psalm 106:19–20, 21–22, 23
Matthew 13:31–35

Tuesday JULY 27

Whoever has ears ought to hear.
—MATTHEW 13:43

Hearing is a complex reality. This becomes all too real when we are in a noisy place. Our brains are bombarded with incoming signals that need to be sorted out. We must filter out unwanted noise to concentrate on the message that is most important to us. In today's Gospel, Jesus reminds us that his voice conveys the message we need to hear and we need to filter out what is simply noise. To truly hear Jesus means much more than just hearing the words: It requires us to listen with the intention of understanding. We must make ourselves available to receive his words and to reflect on their meaning so that we may grow closer to him. Strive today to filter out any distractions that prevent you from hearing—and truly receiving—the Word of God.

Exodus 33:7–11, 34:5b–9, 28
Psalm 103:6–7, 8–9, 10–11, 12–13
Matthew 13:36–43

Wednesday
JULY 28

Then the children of Israel would see that the skin of Moses' face was radiant; so he would again put the veil over his face until he went in to converse with the LORD.
—EXODUS 34:35

We sometimes tell a person who has revealed to us that they've fallen in love or are expecting a baby that they are *glowing*. By this, we mean that they are radiating joy and positivity. They look happy, healthy, and energized. When Moses came down from the mountaintop after his encounter with God, his face was aglow. He was so radiant that people were afraid, and he wore a veil so as not to frighten them. When we encounter God's glory, we too become radiant with joy. While this is a good thing, we may need to veil or temper our radiance so that our encounters with others are not off-putting but allow people to see us as approachable.

Exodus 34:29–35
Psalm 99:5, 6, 7, 9
Matthew 13:44–46

[Jesus said], "Do you believe this?" She said to him, "Yes, Lord. I have come to believe that you are the Christ, the Son of God, the one who is coming into the world."
—JOHN 11:26–27

Throughout the Gospels, various people have their moment when they come to recognize Jesus as the true Messiah. Perhaps the most famous of these is Peter's response when Jesus asked, "Who do you say I am?" In today's Gospel, we find that Martha, the sister of Mary and Lazarus, gave the same response to Jesus that Peter did. Like Peter, she declared that Jesus is indeed the Son of God and the Messiah. Today, we look to Martha for the inspiration to make that profound statement of faith that Jesus is the One in whom we place our complete trust, knowing that he rescues, restores, and reassures us.

Exodus 40:16–21, 34–38
Psalm 84:3, 4, 5–6a and 8a, 11
John 11:19–27 or Luke 10:38–42

• ST. PETER CHRYSOLOGUS, BISHOP AND DOCTOR OF THE CHURCH •

These, therefore, are the festivals of the LORD,
on which you shall proclaim a sacred assembly,
and offer as an oblation to the LORD
burnt offerings and cereal offerings,
sacrifices and libations, as prescribed for each day.
—LEVITICUS 23:37

It's funny how people often characterize God in the Old Testament as being full of wrath. Okay, God does have his wrathful moments. However, in today's first reading, we find Moses telling the people of Israel about all of the holidays and festivals they are required to celebrate throughout the year. If God were an employer, his employees would be thrilled to see all of the holidays they were being granted. God wants us to celebrate the good things he provides for us. These festivals are not intended to appease an angry God. Rather, they are for God's people to recognize just how blessed we are. May every day be a festival of faith!

Leviticus 23:1, 4–11, 15–16, 27, 34b–37
Psalm 81:3–4, 5–6, 10–11ab
Matthew 13:54–58

Saturday

JULY 31

• ST. IGNATIUS OF LOYOLA, PRIEST •

This fiftieth year you shall make sacred
by proclaiming liberty in the land for all its inhabitants.
It shall be a jubilee year for you.
—LEVITICUS 25:10

Today's first reading lays out the criteria for a jubilee year—an opportunity to bring justice to people who have been marginalized in society. The Gospel invites us to reflect on John the Baptist, who called upon leaders like Herod for justice for those who had nothing. On this Feast of St. Ignatius, we are reminded that justice involves living not for ourselves but as *people for others*. This Ignatian principle, coined by the late Fr. Pedro Arrupe, SJ (the Superior General of the Jesuits in 1973), challenges us to use our resources to assist those who are marginalized. In other words, we are to live with a spirit of jubilee each and every day. How can you make today a day of jubilee?

Leviticus 25:1, 8–17
Psalm 67:2–3, 5, 7–8
Matthew 14:1–12

Sunday
AUGUST 1

• EIGHTEENTH SUNDAY IN ORDINARY TIME •

The whole Israelite community grumbled against Moses and Aaron.
—EXODUS 16:2

Scripture tells us that, quite often during their desert experience, the people of Israel grumbled against Moses, forgetting how God had worked through Moses to lead them from slavery to freedom. It would seem they had succumbed to a severe case of spiritual amnesia. The truth is, we are all susceptible to this malady by which we forget God's faithfulness and his marvelous deeds and, instead, doubt God's ability to lead us through the present challenges. This is why gratitude is such an important element of prayer. When we give thanks to God, we recall all the good he has done for us and, in doing so, we reinforce our trust in him to continue his marvelous deeds in the present and future. Reading and praying with Scripture, as you are doing now, is an effective way to combat spiritual amnesia.

Exodus 16:2–4, 12–15
Psalm 78:3–4, 23–24, 25, 54 (24b)
Ephesians 4:17, 20–24
John 6:24–35

Monday

AUGUST 2

• ST. EUSEBIUS OF VERCELLI, BISHOP • ST. PETER JULIAN EYMARD, PRIEST •

When Jesus heard of the death of John the Baptist, he withdrew in a boat to a deserted place by himself.
—MATTHEW 14:13

Even Jesus needed to take a step back from time to time. Scripture reveals to us that Jesus repeatedly went off by himself to a deserted place. This is the essence of a retreat. The notion of retreat can appear as if one is running away from the world's problems. The truth is, there are times when it is healthy to withdraw for a short time, not to run away, but to collect ourselves, seek renewal, and then head right back into doing the Father's work as Jesus did. Each day, we can take mini-retreats—short breaks that enable us to catch our breath—before we jump back into the day's events. Where can you find a *deserted place* each day to withdraw for a short while?

Numbers 11 4b–15
Psalm 81:12–13, 14–15, 16–17
Matthew 14:22–36 or 14:13–21

Tuesday

AUGUST 3

But when he saw how strong the wind was he became frightened; and, beginning to sink, he cried out, "Lord, save me!"
—MATTHEW 14:30

We use the phrase "keep your eye on the prize" to encourage us to maintain focus on a goal, even when the challenge before us is difficult. In today's Gospel, we find that the reason Peter began to sink is because he took his eyes off of Jesus. He became distracted and fearful of the strong winds roaring around him and the waves churning beneath him.

This passage reminds us not to allow ourselves to be distracted by fear or anxiety that tempts us to conclude that we are drowning. Instead, we need to keep our eye on the prize—we need to remain focused on Jesus, who has power over the angry winds and enables us to rise above the swirling waters.

Numbers 12:1–13
Psalm 51:3–4, 5–6ab, 6cd–7, 12–13
Matthew 14:22–36 or 15:1–2, 10–14

Wednesday

AUGUST 4

• ST. JOHN MARY VIANNEY, PRIEST •

She said, "Please, Lord, for even the dogs eat the scraps that fall from the table of their masters."
—MATTHEW 15:27

Polarization is nothing new. In Jesus's time, Jews and Gentiles saw one another as people to be avoided. In fact, it was common for Jewish people to refer to Gentiles as *dogs*. In today's Gospel, however, Jesus and a Gentile woman open the door to a new way of seeing things. Jesus uses the affectionate word for *puppy*, and the woman reminds Jesus that it is commonplace for people and their pet dogs to eat from the same table. This encounter explains Jesus's entrance into Gentile territory, where he will feed four thousand people just as he previously fed five thousand people in Jewish territory. Jesus erases boundaries and invites us each day to recognize those we encounter as brothers and sisters who are invited to sit at the same table.

Numbers 13:1–2, 25—14:1, 26a–29a, 34–35
Psalm 106:6–7ab, 13–14, 21–22, 23
Matthew 15:21–28

Thursday

AUGUST 5

• THE DEDICATION OF THE BASILICA OF ST. MARY MAJOR •

Then, raising his hand, Moses struck the rock twice
with his staff,
and water gushed out in abundance for the people
and their livestock to drink.
—NUMBERS 20:11

Throughout human history, people posing as magicians have sought to convince people that they possess the power to create something out of nothing—to pull a rabbit out of a hat. Scripture, however, reminds us that God alone possesses this power. Moses was no magician. He was an instrument of God's powerful mercy and compassion. Bringing water from the rock for a people dying of thirst was just another way that God showed his love for his people. In our everyday lives, God finds ways where there seems to be no way, and he calls us to help others see possibilities when they see none. God doesn't perform magic. He performs miracles! May your eyes see miracles happening all around you, today and every day.

Numbers 20:1–13
Psalm 95:1–2, 6–7, 8–9
Matthew 16:13–23

Friday

AUGUST 6

• THE TRANSFIGURATION OF THE LORD •

He was transfigured before them, and his clothes became dazzling white, such as no fuller on earth could bleach them.
—MARK 9:2–3

In today's Gospel, Peter, James, and John had a mystical experience—a moment when God's presence burst through the ordinary to reveal the extraordinary. For a fleeting moment, the curtain was lifted and they caught a glimpse of heaven on earth. You and I have mystical experiences—fleeting glimpses of God—in our everyday lives: when we observe a beautiful sunrise or sunset, a full moon, a newborn baby, a rainbow, a flower blooming, a laughing grandchild, an elderly person, a smile, an embrace, a gesture of kindness, or a moment of profound joy or tenderness. Go forth today with eyes wide open, seeking glimpses of God in your day and helping others catch a glimpse of God in a world that too often forgets that God is near.

Daniel 7:9–10, 13–14
Psalm 97:1–2, 5–6, 9
2 Peter 1:16–19
Mark 9:2–10

Saturday

AUGUST 7

• ST. SIXTUS II, POPE, AND COMPANIONS, MARTYRS * ST. CAJETAN, PRIEST •

Take to heart these words which I enjoin on you today.
Drill them into your children.
—DEUTERONOMY 6:6–7

We use the phrase "take to heart" or "learn by heart" to refer to memorizing something. This phrase came about because in earlier times the heart was thought to be the center of all knowledge. While today we know that the brain is the knowledge center, it still makes sense to say that we take things *to heart*—especially when referring to God's law of love—as a reminder that the words we learn must penetrate our very being. Consider making it a regular practice to take to heart words of Scripture or words of the saints. You can start each day with the words from our first reading: "Hear, O Israel! The LORD is our God, the LORD alone!"—words known to the Jewish people as the *Shema* (Hebrew for "hear").

Deuteronomy 6:4–13
Psalm 18:2–3a, 3c–4, 47 and 51
Matthew 17:14–20

Elijah went a day's journey into the desert,
until he came to a broom tree and sat beneath it.
He prayed for death, saying:
"This is enough, O LORD!
Take my life, for I am no better than my fathers."
—1 KINGS 19:4A

Elijah concluded that despite all the powerful works God had accomplished through him, he, Elijah, was a failure whose only reward was a bounty on his head and life as an outcast. He wanted to go to sleep under a broom tree and never wake up again. In contemporary parlance, he was severely depressed. Thankfully, God sent an angel to intervene and set Elijah on the road to renewal and revival. We sometimes have moments in life when despair overwhelms us. Recall with gratitude the various angels that God has sent your way. For whom might you serve as angel this day?

1 Kings 19:4–8
Psalm 34:2–3, 4–5, 6–7, 8–9 (9a)
Ephesians 4:30—5:2
John 6:41–51

Monday

AUGUST 9

• ST. TERESA BENEDICTA OF THE CROSS, VIRGIN AND MARTYR •

Moses said to the people: "And now, Israel, what does the LORD, *your God, ask of you but to fear the* LORD."
—DEUTERONOMY 10:12

The biblical notion of *fear of the Lord* is typically misunderstood and thought of as shaking in our boots, much as Dorothy and her companions trembled before the Wizard of Oz. A good understanding of the concept of fear of the Lord can be drawn from, of all places, the autobiography of Rolling Stones guitarist Keith Richards. In his book *Life*, Richards explains that he always feared his dad, not because his dad was cruel, but rather because he was such a good man that Keith was afraid of doing anything to disappoint him. This is what it means to fear the Lord. We are not afraid of an angry God, but rather we fear doing anything contrary to God's great goodness, mercy, and compassion.

Deuteronomy 10:12–22
Psalm 147:12–13, 14–15, 19–20
Matthew 17:22–27

Tuesday

AUGUST 10

• ST. LAWRENCE, DEACON AND MARTYR •

The one who supplies seed to the sower and bread for food will supply and multiply your seed and increase the harvest of your righteousness.
—2 CORINTHIANS 9:10

God, indeed, provides for us with abundance. Unfortunately, sometimes people mistake abundance in material possessions as a sign of God's favor. This reality, known as the prosperity gospel, couldn't be more contrary to the gospel of Jesus Christ. St. Lawrence, whose feast we celebrate today, demonstrated this powerfully when the emperor commanded him to turn over the abundant treasures of the church. Lawrence showed up with a group of poor, homeless people and said, "These are the true treasures of the church." May we recognize God's abundant grace all around us, recognize others as God's true treasure, and generously share with them the abundance of gifts that God has blessed us with.

2 Corinthians 9:6–10
Psalm 112:1–2, 5–6, 7–8, 9
John 12:24–26

Wednesday

AUGUST 11

• ST. CLARE, VIRGIN •

Where two or three are gathered together in my name, there am I in the midst of them.
—MATTHEW 18:20

While prayer has a very personal dimension, for Catholics it is also a communal reality. It is often through others' words and actions that God's presence and divine will are revealed to us. Praying with others also enables us to be instruments of God's grace for those who are searching for a glimpse of God's presence in their life. Think of *two or three* people in your life in whom you recognize and experience God's grace and presence. Gathering with them may take the shape of a formal prayer group or simply an experience of joy and selfless love that makes manifest God's presence. Ask God to reveal to you *two or three* people with whom you could gather to experience God's loving presence more fully in your life.

Deuteronomy 34:1–12
Psalm 66:1–3a, 5 and 8, 16–17
Matthew 18:15–20

Thursday

AUGUST 12

• ST. JANE FRANCES DE CHANTAL, RELIGIOUS •

Peter approached Jesus and asked him, "Lord, if my brother sins against me, how often must I forgive him? As many as seven times?"
—MATTHEW 18:21

In Scripture, the number seven typically represents fullness or perfection. So Peter thought seven would be the perfect maximum when it comes to forgiveness. Jesus, however, multiplies that number by seventy (a multiple of seven) to emphasize that there is no limit to God's forgiveness that we are expected to emulate. To forgive someone is not to let them off the hook or ignore the wrong they have done and the hurt they have caused. It is, however, a letting go of the burden of anger, resentment, and the desire for vengeance. Take a moment to thank God for his forgiveness, to think of someone who has forgiven you, and to think of someone you need to forgive and ask for the grace to do so.

Joshua 3:7–10a, 11, 13–17
Psalm 114:1–2, 3–4, 5–6
Matthew 18:21—19:1

Friday

AUGUST 13

• ST. PONTIAN, POPE, AND ST. HIPPOLYTUS, PRIEST, MARTYRS •

Joshua addressed all the people: "Thus says the LORD, the God of Israel: in times past . . ."
—JOSHUA 24:2

Many love songs reveal the author reminding their beloved of all the things they've done for them—reasons that the beloved should remain faithful to them. Likewise, many parents remind their children of all that they have done for them when they are feeling taken for granted or unappreciated. In today's first reading from Joshua—similar to other passages throughout the Old Testament—God reminds his people of all that he has done for them. In a sense, God is leading his people through an Examen, a prayer practice in which we reflect on all that God has done for us so that we might respond with gratitude. Take some time each day, through the Daily Examen, to recall all that God has done for you and respond with a grateful heart.

Joshua 24:1–13
Psalm 136:1–3, 16–18, 21–22 and 24
Matthew 19:3–12

Saturday

AUGUST 14

• ST. MAXIMILIAN MARY KOLBE, PRIEST AND MARTYR •

Let the children come to me, and do not prevent them; for the Kingdom of heaven belongs to such as these.
—MATTHEW 19:13–15

Throughout the Gospels, Jesus points to unexpected groups of people—tax collectors, prostitutes, outcasts, sinners, and children—as examples of those who are closest to the kingdom. Children are included in this collection because, like the others, they have no status in society. Children, in particular, are completely dependent on their parents. This realization of complete dependency on a higher power is the key to salvation. People in twelve-step groups understand this all too well: At our deepest level, we are incapable of sustaining ourselves. It is only through divine intervention—the coming of our Savior, Jesus Christ—that we are rescued, restored, and reassured. To get in touch with your *inner child* is to gratefully embrace your total dependence on God's amazing grace for your salvation.

Joshua 24:14–29
Psalm 16:1–2a and 5, 7–8, 11
Matthew 19:13–15

Sunday

AUGUST 15

• THE ASSUMPTION OF THE BLESSED VIRGIN MARY •

But thanks be to God who gives us the victory through our Lord Jesus Christ.
—1 CORINTHIANS 15:57

Given today's technology, it would be almost unheard of for a sports fan not to know immediately of their team's victory and instantly share that good news with others so they can enter into the victory. God wasted no time inviting his children to begin sharing his Son's victory over death. By assuming Mary, the Mother of Jesus, body and soul into heaven, God provides all of us a taste of the victory that we too will share fully in eternity: the resurrection of the body. Today's wonderful feast inspires hope by reminding us that heaven awaits us as long as we remain faithful, as Mary did. While Mary's Assumption anticipates the resurrection of the body at the end of time, it also reminds us of the sacredness of the flesh we embody.

VIGIL:
1 Chronicles 15:3–4, 15–16; 16:1–2
Psalm 132:6–7, 9–10, 13–14
1 Corinthians 15:54b–57
Luke 11:27–28

DAY:
Revelation 11:19a; 12:1–6a, 10ab
Psalm 45:10, 11, 12, 16 (10bc)
1 Corinthians 15:20–27
Luke 1:39–56

Monday

AUGUST 16

• ST. STEPHEN OF HUNGARY •

Jesus said to him, "If you wish to be perfect, go, sell what you have and give to the poor, and you will have treasure in heaven."
—MATTHEW 19:21

Jesus never said that wealth is bad. He did, however, warn of its dangers. Today's Gospel is a good example of just that. Jesus warns us that material possessions and wealth are a mirage. This explains why, throughout Christian history, religious communities have emphasized living in a spirit of poverty. This is not so much a commitment to be poor as much as it is a commitment to be detached from personal ownership of material possessions. In her book *Blessed by Less*, author Susan Vogt relates how, one year for Lent, she committed to giving away one possession each day. She found the practice so refreshing that she continued it as a regular habit. Try being blessed by having less!

Judges 2:11–19
Psalm 106:34–35, 36–37, 39–40, 43ab and 44
Matthew 19:16–22

Tuesday

AUGUST 17

Many who are first will be last, and the last will be first.
—MATTHEW 19:30

It's not usually a compliment to describe someone as being *out of their mind*. And yet, as disciples of Jesus, we are called to put on the mind of Christ, which requires us to get out of our own minds and into his. There, in the mind of Christ, we find things a bit topsy-turvy: The poor are considered blessed; enemies are loved; persecutors are prayed for; the exalted are humbled and the humbled exalted; sins are forgiven (seventy times seven times); feet are washed by the master; and new life is gained through death. Likewise, in the mind of Christ, you will find these percolating: compassion, charity, justice, fortitude, forgiveness, gratitude, patience, kindness, and gentleness, to name a few. Make it your goal today to get *out of your mind* and into the mind of Christ.

Judges 6:11–24a
Psalm 85:9, 11–12, 13–14
Matthew 19:23–30

Wednesday

AUGUST 18

What if I wish to give this last one the same as you? Or am I not free to do as I wish with my own money? Are you envious because I am generous?

—MATTHEW 20:14–15

In today's Gospel, Jesus tells a parable that comments, not on labor practices, but on the fruitlessness of comparing ourselves to others. This cycle of comparison creates a no-win scenario. There are always people around us who have more than we do. The key is to focus on what we have that cannot be taken away, namely, God's grace. When we have no fear of losing what cannot be taken away from us, we become capable of actively seeking and celebrating the good of others. In the Ignatian tradition, this kind of attitude is known as "Ignatian indifference"—not apathy but a liberating detachment from being concerned about what others have that you don't.

Judges 9:6–15
Psalm 21:2–3, 4–5, 6–7
Matthew 20:1–16

Thursday AUGUST 19

• ST. JOHN EUDES, PRIEST •

The feast is ready, but those who were invited were not worthy to come. Go out, therefore, into the main roads and invite to the feast whomever you find.
—MATTHEW 22:8–9

From the time we are young, we begin to play the game of who's *in* and who's *out*. In today's Gospel, Jesus tells a parable of people who were *in* missing their opportunity to attend a banquet and the invitation being expanded to those who were previously *out*. The core message of the parable is that God doesn't play this game of who's in and who's out but rather extends his invitation to all. Likewise, it is not our job to determine who is in and who is out but rather to humbly accept the Lord's invitation and to respond by extending that invitation to others who might otherwise conclude that they are not welcome to God's eternal banquet.

Judges 11:29–39a
Psalm 40:5, 7–8a, 8b–9, 10
Matthew 22:1–14

Friday

AUGUST 20

• ST. BERNARD, ABBOT AND DOCTOR OF THE CHURCH •

But Ruth said, "Do not ask me to abandon or forsake you!
For wherever you go, I will go, wherever you lodge I will lodge,
your people shall be my people, and your God my God."
—RUTH 1:16

In a world that struggles with the notion of commitment, the story of Ruth can serve as an inspiration. Ruth's steadfast commitment to her mother-in-law is beyond expected norms. Her story reveals unwavering loyalty, kindness, selflessness, and faith in the face of hardship and difficult times. Likewise, her trust in God's providence serves as a reminder for us to trust the Lord even in the face of the unknown. Reflect with gratitude on the Ruths of your own life—people who have stood by you with loyalty and selfless love. For whom are you being called to be a Ruth? Ask God for the grace you need to trust in his providence.

Ruth 1:1, 3–6, 14b–16, 22
Psalm 146:5–6ab, 6c–7, 8–9a, 9bc–10
Matthew 22:34–40

Saturday

AUGUST 21

• ST. PIUS X, POPE •

The greatest among you must be your servant. Whoever exalts himself will be humbled; but whoever humbles himself will be exalted.

—MATTHEW 23:11–12

Jesus speaks interchangeably about *serving* others and *laying down one's life* for others. To lay down one's life simply means to set aside one's own needs in favor of someone else's. We are called to do this every day. Parents and spouses set aside their own needs to tend to the needs of their children and one another. Teachers and catechists set aside their own needs to tend to the needs of their students. Doctors and nurses set aside their own needs to tend to the needs of their patients. Many adults set aside their own needs to care for elderly parents. And so on. Such service places one in the ranks of the greatest in the kingdom of God. May we humble ourselves through service to others.

Ruth 2:1–3, 8–11; 4:13–17
Psalm 128:1b–2, 3, 4, 5
Matthew 23:1–12

Sunday

AUGUST 22

• TWENTY-FIRST SUNDAY IN ORDINARY TIME •

Simon Peter answered him, "Master, to whom shall we go? You have the words of eternal life. We have come to believe and are convinced that you are the Holy One of God."
—JOHN 6:69

It can be easy to cave in to peer pressure, no matter what your age. It takes courage to take a stand that may not be popular with the rest of the crowd. We know that Peter didn't always exhibit this courage. He actually denied knowing Jesus when the crowds had turned against him. In today's Gospel, however, Peter got it right. While many were rejecting Jesus's teachings as too difficult and turning away from him, Peter asserted that Jesus is the One to stick with. Each day, in small or large ways, we need the grace to stand up for what we believe in, even when it is unpopular.

Joshua 24:1–2a, 15–17, 18b
Psalm 34:2–3, 16–17, 18–19, 20–21, 22–23 (9a)
Ephesians 5:21–32 or 5:2a, 25–32
John 6:60–69

Monday

AUGUST 23

• ST. ROSE OF LIMA, VIRGIN •

We give thanks to God always for all of you, remembering you in our prayers, unceasingly calling to mind your work of faith and labor of love and endurance in hope of our Lord Jesus Christ.
—1 THESSALONIANS 1:2–3

It is a powerful thing to know that someone is praying for you. On Cursillo retreats, it is common practice for people to send "palanca letters" (*palanca* means "lever") to retreatants, expressing their support, prayers, and promises of works of mercy done in their name while they are on retreat. When retreatants receive and read these letters from family, loved ones, and friends, it is an extremely moving experience. In today's first reading, Paul tells the people of Thessalonica that he and others are praying for them. As you encounter people who are going through difficult challenges, take a moment to assure them that you are praying for them.

1 Thessalonians 1:1–5, 8b–10
Psalm 149:1b–2, 3–4, 5–6a and 9b
Matthew 23:13–22

Tuesday

AUGUST 24

• ST. BARTHOLOMEW, APOSTLE •

But Nathanael said to him, "Can anything good come from Nazareth?" Philip said to him, "Come and see."
—JOHN 1:46

In one of the more humorous passages in the Bible, Nathanael (also known as Bartholomew) pokes fun at the seemingly insignificant town of Nazareth. Jesus's response is equally humorous as he says the equivalent of "Whoa, we've got a live one here!" This is a good example of how humor can serve a theological purpose: It emphasizes God's penchant for confounding human expectations by choosing the humble and unexpected to reveal his greatness. On this feast of St. Bartholomew, may we remember and appreciate how Jesus called ordinary people like you and me to follow him and to participate in his mission. Ordinary people are capable of accomplishing extraordinary things. This feast also reminds us that we can find God in the places where we least expect him.

Revelation 21:9b–14
Psalm 145:10–11, 12–13, 17–18
John 1:45–51

Wednesday

AUGUST 25

• ST. LOUIS OF FRANCE * ST. JOSEPH CALASANZ, PRIEST •

And for this reason we too give thanks to God unceasingly, that, in receiving the word of God from hearing us, you received not a human word but, as it truly is, the word of God, which is now at work in you who believe.

—1 THESSALONIANS 2:13

Anyone who proclaims the gospel should be thin. Now, before you send in letters of complaint, let me clarify—I'm not referring to physical size. Rather, I'm referring to the idea that, just as a place or a moment can be considered "thin," so too should those who proclaim the gospel be "thin." In other words, those who proclaim the gospel must not obstruct others' view of God but rather should make God's presence more visible to others. Our role as followers of Jesus is not to draw attention to ourselves but to the presence of God in the moments of everyday living.

1 Thessalonians 2:9–13
Psalm 139:7–8, 9–10, 11–12ab
Matthew 23:27–32

Thursday

AUGUST 26

Jesus said to his disciples: "Stay awake! For you do not know on which day your Lord will come."
—MATTHEW 24:42

When we get sleepy, we become less conscious of the world around us. Our responsiveness to external stimuli diminishes. Our ability to process and respond to sounds and sights is switched off. In today's Gospel, Jesus warns that this sleepiness can happen to us on a spiritual level. To stay awake spiritually is to remain conscious of God's presence, listening and looking for signs of that presence, and respond appropriately. When Jesus says that we cannot know the day that our Lord is coming, he is not solely referring to the second coming. Instead, he reminds us that the Lord comes to us over and over again in big and small ways. As you shake off last night's sleep, be sure to shake off spiritual sleepiness as well.

1 Thessalonians 3:7–13
Psalm 90:3–5a, 12–13, 14 and 17
Matthew 24:42–51

This is the will of God, your holiness
—1 THESSALONIANS 4:3

Some years back, when I attended the graduation ceremony for my doctorate, I stood proudly in line as the various diplomas were being awarded. When it came time for the doctorate diplomas, the emcee announced, "And now for the doctorate degree, the terminal degree." Terminal! This made it sound like there was no more learning or growth to occur. Just as we can always continue growing and learning with regard to knowledge and wisdom, we can always continue growing spiritually. Holiness is not something that is achieved like a diploma and then displayed in a frame. It is a way of life. Today's first reading reminds us to continue making greater progress in our quest to be holy. And holiness is nothing other than resembling God in whose image and likeness we are made.

1 Thessalonians 4:1–8
Psalm 97:1 and 2b, 5–6, 10, 11–12
Matthew 25:1–13

Saturday

AUGUST 28

• ST. AUGUSTINE, BISHOP AND DOCTOR OF THE CHURCH •

For to everyone who has, more will be given and he will grow rich; but from the one who has not, even what he has will be taken away.
—MATTHEW 25:29

Investors know that the goal for any investment is growth. Keeping money in our mattress may help us to feel safe, however, we are losing the opportunity for that money to grow. Growth always involves some degree of risk, whether it is growing an investment or growing as a human being. Today's readings continue the theme of growing in holiness which we do, not by sitting still and avoiding risk, but by taking the gifts that God has given us and putting them to work in the service of others. As we share our gifts with others, they grow and multiply. Think of it this way: Sharing your gifts with others is a way of investing in them and their well-being. May you grow rich in the gifts of the Spirit.

1 Thessalonians 4:9–11
Psalm 98:1, 7–8, 9
Matthew 25:14–30

Sunday

AUGUST 29

• TWENTY-SECOND SUNDAY IN ORDINARY TIME •

Humbly welcome the word that has been planted in you and is able to save your souls. Be doers of the word and not hearers only, deluding yourselves.

—JAMES 1:21–22

Cliches are cliches for a reason: They capture a simple truth in a few words. Two such examples are "talk is cheap" and "actions speak louder than words." Both of these emphasize the need to be consistent between our words and our actions. This is the heart of today's second reading from the Letter of James. We are called to be not only hearers of the word but also doers of the word. We have opportunities every day to put our beliefs into action, whether at home, work, or play. The word that has taken root in us calls us to selfless love and compassion for all, especially those who are struggling. Strive today to be a doer of God's word.

Deuteronomy 4:1–2, 6–8
Psalm 15:2–3, 3–4, 4–5 (1a)
James 1:17–18, 21b–22, 27
Mark 7:1–8, 14–15, 21–23

Monday

AUGUST 30

Today this Scripture passage is fulfilled in your hearing.
—LUKE 4:21

When Jesus got up in the synagogue to read from the prophet Isaiah, he proclaimed a passage that could only be fulfilled by the coming of the Messiah. You can imagine why folks were a bit dismayed that Jesus was pointing to himself as the fulfillment of this promise. How could the carpenter's son be the Messiah? And yet, Jesus fulfilled the promise spoken through Isaiah: He brought glad tidings to the poor, proclaimed liberty to captives, recovered the sight of the blind. It is this good news that we are called to proclaim in Jesus's name as we encounter people who are being held captive by poverty, despair, loneliness, sickness, and many other evils. Each day, we have opportunities to show that Jesus is indeed the fulfillment of the promise that God gave long ago.

1 Thessalonians 4:13–18
Psalm 96:1 and 3, 4–5, 11–12, 13
Luke 4:16–30

Tuesday

AUGUST 31

Jesus rebuked him and said, "Be quiet! Come out of him!"
—LUKE 4:35

The Gospels show us that Jesus had power over the wind and the waves, over blindness and paralysis, and even over death. One area that is often overlooked or misunderstood is Jesus's power over demons. Perhaps it is because the concept of demons has been trivialized by Hollywood. We dismiss the notion of evil spirits and demons as something that only happens in stories and movies. And yet, we continue to grapple with the demons of despair, anxiety, depression, loneliness, and fear. It is good to remind ourselves, as today's Gospel does, that Jesus has power over these demons. Whenever we find ourselves struggling with the voices of demons that will not allow us to rest, we can recall the words of Jesus—"Be quiet! Come out!"—and use these words to be freed from their control.

1 Thessalonians 5:1–6, 9–11
Psalm 27:1, 4, 13–14
Luke 4:31–37

Wednesday

SEPTEMBER 1

Simon's mother-in-law was afflicted with a severe fever. . . .
[Jesus] stood over her, rebuked the fever, and it left her.
—LUKE 4:38–39

In today's Gospel, as daylight fades, people bring the sick to him, and he lays his hands on each one. Jesus's care is not distant, but personal; not rushed, but compassionate. After laying hands on the people brought to him, he withdraws to a deserted place to pray, showing that his strength flows from quiet, intimate communion with the Father. This Gospel invites us to trust that Jesus will heal us and follow him with confidence into the stillness where God restores our hearts. We often try to push through difficulties with sheer stubborn effort, convincing ourselves that we should be stronger, more faithful, more capable. Yet the Gospel reminds us that a special grace begins when we allow Jesus to meet us in our need.

Colossians 1:1–8
Psalm 52:10, 11
Luke 4:38–44

Thursday

SEPTEMBER 2

When Simon Peter saw this, he fell at the knees of Jesus and said, "Depart from me, Lord, for I am a sinful man."
—LUKE 5:8

Soon after Cardinal Jorge Bergoglio became Pope Francis, an interviewer asked him, "Who is Jorge Bergoglio?" Without hesitation, Pope Francis replied, "I am a sinner." This was not a display of false humility or self-loathing. Rather, it was the acknowledgment of our human condition that requires the intervention of a savior—and opens the door to accepting the forgiveness offered to us through Jesus Christ. When we come face-to-face with the overwhelming goodness of God, we can't help but become aware of our shortcomings, much as someone with an ordinary body shape becomes aware of physical flaws when standing next to someone whose build is statuesque. Embracing our sinfulness is actually liberating because it opens us up to saving grace on which we truly thrive.

Colossians 1:9–14
Psalm 98:2–3ab, 3cd–4, 5–6
Luke 5:1–11

Friday

SEPTEMBER 3

• ST. GREGORY THE GREAT, POPE AND DOCTOR OF THE CHURCH •

Likewise, no one pours new wine into old wineskins. Otherwise, the new wine will burst the skins, and it will be spilled, and the skins will be ruined. Rather, new wine must be poured into fresh wineskins.

—LUKE 5:37–38

Our brains are wired to rely on familiarity, so when our rapidly changing world bombards us with new ways of doing things, we can sometimes feel uneasy and even distrustful of what is new. In today's Gospel, Jesus reminds us that sometimes the healthiest thing for us to do is let go of the old, recognizing that old patterns, habits, and mindsets are sometimes incapable of supporting new ones. This does not mean that we must abandon traditions or time-tested beliefs and practices. It does, however, encourage us to be open to what is new, namely the new life offered to us through Jesus Christ who makes all things new.

Colossians 1:15–20
Psalm 100:1b–2, 3, 4, 5
Luke 5:33–39

Saturday

SEPTEMBER 4

God has now reconciled you
in the fleshly Body of Christ through his death,
to present you holy, without blemish,
and irreproachable before him
—COLOSSIANS 1:22–23

When something is successfully repaired, it feels as though order has been restored to the universe. Perhaps because, in some way, that's exactly what occurs: Things go back to the way they should be. And this, I believe, is one of God's most attractive qualities: God repairs things, beginning with us. Today's first reading reminds us that through Jesus Christ we have been reconciled with God—a hard reset that erases all of our sins and enables us to start anew. What a great thought to wake up to! Today is another opportunity to give thanks for this reset and to live as a new creation, inviting others to enjoy the gift of reconciliation God offers us through his Son, Jesus Christ.

Colossians 1:21–23
Psalm 54:3–4, 6 and 8
Luke 6:1–5

Sunday

SEPTEMBER 5

• TWENTY-THIRD SUNDAY IN ORDINARY TIME •

Thus says the LORD*:*
Say to those whose hearts are frightened:
Be strong, fear not!
—ISAIAH 35:4

Fear is a natural human condition. The following are considered some of the most common fears. Which do you share? Spiders, snakes, heights, closed spaces, lightning, injections, social situations, flying, germs/dirt, public speaking, darkness. It often seems as though we have many things to fear. Perhaps this is why one of the most commonly used phrases in the Bible (appearing over 150 times) is the phrase, "Do not fear" or variations such as "do not be afraid," "fear not," "be not afraid." Today's first reading from Isaiah boldly proclaims that we have no reason to fear with God at our side. The problem is, we too often forget that God is at our side! Isaiah says, "Here is your God!" as opposed to, "There is your God, over there!" God's nearness enables us to fear not.

Isaiah 35:4–7a
Psalm 146:7, 8–9, 9–10 (1b)
James 2:1–5
Mark 7:31–37

Monday

SEPTEMBER 6

• LABOR DAY •

It is Christ in you, the hope for glory. It is he whom we proclaim.
—COLOSSIANS 1:27–28

In speaking to a group of parents whose children were preparing for First Holy Communion, I ruffled a few feathers by saying, "Keep in mind that your child's First Holy Communion is not about your child." After pausing for a little dramatic effect, I added, "It's about what God is doing in the life of your child." Thankfully, the feathers unruffled.

This was an important distinction I wanted them to understand, and it is the same one Paul makes in his Letter to the Colossians: It is Christ in you whom we proclaim. It is not about us. This can be a difficult lesson to learn, especially in a culture that says, "It's all about you!" We go forth into the world glorifying God by our lives!

Colossians 1:24—2:3
Psalm 62:6–7, 9
Luke 6:6–11

Tuesday

SEPTEMBER 7

See to it that no one captivate you with
an empty, seductive philosophy.
—COLOSSIANS 2:8

My friend, author Tom McGrath, taught me an important lesson when we worked together at a Catholic publishing company. Tom said that it was critical that we populate the imaginations of young people with stories and images of a loving, compassionate, merciful, and just God, because if we don't, our culture will be happy to populate their imaginations with vapid and even destructive philosophies. This is true for people of all ages. In today's first reading, St. Paul warns that we must not allow ourselves to be captivated with an empty, seductive philosophy. Instead, we turn to Scripture and Tradition for a healthy and fortifying narrative of a God who rescues, restores, and reassures us. Our goal each day is to live within this life-giving narrative and project it outward to those we encounter.

Colossians 2:6–15
Psalm 145:1b–2, 8–9, 10–11
Luke 6:12–19

Wednesday

SEPTEMBER 8

• THE NATIVITY OF THE BLESSED VIRGIN MARY •

The Book of the genealogy of Jesus Christ,
the son of David, the son of Abraham.
—MATTHEW 1:1

For most people, biblical genealogies may not seem like the most inspiring passages to use for prayer and reflection. And yet, today people are increasingly using services that trace our family trees as far back as we can go. Family trees and genealogies tell us a story and paint a picture of how we got to be the person we are today. As we celebrate the Nativity of the Blessed Virgin Mary, we are reminded of Jesus's human origins, his flawed ancestors, his lineage to royalty, and God's providence. This is a story of grace and redemption and how God uses ordinary people like you and me for extraordinary purposes. As you reflect on your own family story—warts and all—be grateful for the grace of God that sustains you each day.

Micah 5:1–4a or Romans 8:28–30
Psalm 13:6ab, 6c
Matthew 1:1–16, 18–23 or, for shorter form,
Matthew 1:18-23

Thursday

SEPTEMBER 9

• ST. PETER CLAVER, PRIEST •

Brothers and sisters: Put on, as God's chosen ones, holy and beloved, heartfelt compassion, kindness, humility, gentleness, and patience.
—COLOSSIANS 3:12

At professional sporting events, many fans don their favorite team's jersey or regalia. We wear these to identify with the team and embody what the team stands for, which is usually a fighting spirit, determination, and quest for victory. In today's first reading, St. Paul uses the imagery of *putting on* a piece of clothing or armor that signifies our own embodiment of the Lord's saving qualities. As Catholics, this notion of *putting on Christ* is etched into our sacramental life when we put on a baptismal garment and commit to follow Christ. We wear that ritual garment only once, but each day as we get dressed, we can remind ourselves to *put on* Christ so that others may see the good we do and give glory to God.

Colossians 3:12–17
Psalm 150:1b–2, 3–4, 5–6
Luke 6:27–38

Friday

SEPTEMBER 10

"Remove the wooden beam from your eye first; then you will see clearly to remove the splinter in your brother's eye."
—LUKE 6:42

Author and speaker Mel Robbins explains in her book *Let Them* that the quest to change others is futile unless they themselves want to change. Instead, she advises that we save that energy by shifting our focus from managing others to prioritizing our own growth and well-being. In today's Gospel, Jesus tells us much the same and emphasizes the need to honestly confront and acknowledge our own shortcomings, not to dwell on them and wallow in misery, but to accept the reality that we need God's grace. To do so opens us to receiving God's redeeming grace, which is blocked by self-righteousness. If you find yourself today focused on correcting someone else's behavior, do yourself a favor and shift your focus to your own need for saving grace.

1 Timothy 1:1–2, 12–14
Psalm 16:1b–2a and 5, 7–8, 11
Luke 6:39–42

Saturday

SEPTEMBER 11

That one is like a person building a house, who dug deeply and laid the foundation on rock; when the flood came, the river burst against that house but could not shake it because it had been well built.

—LUKE 6:48

I grew up in an apartment building that was not built well—and, in fact, literally began to crumble. It was unable to stand the test of time. We tenants were all forced to leave, and the building was demolished. Jesus uses this metaphor in today's Gospel to remind us to lay a solid foundation for our lives, which will involve no shortage of storms and challenges. Just as a builder digs deep to lay a firm foundation, we are called this day to dig deep into the word of God and to put his word into action. A life built on faith in Jesus will withstand life's storms.

1 Timothy 1:15–17
Psalm 113:1b–2, 3–4, 5a and 6–7
Luke 6:43–49

Sunday

SEPTEMBER 12

• TWENTY-FOURTH SUNDAY IN ORDINARY TIME •

And he asked them, "But who do you say that I am?" Peter said to him in reply, "You are the Christ."
—MARK 8:29

Ultimately, we are called to answer the question Jesus asked of his disciples: "Who do you say that I am?" In the early centuries of the church, councils were held to answer this question in the face of heresies that portrayed Jesus as less than he is: fully human and fully divine. Today, these heresies subtly linger as we can be tempted to think that Jesus is just a great teacher, a wise philosopher, even a miracle worker. And yet, while Jesus is all of these, he is so much more: He is the Christ, the Son of God, our Savior. To proclaim Jesus as the Christ is to acknowledge our inability to save ourselves. Thank God for that because trying to save ourselves is exhausting!

Isaiah 50:5–9a
Psalm 116:1–2, 3–4, 5–6, 8–9 (9)
James 2:14–18
Mark 8:27–35

Monday

SEPTEMBER 13

• ST. JOHN CHRYSOSTOM, BISHOP AND DOCTOR OF THE CHURCH •

The centurion sent friends to tell him, "Lord, do not trouble yourself, for I am not worthy to have you enter under my roof; . . . but say the word and let my servant be healed."
—LUKE 7:6–7

These words, which we echo right before coming forward to receive Holy Communion, are key to our salvation. Like the centurion, we acknowledge our unworthiness, which Jesus seeks to heal, and we trust that Jesus alone can bring about that healing. These words can be spoken in prayer at the start of each day as a way of humbly placing ourselves before God and praising him for his greatness as we ask for the grace we need to bring the healing—physical, emotional, mental, spiritual—that we and others need. It is also an act of faith as we trust that Jesus need only *say the word* to bring about healing.

1 Timothy 2:1–8
Psalm 28:2, 7, 8–9
Luke 7:1–10

Tuesday

SEPTEMBER 14

• THE EXALTATION OF THE HOLY CROSS •

He humbled himself,
becoming obedient to death,
even death on a cross.
—PHILIPPIANS 2:8

When my beloved Chicago Blackhawks hockey team ended a forty-nine-year drought to win the Stanley Cup in 2010, I, along with a few million other fans, gathered to celebrate the victory and see the prestigious trophy paraded through the city because we all long to be associated with a winner. For Christians, the cross of Jesus Christ is our unlikely symbol of God's victory over death. Today, we celebrate the Exaltation of the Holy Cross, and we glory in the cross, not because we like to see suffering, but because we know that Jesus's death on the cross was transformed into new life through the Resurrection, a victory in which we share. Today we pray, "We adore you, O Christ, and we bless you, because by your Cross you have redeemed the world." (Gospel Acclamation)

Numbers 21:4b–9
Psalm 78:1bc–2, 34–35, 36–37, 38
Philippians 2:6–11
John 3:13–17

Wednesday

SEPTEMBER 15

• OUR LADY OF SORROWS •

Standing by the cross of Jesus were his mother and his mother's sister, Mary the wife of Clopas, and Mary Magdalene.
—JOHN 19:25

For decades, I have lived just a mile away from Little Company of Mary Hospital. For many of those years, however, I had no idea what the name of the hospital—Little Company of Mary—meant. Thankfully, I eventually learned that the hospital was established by the Little Company of Mary Sisters and that the *little company of Mary* referred to the small group of people, mostly women, who stood with Mary at the foot of her son's cross at her time of great sorrow. Today, as we celebrate the Feast of Our Lady of Sorrows, may we join Mary and her little company by accompanying those who are sick with our visits and prayers and by being a compassionate presence to all we encounter.

1 Timothy 3:14–16
Psalm 111:1–2, 3–4, 5–6
John 19:25–27 or Luke 2:33–35

Thursday

SEPTEMBER 16

• ST. CORNELIUS, POPE, AND ST. CYPRIAN, BISHOP, MARTYRS •

I tell you, her many sins have been forgiven; hence, she has shown great love. But the one to whom little is forgiven, loves little.
—LUKE 7:47

In the great Dr. Seuss's Christmas classic *The Grinch Who Stole Christmas*, we are told that the Grinch's heart grew three sizes larger after he learned the true meaning of Christmas. We often describe very loving people as having a big heart. A bighearted person is someone who is kind, generous, compassionate, and helpful toward others. In today's Gospel, we meet a bighearted woman who went out of her way to show love for Jesus, who says her great love is evidence that she has been forgiven. We can all grow the size of our hearts each day and resist the forces in our world that seek to shrink them. As our hearts grow, so too will our experience of God's mercy and forgiveness.

1 Timothy 4:12–16
Psalm 111:7–8, 9, 10
Luke 7:36–50

Friday

SEPTEMBER 17

• ST. ROBERT BELLARMINE, BISHOP AND DOCTOR OF THE CHURCH •

Accompanying him were the Twelve and some women who had been cured of evil spirits and infirmities.
—LUKE 8:1–2

In his Gospel, Luke goes out of his way to mention people who were too often not considered central to God's plan: Gentiles, outcasts, sinners, children, and, in the case of today's Gospel, women. This short reference to women accompanying Jesus is extraordinary in a world where women were not seen as disciples of master teachers. Jesus breaks down these barriers and welcomes women into his inner circle. We, too, are called to break down barriers that exclude people from full participation in many aspects of life and work. Likewise, today's Gospel invites us to pause and give thanks for the many great women who have used their gifts selflessly and bravely to do God's work and to bring us and others closer to Christ.

1 Timothy 6:2c–12
Psalm 49:6–7, 8–10, 17–18, 19–20
Luke 8:1–3

Saturday

SEPTEMBER 18

Come with joy into the presence of the Lord.
—PSALM 100:1

Psalm 100 is among the shortest psalms in the Bible, which makes it one of the easiest to take to heart (memorize). As a psalm of thanksgiving, it is one of the most joyful psalms in the Bible as well. This is a wonderful psalm to begin your day with since it gives praise to God for his enduring goodness, love, and faithfulness while reminding us that God is our creator to whom we belong. Whether you memorize it or just keep a copy handy, praying Psalm 100 at the beginning of the day is a great way to spiritually reboot as you prepare to go forth into the world, knowing that, wherever we go, we are entering his gates and will encounter his goodness. That, indeed, calls for shouts of joy!

1 Timothy 6:13–16
Psalm 100:1b–2, 3, 4, 5
Luke 8:4–15

Sunday

SEPTEMBER 19

• TWENTY-FIFTH SUNDAY IN ORDINARY TIME •

But they remained silent. They had been discussing among themselves on the way who was the greatest.
—MARK 9:34

Today's readings remind us that human pettiness is nothing new. In fact, in today's Gospel, Jesus's disciples are caught in the act of arguing about which of them was the greatest. These readings should accomplish two things: First, they challenge us to reflect on the worthiness of our own thoughts and actions. Second, they reassure us: Even Jesus's disciples were not immune from such behavior, which means there is indeed hope for all of us. Jesus reminds us today that we need to be vigilant against temptations to lower ourselves to pettiness. We can overcome these tendences by focusing on love for others, treating others as more important than ourselves, and adopting a selfless, service-oriented attitude. We can do this knowing that, as today's Psalm reminds us, God is our helper.

Wisdom 2:12, 17–20
Psalm 54:3–4, 5, 6–8 (6b)
James 3:16—4:3
Mark 9:30–37

Monday

SEPTEMBER 20

• ST. ANDREW KIM TAE-GŎN, PRIEST, AND ST. PAUL CHŎNG HA-SANG, CATECHIST, AND COMPANIONS, MARTYRS •

Jesus said to the crowds: "No one who lights a lamp conceals it with a vessel or sets it under a bed; rather, he places it on a lampstand so that those who enter may see the light."
—LUKE 8:16

The challenge we face as humble disciples of Christ is to figure out how to *let our light shine* without *tooting our own horn*. Today, it is common to hear the phrase *virtue signaling* when someone publicly makes a show of moral correctness to gain social approval or standing. Letting our light shine is not to draw attention to ourselves but to the goodness of God working through us. Our hope is that others will see our witness and be inspired to live according to God's way of mercy, compassion, and justice. Let your good works today be a light to others, guiding them to follow the way of Jesus.

Ezra 1:1–6
Psalm 126:1b–2ab, 2cd–3, 4–5, 6
Luke 8:16–18

Tuesday

SEPTEMBER 21

• ST. MATTHEW, APOSTLE AND EVANGELIST •

Go and learn the meaning of the words, "I desire mercy, not sacrifice." I did not come to call the righteous but sinners.
—MATTHEW 9:13

A child finds a special tenderness in the arms of his or her mother. For this reason, the notion of a "mother and child reunion" provokes an image of incredible tenderness. Well, it might surprise you to know that the Hebrew word for mercy—*rechem*—has a double meaning. It also can be translated as *womb*. In other words, when Jesus says that he desires mercy and not sacrifice, he is saying that his greatest desire is that we treat others as though they were our own children, which, of course, involves tenderness. The world could use more tenderness of the kind that a loving mother shows her child—the kind of love that God shows each of us. Go forth today with tenderness toward others.

Ephesians 4:1–7, 11–13
Psalm 19:2–3, 4–5
Matthew 9:9–13

Wednesday

SEPTEMBER 22

Thus he has given us new life to raise again the house of our God and restore its ruins, and has granted us a fence in Judah and Jerusalem.

—EZRA 9:9

When the Jewish people returned from their exile in Babylon, Ezra, a priest and prophet, led them in a spiritual renewal—teaching the Torah, renewing their covenant with God, and rebuilding the temple that had been destroyed. This restoration mirrors what God does for us. God creates and God restores. Throughout Scripture, God seeks to repair the relationship that his people have damaged. In his book *Simply Christian*, Bible scholar and Anglican bishop N. T. Wright tells us that God's intention is not to abandon this world in favor of heaven but rather to remake it. Each day, we have the opportunity to remake this world to reflect God's wonderful plan more closely.

Ezra 9:5–9
Tobit 13:2, 3–4a, 4befghn, 7–8
Luke 9:1–6

Thursday

SEPTEMBER 23

• ST. PIUS OF PIETRELCINA, PRIEST •

(Then this word of the LORD
came through Haggai, the prophet:)
Is it time for you to dwell in your own paneled houses,
while this house lies in ruins?
—HAGGAI 1:3–4

In today's first reading, Haggai the prophet calls for the rebuilding of the temple in Jerusalem that had been destroyed during their exile in Babylon. Throughout history, we human beings have been compelled to build altars, temples, and cathedrals as tangible reminders of God's presence in our midst. While these beautiful edifices provide us with inspiring places to worship God, remember that you are a *temple of the Holy Spirit* and a *living stone.* Today, through your encounters with others, you will have ample opportunities to serve as a living reminder that God is in our midst, inspired by the knowledge that every person you meet is also a temple of the Holy Spirit, and thus sacred.

Haggai 1:1–8
Psalm 149:1b–2, 3–4, 5–6a and 9b
Luke 9:7–9

Friday

SEPTEMBER 24

He said, "The Son of Man must suffer greatly and be rejected by the elders, the chief priests, and the scribes, and be killed and on the third day be raised."
—LUKE 9:22

A friend of mine related how he was participating in an interreligious dialogue taking place at his own home. During a break, a Buddhist man came up to him, pointed at the crucifix on the wall, and asked, "Why do you Catholics like to remind yourself of suffering?" Buddhists believe that while suffering is inevitable, it can be ended. Christians, on the other hand, believe that suffering is something that can be transformed—it is a part of the Paschal mystery that leads to new life. Ask God today for the grace to navigate through the suffering that is present in your life and in the lives of others and to transform that suffering into new life.

Haggai 2:1–9
Psalm 43:1, 2, 3, 4
Luke 9:18–22

Saturday

SEPTEMBER 25

Sing and rejoice, O daughter Zion!
See, I am coming to dwell among you, says the LORD.
Many nations shall join themselves to the LORD on that day,
and they shall be his people and he will dwell among you.
—ZECHARIAH 2:14–15

What a joyful day it is when a newborn is brought home, when a loved one returns after convalescence, when a child return home from college, when a parent returns after a long trip. We long to have our loved ones present with us. Knowing this, God comes to dwell among us! The promise given in the Old Testament, recounted in today's first reading, was fulfilled in the coming of Jesus Christ, who dwells among us. Too many people are unable to see, feel, and experience the nearness of God because of fear, anxiety, or despair. Through your words and actions, you can be a living reminder that God's mercy and compassion are in our midst. We are not alone.

Zechariah 2:5–9, 14–15a
Jeremiah 31:10, 11–12ab, 13
Luke 9:43b–45

Sunday

SEPTEMBER 26

• TWENTY-SIXTH SUNDAY IN ORDINARY TIME •

The LORD then came down in the cloud and spoke to Moses. Taking some of the spirit that was on Moses, the LORD bestowed it on the seventy elders.

—NUMBERS 11:25

The ordination of a Catholic bishop involves anointing with sacred chrism. This is no ordinary anointing, however—this is a *pouring* of oil! As the oil is poured over the head of the new bishop, it drips down his face and neck. The symbolism is powerful: The gifts of the Holy Spirit are poured out in abundance. In today's first reading, God spreads his spirit beyond Moses to the seventy elders, including two—Eldad and Medad—who were outside of the camp. The Holy Spirit knows no boundaries! This same Holy Spirit has been poured out into your heart so that you, too, can share this anointing with others by embodying Christ's values and sharing your gifts in service to others.

Numbers 11:25–29
Psalm 19:8, 10, 12–13, 14 (9a)
James 5:1–6
Mark 9:38–43, 45, 47–48

Monday

SEPTEMBER 27

• ST. VINCENT DE PAUL, PRIEST •

Thus says the LORD of hosts:
Lo, I will rescue my people from the land of the rising sun,
and from the land of the setting sun.
—ZECHARIAH 8:7

Think for a moment about rescuers that you see on the news: first responders who dramatically run toward and reach out to grasp the hands of those in danger and lead them to safety, as God did for his people Israel after their exile in Babylon. Today, we celebrate the feast of St. Vincent de Paul, whose legacy includes an organization—the St. Vincent de Paul Society—dedicated to rescuing people through outreach programs that feed, clothe, house, and heal individuals and families who have nowhere else to turn for help. You can participate in this rescue program by volunteering your time, making financial donations, donating goods to thrift stores or drives, and shopping at St. Vincent de Paul thrift stores.

Zechariah 8:1–8
Psalm 102:16–18, 19–21, 29 and 22–23
Luke 9:46–50

Tuesday

SEPTEMBER 28

• ST. WENCESLAUS, MARTYR • ST. LAWRENCE RUIZ AND COMPANIONS, MARTYRS •

When the disciples James and John saw this they asked, "Lord, do you want us to call down fire from heaven to consume them?"
—LUKE 9:54

When James and John saw that the Samaritan people would not welcome Jesus, they wanted to impulsively punish them. For this outburst, they earned the nickname "Sons of Thunder." We too can react impulsively when something or someone angers us. When we express anger impulsively, three things tend to happen: Our response is hasty and unmeasured, it is usually excessive, and its effects linger far too long. Strong emotions like anger lack judgment. Left alone, anger is reactive and unreflective, aimed at destruction of the object or person who has aroused it. This is why anger management strategies almost always include taking a few deep breaths and counting to ten before responding. Be sure to breathe deeply as you encounter frustrations today!

Zechariah 8:20–23
Psalm 87:1b–3, 4–5, 6–7
Luke 9:51–56

Wednesday

SEPTEMBER 29

• ST. MICHAEL, ST. GABRIEL, AND ST. RAPHAEL, ARCHANGELS •

I will give thanks to you, O LORD, with all my heart,
for you have heard the words of my mouth;
in the presence of the angels I will sing your praise.
—PSALM 138:1

With reference to angels, St. Augustine wrote: "'Angel' is the name of their office, not of their nature. If you seek the name of their nature, it is 'spirit'; if you seek the name of their office, it is 'angel': from what they are, 'spirit,' from what they do, 'angel'" (*City of God*). In other words, when Scripture refers to angels, it is emphasizing their function: to be a messenger of God, performing tasks for God. As we celebrate today's feast of the archangels, may we be inspired to serve as angels for others, being messengers of God's mercy, charity, compassion, and justice, while also performing tasks for God such as the Corporal and Spiritual Works of Mercy.

Daniel 7:9–10, 13–14 or Revelation 12:7–12ab
Psalm 138:1–2ab, 2cde–3, 4–5
John 1:47–51

Thursday

SEPTEMBER 30

• ST. JEROME, PRIEST AND DOCTOR OF THE CHURCH •

Ezra read plainly from the book of the law of God, interpreting it so that all could understand what was read.
—NEHEMIAH 8:8

In today's first reading, a dramatic event unfolds as the people of Israel return from their exile in Babylon. Some years before, the scrolls of the Torah (the law of Moses) were found in the ruins of the temple. Now, Ezra, a scribe, gathers the people who have returned from Exile, dramatically shows and unrolls the scroll, and then reads and interprets Scripture for them, leading to a great spiritual renewal. Today, we celebrate the feast of St. Jerome, who is known for translating the Bible into Latin at a time when Latin was the language of the people. Today is a good day to renew your commitment to reading and reflecting on God's word and to pray that this practice leads to your own spiritual renewal.

Nehemiah 8:1–4a, 5–6, 7b–12
Psalm 19:8, 9, 10, 11
Luke 10:1–12

Friday

OCTOBER 1

• ST. THÉRÈSE OF THE CHILD JESUS, VIRGIN AND DOCTOR OF THE CHURCH •

Whoever listens to you listens to me. Whoever rejects you rejects me. And whoever rejects me rejects the one who sent me.
—LUKE 10:16

It is a profound responsibility to speak on someone's behalf. At the same time, it is a great honor to have someone trust us enough to allow us to speak on their behalf. In today's Gospel, Jesus reminds us that we have been sent forth to speak on his behalf. How can we possibly speak on behalf of Jesus? In simple terms, we do so by speaking and acting with compassion, goodness, mercy, and justice—all qualities that are available to us through the power of the Holy Spirit and by virtue of the fact that we are made in the image and likeness of God. We pray for the grace to *get out of the way* and allow Jesus to speak and act through us.

Baruch 1:15–22
Psalm 79:1b–2, 3–5, 8, 9
Luke 10:13–16

Fear not, my children; call out to God!
—BARUCH 4:21

The spiritual hymn "Sometimes I Feel Like a Motherless Child" came out of the oral traditions of enslaved African Americans in the 1800s. Originally, the hymn expressed the devastation of the enslaved person's separation from their African homeland and family. The image is poignant because when a child experiences fear, he or she instinctively calls "Mama!" knowing that she will respond. How devastating it is to be separated from one's mother! In today's first reading, God reassures us, through the prophet Baruch, that he hears our pleas and is near to us, responding to our needs just as a mother responds to her child's cries. Knowing this, we are told to fear not and to call out to God, confident that we are not alone and that God is embracing us like a mother holds her child close to her heart.

Baruch 4:5–12, 27–29
Psalm 69:33–35, 36–37
Matthew 18:1–5, 10

Sunday OCTOBER 3

• TWENTY-SEVENTH SUNDAY IN ORDINARY TIME •

The LORD God said: It is not good for the man to be alone.
—GENESIS 2:18

In the book of Genesis, shortly after God creates Adam, he comments that it is not good for Adam to be alone. This teaches us that one of the very first things God provides for Adam is a relationship. The creation of Adam, then of Eve as his companion reveals that God considers relationships to be necessary for our human welfare. God knew something that humankind has learned over time: It is not good for us humans to be alone—that is, isolated from others. Even introverts need relationships! Research reveals that people with healthy relationships have fewer doctor visits, shorter hospital stays, and more positive emotions. We become more like our God—who is a divine relationship of Father, Son, and Holy Spirit—when we build, sustain, and celebrate our relationships.

Genesis 2:18–24
Psalm 128:1–2, 3, 4–5, 6
Hebrews 2:9–11
Mark 10:2–16 or, for shorter form, Mark 10:2–12

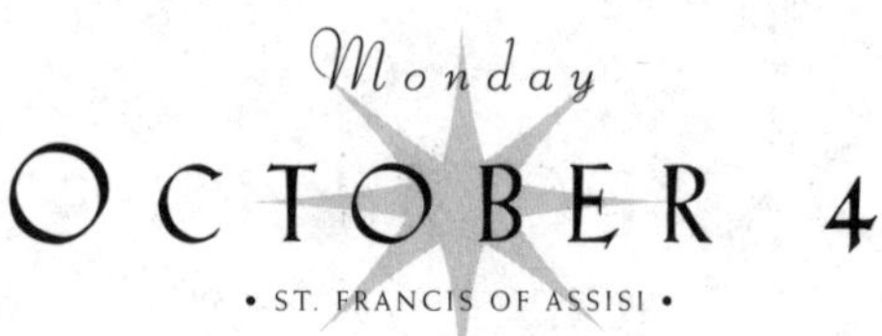

Monday OCTOBER 4

• ST. FRANCIS OF ASSISI •

But the LORD sent a large fish, that swallowed Jonah;
and Jonah remained in the belly of the fish
three days and three nights.
—JONAH 2:1

While the story of Jonah belongs to the category of mythology, it is nonetheless a *true* story because it teaches a central truth of our faith: We can run, but we cannot hide. This became powerfully evident to me at a presentation I was giving when a tearful young woman came up to me and said, "This story of Jonah—this is my story! I've been in the belly of the whale!" She explained that she is in a twelve-step program and that hitting rock bottom is akin to being in the belly of the whale. She credited her sobriety to the intervention of God's saving grace—the same amazing grace that saves us all from the darkness and enables us to see the light.

Jonah 1:1—2:1–2, 11
Jonah 2:3, 4, 5, 8
Luke 10:25–37

Tuesday

OCTOBER 5

The Lord said to her in reply, "Martha, Martha, you are anxious and worried about many things."
—LUKE 10:41

The encounter with Martha and Mary has long caused many people to come to the defense of Martha, saying that Jesus seems to be dismissing the importance of housework. Upon closer inspection, however, we find that Jesus never mentions the work she is doing but points out her anxiousness. Anyone sitting at the feet of Jesus, like her sister Mary, could just as easily have been overwhelmed with anxiety. Jesus is encouraging us to approach whatever we do with a sense of calm and a dismissal of fear and anxiety, which can too often cause us to lose focus. Like Mary, we are called to prioritize our spiritual connection and allow it to bring a sense of calm to all that we do, whether we are doing chores or sitting still.

Jonah 3:1–10
Psalm 130:1b–2, 3–4ab, 7–8
Luke 10:38–42

Wednesday

OCTOBER 6

• ST. BRUNO, PRIEST • BL. MARIE-ROSE DUROCHER, VIRGIN •

Jesus was praying in a certain place,
and when he had finished,
one of his disciples said to him,
"Lord, teach us to pray just as John taught his disciples."
—LUKE 11:1B

When my daughter was in her first year at a Catholic high school, she was struggling to compose a prayer for her religion class the next day. "I can't think of the right words," she said. Realizing that she was trying to compose a piece of poetry, I told her St. Ignatius taught that prayer should resemble one friend speaking to another and asked her to think about what she would text to a good friend about her day—her joys, her worries, and so on—and do the same with God. When Jesus taught his disciples to pray the Our Father, he wasn't so much telling them to use those exact words. He was saying, "Talk to God as if you were talking to your Papa."

Jonah 4:1–11
Psalm 86:3–4, 5–6, 9–10
Luke 11:1–4

For everyone who asks, receives; and the one who seeks, finds; and to the one who knocks, the door will be opened.
—LUKE 11:10

Typically, when we enter a large, unfamiliar place like an airport, museum, or corporate headquarters, we are relieved to find an information desk where someone can help us navigate through the confusion. In a comparable way, we often find ourselves looking for help to navigate life's complexities. Jesus reminds us today that this help comes from the Lord, who knows what we are asking for, what we seek, and where we are trying to go in life. How reassuring it is to know that God is nearby and accessible through prayer, eager to show us the way to fullness of life. God also works through us to help others navigate through life. Your help may very well be the answer to someone's prayerful plea for divine assistance.

Malachi 3:13–20b
Psalm 1:1–2, 3, 4 and 6
Luke 11:5–13

Friday
OCTOBER 8

Alas, the day!
for near is the day of the L*ORD,*
and it comes as ruin from the Almighty.
—JOEL 1:15

In psychology, the term approach/avoidance refers to our tendency to be simultaneously excited but hesitant about something. We may be excited about the possibility of accepting a new job offer or new responsibility while at the same time fearful of it. In Scripture, the *day of the Lord* provokes this kind of feeling. The coming of the Lord is exciting, yet also frightening. This is because, while we are eager to encounter God's great goodness, we know that, next to God's goodness, our own shortcomings will be all too obvious. It might feel like our *destruction*. This realization, however, is purifying, much like fire purifies metal. This is why we pray, each day, to be purged of our offenses so that we may fully enjoy the goodness of God's grace.

Joel 1:13–15; 2:1–2
Psalm 9:2–3, 6 and 16, 8–9
Luke 11:15–26

Saturday
OCTOBER 9

• ST. DENIS, BISHOP, AND COMPANIONS, MARTYRS *
ST. JOHN LEONARDI, PRIEST •

Then you will know that I, the LORD, am your God, dwelling on Zion, my holy mountain.
—JOEL 4:17

Sometimes, in order to get our attention, people may assert themselves, speak more forcefully, or even physically touch us to remind us, "Hey, I'm talking to you." They do this because we sometimes lose our focus, or our attention may be grabbed by something or someone else. In today's first reading, God reminds us that from time to time he will make his presence known in an extraordinary way so that we refocus our attention on him and away from those things that distract us from him. At those moments, we know that God is God and that nothing should turn us from him. What helps you to keep your focus on God? What can you do to help others overcome distractions and turn their attention to God?

Joel 4:12–21
Psalm 97:1–2, 5–6, 11–12
Luke 11:27–28

Sunday

OCTOBER 10

• TWENTY-EIGHTH SUNDAY IN ORDINARY TIME •

I prayed, and prudence was given me;
I pleaded and the spirit of wisdom came to me.
—WISDOM 7:7

Prayer can sometimes be mistakenly thought of as sitting on Santa's lap and asking him to bring us what we want because we've been a good boy or girl. Too often, the things we want are just grown-up versions of the shiny new toys we asked for as children. Today's first reading reminds us that God's blessing is not measured by material possessions. Rather, we are to pray for what we need to be a better person. Scripture teaches us that Solomon, when told by the Lord he could ask for anything, asked for wisdom instead of riches and was rewarded by God with this very gift. In your prayer today, ask God for the gifts and the grace you need to be a better, more loving, caring, and compassionate person.

Wisdom 7:7–11
Psalm 90:12–13, 14–15, 16–17 (14)
Hebrews 4:12–13
Mark 10:17–30 or, for shorter form, Mark 10:17–27

Monday

October 11

Paul, a slave of Christ Jesus, called to be an Apostle and set apart for the Gospel of God, which he promised previously through his prophets.
—Romans 1:1–2

Some family heirlooms are actually ordinary, everyday objects that we've set apart because of their age, significance, or connection to someone important to us. When that happens, the object is no longer used for its original mundane purpose but now takes on a new more meaningful purpose. To be holy is to be set apart for God's purposes. St. Paul refers to himself in today's first reading as someone who has been set apart to proclaim the Good News. As followers of Christ, we are all called to holiness—to be set apart—so that through our words and actions, others may come to see the transforming power of the Good News of Jesus Christ.

Romans 1:1–7
Psalm 98:1, 2–3ab, 3cd–4
Luke 11:29–32

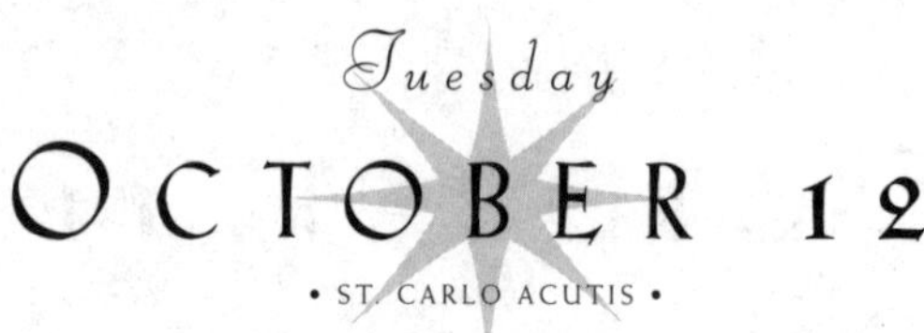

Tuesday OCTOBER 12

• ST. CARLO ACUTIS •

The Lord said to him: "Oh you Pharisees! Although you cleanse the outside of the cup and the dish, inside you are filled with plunder and evil."
—LUKE 11:39

Jesus did not mince words when he spoke to the Pharisees. Rather, he challenged them with brutal honesty in an attempt to break through their self-righteousness and arrogance. Sometimes, the truth hurts, and sometimes speaking in brutal honesty is the most loving thing we can do for someone who has closed their mind and heart to correction. We call this kind of anger righteous anger because it is attempts to break through to someone who refuses to acknowledge that they are hurting themselves or others. Righteous anger is not impulsive or random: It is measured and targeted. Pray for the grace to avoid impulsive anger and to rely on righteous anger only when needed to bring about good, not to hurt someone.

Romans 1:16–25
Psalm 19:2–3, 4–5
Luke 11:37–41

Wednesday

OCTOBER 13

Or do you hold his priceless kindness, forbearance, and patience in low esteem, unaware that the kindness of God would lead you to repentance?
—ROMANS 2:4

We don't tend to associate the words *kindness* and *repentance*. On the surface, it would seem that these two words have little in common. And yet, St. Paul tells the Romans that repentance is something we do in response to God's kindness. God does not go around wagging his finger at us and telling us how naughty we've been in hopes that we will be goaded into repenting. Rather, it is God's loving kindness that melts our hearts and creates in us a desire to repent—to have a change of heart and to start over again, attempting to imitate Christ more closely. In your encounters today, surprise people with your kindness: You just might help God transform hearts and open the door for repentance.

Romans 2:1–11
Psalm 62:2–3, 6–7, 9
Luke 11:42–46

Thursday

October 14

• ST. CALLISTUS I, POPE AND MARTYR •

Does God belong to Jews alone? Does he not belong to Gentiles, too? Yes, also to Gentiles, for God is one.
—ROMANS 3:29–30

When we fall in love, we can react in one of two ways: We can become possessive and seek to keep our beloved to ourselves, not sharing them with others, or we can be so smitten that we want to tell the whole world how great our beloved is. St. Paul teaches us that, when it comes to loving God, it is the latter rather than the former that God desires: We cannot place limits on God's love—it is a love that transcends any one person and any one group of people. It is an expansive love that always reaches out to others. We are to joyfully and eagerly proclaim this love to the world, not keep it to ourselves.

Romans 3:21–30
Psalm 130:1b–2, 3–4, 5–6ab
Luke 11:47–54

Friday

OCTOBER 15

• ST. TERESA OF AVILA, VIRGIN AND DOCTOR OF THE CHURCH •

Even the hairs of your head have all been counted. Do not be afraid. You are worth more than many sparrows.
—LUKE 12:7

At Mass, after the Lord's Prayer, the priest prays that we might be "free from all distress." How urgently we need to hear these words! We live in a very stressful world, and it is common for our lives to become filled with anxiety. Yet Jesus tells us in today's Gospel to fear nothing. This message is central to the Good News of Jesus, which is why it is echoed in the Mass: We are not to be filled with fear or troubled by distress. We know that because Jesus Christ has conquered sin and death, his grace will overcome any challenge that we may face. Pray for the grace to overcome your fears and to help others conquer the things that are causing them distress.

Romans 4:1–8
Psalm 32:1b–2, 5, 11
Luke 12:1–7

Saturday

OCTOBER 16

• ST. HEDWIG, RELIGIOUS • ST. MARGARET MARY ALACOQUE, VIRGIN •

The Holy Spirit will teach you at that moment what you should say.
—LUKE 12:12

I used to get tongue-tied and cotton-mouthed whenever I had to speak in front of people. For some reason, God saw fit to call me to a ministry that often involved public speaking! I still get nervous when I get in front of an audience, but I have learned how to minimize my fear and calm my nerves: I pray confidently and calmly to the Holy Spirit to teach me all I should say at that moment. I look at the faces of those I am about to speak to and ask God to help me to love them, not impress them. In doing so, I find that my fears diminish and often a deep calm comes over me, allowing words to gently float up from deep within and pass through my lips.

Come, Holy Spirit!

Romans 4:13, 16–18
Psalm 105:6–7, 8–9, 42–43
Luke 12:8–12

Sunday

OCTOBER 17

• TWENTY-NINTH SUNDAY IN ORDINARY TIME •

So let us confidently approach the throne of grace to receive mercy and to find grace for timely help.
—HEBREWS 4:16

A friend of mine from my alma mater, St. Ignatius High School, once asked me to pray for a special intention. Knowing that I was in pastoral ministry, he said, "You have a special connection with God." After assuring him of my prayers, I said, "You know, St. Ignatius taught that every one of us can pray to God in a way that resembles one friend speaking to another, and that we can find God in all things." We are told in the Letter to the Hebrews that our God is accessible and that we can easily and confidently approach him to ask and receive his mercy and assistance. You don't need a special title or status or any special knowledge or gift to gain access to God.

Isaiah 53:10–11
Psalm 33:4–5, 18–19, 20, 22 (22)
Hebrews 4:14–16
Mark 10:35–45 or, for shorter form, Mark 10:42–45

Monday
OCTOBER 18

• ST. LUKE, EVANGELIST •

He said to them, "The harvest is abundant but the laborers are few; so ask the master of the harvest to send out laborers for his harvest."
—LUKE 10:2

God does not force his kingdom upon us. Rather, he invites us. That invitation often comes through another person who so authentically embodies the values of the kingdom that we desire to emulate them. Think of people in your life who, through words, actions, or both, brought you closer to Jesus. Now, it's your turn. Jesus sends us out into the fields to reap the harvest—that is, he relies on us to invite others to follow his Son, Jesus Christ. What an honor it is to be called by God to be one of his workers. Today, give thanks for those who have brought you closer to Christ and pray for the grace to invite others to follow him more closely.

2 Timothy 4:10–17b
Psalm 145:10–11, 12–13, 17–18
Luke 10:1–9

Tuesday OCTOBER 19

• ST. JOHN DE BRÉBEUF AND ST. ISAAC JOGUES, PRIESTS, AND COMPANIONS, MARTYRS •

Blessed are those servants whom the master finds vigilant on his arrival.
—LUKE 12:37

Spirituality is about cultivating a deeper awareness of the presence of God in our lives. Sometimes we can suffer from spiritual drowsiness or a lack of awareness of God's presence and action. In today's Gospel, Jesus exhorts us to remain awake lest we miss the opportunity to encounter him. To remain physically awake, we need to engage in strategies that stimulate the body and mind: through physical activity, time spent outdoors, good sleep and nutrition, and so on. Similarly, to remain spiritually awake, we need to engage in strategies to stimulate our heart and spirit: prayer, meditation, reading Scripture, and engaging in Corporal and Spiritual Works of Mercy.

Romans 5:12, 15b, 17–19, 20b–21
Psalm 40:7–8a, 8b–9, 10, 17
Luke 12:35–38

Wednesday OCTOBER 20

• ST. PAUL OF THE CROSS, PRIEST •

Present yourselves to God as raised from the dead to life.
—ROMANS 6:13

There are times when we are so physically depleted that we describe it as feeling dead. After some rest and rehydration, we feel restored to life. St. Paul uses this metaphor to describe what it should look and feel like to live in Christ: It is like coming back from the dead! Indeed, in the sacrament of baptism, we are plunged into water to simulate death and emerge, filling our lungs with air and being alive again, now in Christ. In our prayer each day, we can ask the Lord for his renewing grace, to enable us to live in the new life of the resurrection of Jesus and to bring hope of new life to those we encounter, especially those who are burdened by loneliness, difficulties, or despair.

Romans 6:12–18
Psalm 124:1b–3, 4–6, 7–8
Luke 12:39–48

Thursday

OCTOBER 21

Jesus said to his disciples, "I have come to set the earth on fire, and how I wish it were already blazing!"
—LUKE 12:49

Back in the day, when apprentice chimney sweeps were nervous about climbing up and out of a narrow chimney, their boss would light a fire under them to motivate them to get moving. We continue to use this phrase when we talk about wanting to motivate someone to action. In today's Gospel, Jesus says that he has come to light a fire. St. Ignatius used similar imagery when he told his fellow Jesuits to "go forth and set the world on fire!" By that, he meant that they should ignite hearts with passionate love for God and the world through faith, service, and justice. We can do the same by allowing our hearts to be ignited with passionate love for God and kindling the flame in the hearts of others.

Romans 6:19–23
Psalm 1:1–2, 3, 4 and 6
Luke 12:49–53

I do not do the good I want, but I do the evil I do not want.
—ROMANS 7:19

Parents spend a good amount of time and energy teaching their children to become autonomous so that they do not have to rely on others for everything. Autonomy is crucial since it encourages children to make their own choices, face up to tasks independently, build confidence, solve problems, and develop a strong sense of self-worth. This is all good. The only problem is that in the spiritual life, we never become autonomous—we are fully dependent on the grace of God. St. Paul admits this powerlessness by confessing that he is unable to independently overcome temptation. None of us have this capability. It is only through the grace of God—divine intervention—that we are saved from sin. And that grace is offered to us freely!

Romans 7:18–25a
Psalm 119:66, 68, 76, 77, 93, 94
Luke 12:54–59

Saturday

OCTOBER 23

• ST. JOHN OF CAPISTRANO, PRIEST •

If the Spirit of the one who raised Jesus from the dead dwells in you, the one who raised Christ from the dead will give life to your mortal bodies also, through his Spirit that dwells in you.
—ROMANS 8:11

Hollywood loves to depict stories of body-swapping and possession in which a person is somehow inhabited by another force or being. St. Paul invites us to consider another type of indwelling: the possibility of the Spirit of God dwelling within us. Such an indwelling is not forced upon us. It is not a *possession* that results in the loss of free will but the sharing of God's life within us. It is the very real presence of divine life within us that we can draw from to more fully reach our potential as children of God. Come, Holy Spirit, and fill the hearts of your faithful people.

Romans 8:1–11
Psalm 24:1b–2, 3–4ab, 5–6
Luke 13:1–9

Sunday

October 24

• THIRTIETH SUNDAY IN ORDINARY TIME •

Jesus said to him in reply, "What do you want me to do for you?" The blind man replied to him, "Master, I want to see."
—MARK 10:51

When I was growing up, my siblings and I worked in our dad's drugstore, where we were taught to ask customers, "Can I help you?" to show that we were ready to listen, understand their specific needs, and provide an effective, personalized solution. In today's Gospel account of Jesus's encounter with the blind man, Jesus asks the man, "What do you want me to do for you?" Know that every time we pause to pray, Jesus is asking us this same question. Our prayer is a response to this question as we share our needs with Jesus and ask him to assist us with his saving grace. Speak to Jesus today and tell him what you need, knowing that God hears and provides.

Jeremiah 31:7–9
Psalm 126:1–2, 2–3, 4–5, 6 (3)
Hebrews 5:1–6
Mark 10:46–52

Monday

OCTOBER 25

The Spirit himself bears witness with our spirit that we are children of God, and if children, then heirs, heirs of God and joint heirs with Christ.
—ROMANS 8:16–17

People waiting in line to purchase lottery tickets for mega jackpots often talk about what they will do with their incredible fortune once they win. It's fun to dream about what we might be able to do with an extraordinary infusion of wealth. St. Paul teaches us today that, as heirs of God, we have indeed inherited extraordinary spiritual riches in the form of saving grace. As heirs, this means we can live with a sense of security. It also means that we have the ability to use our abundance to invest in others and to be philanthropic, sharing our spiritual wealth with those need an infusion of divine grace. What will you do with your inheritance?

Romans 8:12–17
Psalm 68:2 and 4, 6–7ab, 20–21
Luke 13:10–17

Tuesday

OCTOBER 26

It became a large bush and "the birds of the sky dwelt in its branches."
—LUKE 13:19

Birds nest in the branches of large shrubs and trees to find protection, stability, and a good view of approaching threats. In short, a nest in the branches of a tree provides refuge. Jesus knows that we, too, need to find refuge from life's challenges—we need protection, stability, and a good perspective. This is why Jesus compares the reign of God to the mustard seed, which, though small, grows into a place of refuge. To live in the reign of God is to place ourselves within God's protection and find refuge in his loving arms. Just as birds take refuge by engaging in the active process of building a nest, we must likewise engage in an active process that includes prayer, reliance on the Word of God, and engagement in works of mercy.

Romans 8:18–25
Psalm 126:1b–2ab, 2cd–3, 4–5, 6
Luke 13:18–21

Wednesday

OCTOBER 27

And the one who searches hearts knows what is the intention of the Spirit, because it intercedes for the holy ones according to God's will.

—ROMANS 8:27

We all treasure that friend or family member who knows our heart—someone who understands our true inner self, beyond outward appearances. St. Paul consoles us with the knowledge that God *searches hearts*, meaning that God knows our deepest thoughts, desires, fears, and unspoken prayers. This means that we should be comfortable spending time with God in prayer even when we are unable to think of words to say. Sitting in silence with God reassures us that we are spending time with a God who knows our heart and can reveal to us our own deepest thoughts and feelings. Nothing is hidden from God, who helps us to see ourselves as we really are and to see others as he sees them.

Romans 8:26–30
Psalm 13:4–5, 6
Luke 13:22–30

Thursday
OCTOBER 28

• ST. SIMON AND ST. JUDE, APOSTLES •

Jesus went up to the mountain to pray, and he spent the night in prayer to God. When day came, he called his disciples to himself, and from them he chose Twelve, whom he also named Apostles.
—LUKE 6:12–13

In 1987, Fr. Richard Rohr, OFM, founded the Center for Action and Contemplation in Albuquerque, New Mexico. He has said that the most important word in the Center's title is the word *and*, explaining that we need both compassionate action and contemplative practice for the spiritual journey to ensure that our actions flow not from our ego but rather from true compassion. The two are reliant on each other: Before Jesus took the action of choosing his apostles, he spent the night in prayer, modeling the connection. When we turn to God in prayer and contemplation, we become more capable of seeing ourselves and others as God sees us and acting accordingly.

Ephesians 2:19–22
Psalm 19:2–3, 4–5
Luke 6:12–16

Friday

October 29

He took the man and, after he had healed him, dismissed him.
—Luke 14:4

At the time of Jesus, medical knowledge was much more rudimentary than it is today. Even so, physicians had remedies for certain ailments. Other ailments were seen as beyond their capacity and could only be remedied by divine intervention. Dropsy, today known as edema, was one such condition. By healing the man with dropsy, Jesus once again revealed that he indeed is the divine intervention that we need. In today's world, technological advances have enabled us to gain control over many realities that once mystified and stymied us. Sin, however, continues to be beyond our ability to cure. We need divine intervention to overcome this spiritual malady. We pray each day for Jesus, our Divine Physician, to bring healing to our souls so that, like the man healed from dropsy, we may be sent on our way.

Romans 9:1–5
Psalm 147:12–13, 14–15, 19–20
Luke 14:1–6

Saturday

OCTOBER 30

When you are invited, go and take the lowest place so that when the host comes to you he may say, "My friend, move up to a higher position."

—LUKE 14:10

Showing humility is not in vogue today. As such, we could all use some tips on how to show humility. In today's Gospel, Jesus offers a parable to illustrate the mindset of humility as an attitude that eschews worldly status, attention, or prestige. Instead, we cultivate the practice of humility by devoting attention to others, actively listening to them, expressing gratitude, being of service to others, admitting our mistakes, gracefully accepting constructive criticism, and celebrating the success of others. Practicing humility is a shift of mindset that enables us to shift ourselves from the center of attention to the periphery. The benefits of practicing humility are many, but most of all, it opens up space for God in our lives.

Romans 11:1–2a, 11–12, 25–29
Psalm 94:12–13a, 14–15, 17–18
Luke 14:1, 7–11

Sunday

OCTOBER 31

• THIRTY-FIRST SUNDAY IN ORDINARY TIME •

"You shall love the Lord your God with all your heart, with all your soul, with all your mind, and with all your strength." The second is this: "You shall love your neighbor as yourself."
—MARK 12:30–31

When attending church as a child, I recall gazing often at the colorful stained-glass window that depicted Moses with the stone tablets of the law. I was mystified that it showed the first tablet with the Roman numerals one through three and the second tablet with the Roman numerals four through ten. Why not five and five? Years later I was taught that the first three commandments are about loving God, while the remainder are about love of neighbors—two types of love that cannot be separated. In fact, God is telling us that the best way to show love for him is to love our neighbor—something we can do each day.

Deuteronomy 6:2–6
Psalm 18:2–3, 3–4, 47, 51 (2)
Hebrews 7:23–28
Mark 12:28b–34

Monday

NOVEMBER 1

• ALL SAINTS •

When Jesus saw the crowds, he went up the mountain, and after he had sat down, his disciples came to him. He began to teach them.
—MATTHEW 5:1–2

It is interesting that the Gospel for the Feast of All Saints is the beginning of the Sermon on the Mount, specifically, the section we know as the Beatitudes. What do the Beatitudes have to do with the saints? Everything! The Beatitudes are the *blueprint* for leading a saintly life—they are the path to holiness that the saints followed and that we are called to follow. The saints are models of humility, meekness, compassion, and justice—all virtues taught in the Beatitudes. In fact, the Beatitudes have sometimes been referred to as a *gospel within the Gospel*. On this Feast of All Saints, recall the words attributed to Oscar Wilde: "Every saint has a past, and every sinner has a future."

Revelation 7:2–4, 9–14
Psalm 24:1b–2, 3–4ab, 5–6
1 John 3:1–3
Matthew 5:1–12a

Tuesday

NOVEMBER 2

• THE COMMEMORATION OF ALL THE FAITHFUL DEPARTED (ALL SOULS' DAY) •

*The souls of the just are in the hand of God,
and no torment shall touch them.*
—WISDOM 3:1

In the movie *The Sixth Sense*, the young boy at the center of the story (played by Haley Joel Osment) famously says the line, "I see dead people." Sadly, he fears that he is crazy. Over the years, I have often told audiences, "If you see dead people or at least talk to dead people, you're not crazy. You're Catholic." Catholics believe that those who have died are not gone but only separated from us by a thin veil. On All Souls Day, we honor and pray for all the faithful departed who comprise the communion of saints. How comforting to know that our deceased loved ones are not out of reach but are in the hands of God! Today, we pray: "Eternal rest grant unto them, O Lord, and let perpetual light shine upon them."

Wisdom 3:1–9
Romans 5:5–11 or 6:3–9
John 6:37–40
Other readings may be selected.

Wednesday

NOVEMBER 3

• ST. MARTIN DE PORRES, RELIGIOUS •

Or what king marching into battle would not first sit down and decide whether with ten thousand troops he can successfully oppose another king advancing upon him with twenty thousand troops?

—LUKE 14:31

Jesus's parable today reminds us of the importance of *discernment*—a type of thinking that puts the brain and the heart in dialogue with one another. Discernment is a vital part of a healthy spirituality. St. Ignatius of Loyola used the word *discernment* to describe the process of thinking before acting: a process that seeks to align our own will with the will of God so we can learn what God is calling us to do and to become. Every choice we make, no matter how small, is an opportunity to get in touch with our spiritual life, as long as we bring thinking and feeling into dialogue.

Romans 13:8–10
Psalm 112:1b–2, 4–5, 9
Luke 14:25–33

Thursday

NOVEMBER 4

• ST. CHARLES BORROMEO, BISHOP •

What man among you having a hundred sheep and losing one of them would not leave the ninety-nine in the desert and go after the lost one until he finds it?

—LUKE 15:4

I can only imagine that when Jesus asked the above question about going after the lost sheep, some people might have responded, "Not me! Are you serious? What kind of shepherd would do that?" Jesus, however, is not talking about normal shepherding procedures. He is illustrating for us how God feels about the repentant sinner who is lost but hopes to be found. God's mercy is boundless. Every one of us is of immense value to God, and he takes great joy in our return to him when we repent from sin. To repent means to change our minds—to think and believe differently. Change your mind, today, where needed, and return to the Lord.

Romans 14:7–12
Psalm 27:1bcde, 4, 13–14
Luke 15:1–10

Friday

November 5

For the children of this world are more prudent in dealing with their own generation than the children of light.
—Luke 16:8

Today's Gospel tells the story of a dishonest businessman. To avoid the inference that Jesus was promoting dishonesty, many preachers over the centuries have referred to the character as the *shrewd* or *wily* manager. Let's not mince words: He was dishonest! Jesus does not make this point to promote dishonest practices, but to show how far people will go to look out for their own interests, especially when those interests are less than honorable. Jesus encourages us to be just as shrewd in using the resources God has entrusted to us not for personal, short-term gain but for that which has eternal value. In other words, discipleship demands resourcefulness and intentionality. To follow Jesus, we must be proactive and use all the gifts God has blessed us with.

Romans 15:14–21
Psalm 98:1, 2–3ab, 3cd–4
Luke 16:1–8

Saturday

NOVEMBER 6

He said to them: "You justify yourselves in the sight of others, but God knows your hearts; for what is of human esteem is an abomination in the sight of God."

—LUKE 16:15

The first commandment warns us not to worship false gods. We sometimes think that this commandment is anachronistic, hearkening back to a time when people created images of gods to worship. Today, however, our priorities can still get out of whack, and we end up prioritizing things that are not life-giving and even unhealthy. Jesus reminds us that sometimes the things that we think are important or of value may not be so in God's eyes. Repentance is when we rearrange our priorities to things that are valuable in God's eyes such as family, friends, work, love, mercy, justice, understanding, compassion, and forgiveness. And with God's help, we can rearrange our priorities any time we want.

Romans 16:3–9, 16, 22–27
Psalm 145:2–3, 4–5, 10–11
Luke 16:9–15

Sunday

NOVEMBER 7

• THIRTY-SECOND SUNDAY IN ORDINARY TIME •

For they have all contributed from their surplus wealth, but she, from her poverty, has contributed all she had, her whole livelihood.
—MARK 12:44

Over the years, I have talked with many people who have spent time living among and serving people in deeply impoverished areas. When they describe their experience, they consistently describe the same thing: They have never seen such dire poverty but have also never seen people who were so joyful and so generous. This seems counterintuitive. Logic suggests that those with more wealth would experience greater joy and would likewise be the most generous. Yet it is actually the other way around. Jesus reminds us that joy and generosity do not flow from material abundance but rather from a spirit of abundance that refuses to see or submit to a scarcity mentality. Grateful for all that we have, we eagerly seek to share with others.

1 Kings 17:10–16
Psalm 146:7, 8–9, 9–10 (1b)
Hebrews 9:24–28
Mark 12:38–44 or 12:41–44

Monday

NOVEMBER 8

Love justice, you who judge the earth;
think of the Lord in goodness,
and seek him in integrity of heart.
—WISDOM 1:1

It has been said that integrity is doing the right thing even when there's no one around to see it. With that definition in mind, I'm sure we can each think of people in our lives who exhibit great integrity. Today's first reading from the book of Wisdom teaches us that living with integrity of heart is one of the ways we seek and find God, along with loving justice and goodness. It goes without saying, then, that each time we witness justice, goodness, and integrity, we are seeing God in action among his people. It also means that we can reveal God's presence to others by living lives of justice, goodness, and integrity. This is especially important for people who have been victimized by those who lack these virtues.

Wisdom 1:1–7
Psalm 139:1b–3, 4–6, 7–8, 9–10
Luke 17:1–6

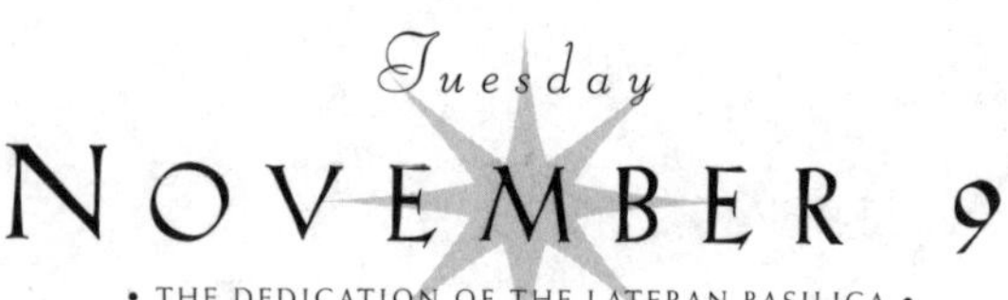

He made a whip out of cords and drove them all out of the temple area, with the sheep and oxen, and spilled the coins of the money-changers and overturned their tables.
—JOHN 2:15

When Jesus cleansed the temple, his action was not about the impropriety of money-changing in the shadow of the Holy of Holies. Rather, he was announcing that it was an abomination for the people of Israel to believe that worship was the extent of their duties and that temple worship somehow granted them license to behave in contradictory ways outside the temple walls. The *Catechism* reminds us that "the moral life is spiritual worship" (2031). In other words, one of the most profound ways to worship God is to live a moral life. Love of God is shown most powerfully through love of neighbor. Commit to worshipping God today by practicing the virtues of a moral life.

Ezra 47:1–2, 8–9, 12
Psalm 46:2–3, 5–6, 8–9
1 Corinthians 3:9c–11, 16–17
John 2:13–22

Wednesday

NOVEMBER 10

• ST. LEO THE GREAT, POPE AND DOCTOR OF THE CHURCH •

Jesus said in reply, "Ten were cleansed, were they not? Where are the other nine? Has none but this foreigner returned to give thanks to God?"
—LUKE 17:17–18

Throughout Luke's Gospel, foreigners play a crucial role in highlighting the theme of God's inclusive love. Today's Gospel is no exception as Jesus heals ten lepers but is only thanked by the foreigner. It was the outsider who truly embraced God's grace as opposed to those who considered themselves to be religious or holy but showed no gratitude to God. God has indeed made us whole. For this, the proper spiritual response is gratitude shown and expressed in tangible ways. Take some time today to reflect on all the ways God has brought wholeness into your life, and then, find tangible ways to show gratitude to God not only through prayer but also by paying it forward through acts of kindness to others.

Wisdom 6:1–11
Psalm 82:3–4, 6–7
Luke 17:11–19

Thursday

NOVEMBER 11

• ST. MARTIN OF TOURS, BISHOP •

Behold, the Kingdom of God is among you.
—LUKE 17:21

Christians often equate the kingdom or reign of God with the afterlife—namely, heaven. Perhaps this is because the Gospels sometimes use the phrase *kingdom of heaven* in place of *kingdom of God*. Even so, it is misleading to think of the kingdom as a reward awaiting us in the afterlife—something we can earn by gritting our teeth and surviving this hell on earth until we earn our reward. Jesus's message was not about "later"; it was about *now*. Jesus states in no uncertain terms that the kingdom of God is a present reality—already in our midst—and that we can participate in the reign of God now and then fully in the afterlife. Whenever we live according to the teachings of Jesus, we are participating in the reign of God and revealing its presence to others.

Wisdom 7:22b—8:1
Psalm 119:89, 90, 9200 1, 130, 135, 175
Luke 17:20–25

Friday

NOVEMBER 12

• ST. JOSAPHAT, BISHOP AND MARTYR •

For from the greatness and the beauty of created things
their original author, by analogy, is seen.
—WISDOM 13:5

Catholic sacramental sensibility is characterized by a recognition of God's presence being reflected in all things. This is not to be confused with *pantheism*, the belief that God is actually *in* every aspect of creation and that creation itself is divine. Today's psalm states quite clearly that the greatness and beauty of creation enable us, *by analogy*, to see the greatness and beauty of God. This can be compared to gazing upon a work of art and, in its beauty, recognizing the unique touch of the artist. This is why spiritual experts of all religions recommend communing with nature as one of the most profound ways of experiencing the divine in our midst. Take a moment today to appreciate the goodness and beauty of God's creation and know that God is near.

Wisdom 13:1–9
Psalm 19:2–3, 4–5ab
Luke 17:26–37

Saturday

NOVEMBER 13

• ST. FRANCES XAVIER CABRINI, VIRGIN •

Will not God then secure the rights of his chosen ones who call out to him day and night?
—LUKE 18:7

Jesus asks a rhetorical question in today's Gospel. The answer is obvious: *Of course* God will do justice to his chosen who call out to him day and night! The first thing that is striking about this passage is that Jesus affirms that we are God's chosen ones. Next, is the description of his chosen ones calling out to him *day and night*, which is what a child does when in need. Finally, the assurance of God doing justice on our behalf reminds us of why we call out to him in the first place. Let us be thankful that God has chosen us to be his own. Let us call out to him day and night. And let us pray confidently for his justice to roll down like waters.

Wisdom 18:14–16; 19:6–9
Psalm 105:2–3, 36–37, 42–43
Luke 18:1–8

Sunday

NOVEMBER 14

• THIRTY-THIRD SUNDAY IN ORDINARY TIME •

But of that day or hour, no one knows, neither the angels in heaven, nor the Son, but only the Father.
—MARK 13:32

People have been predicting the end of the world for millennia, and up to now, they've all been wrong! You might think we would know by now not to fall for any of these types of predictions. It is especially ridiculous when such predictions come from Christian sources, since Jesus himself told us that nobody knows when this will occur and that we should not be preoccupied with it. This means that our preoccupation should be with the present moment, which is infused with hope for the promise of eternal life with God and is buoyed by the knowledge of God's faithfulness in the past. Strive today to live in the moment, knowing that God's presence is most needed in the present.

Daniel 12:1–3
Psalm 16:5, 8, 9–10, 11 (1)
Hebrews 10:11–14, 18
Mark 13:24–32

Monday

NOVEMBER 15

• ST. ALBERT THE GREAT, BISHOP AND DOCTOR OF THE CHURCH •

But many in Israel were determined and resolved in their hearts not to eat anything unclean; they preferred to die rather than to be defiled with unclean food or to profane the holy covenant.
—1 MACCABEES 1:62–63

We tend to think of peer pressure as an adolescent reality, but the fact is that, as adults, we continue to be affected. The pressure to conform can affect our decisions in aspects of life such as drinking and spending habits and other lifestyle expectations. Peer pressure can, however, be both negative and positive. Today's first reading tells us about brave people who refused to conform to pagan ways but remained faithful to God's covenant. We may not be facing life-and-death decisions when it comes to pressure to conform to society's whims, but we do need God's grace and the gift of fortitude each and every day to live with virtue as followers of Christ.

1 Maccabees 1:10–15, 41–43, 54–57, 62–63
Psalm 119:53, 61, 134, 150, 155, 158
Luke 18:35–43

Tuesday

NOVEMBER 16

• ST. MARGARET OF SCOTLAND • ST. GERTRUDE THE GREAT, VIRGIN •

The Son of Man has come to seek and to save what was lost.
—LUKE 19:10

Getting lost is no fun. Thanks to today's GPS technology, we do not often get lost. Likewise, in our spiritual lives, we also need something to keep us from wandering away from the path that Jesus has laid out for us. That help comes to us in the form of the gospel, which, like a GPS, guides us on a path toward God's will and helps us navigate unexpected turns or wrong paths while also providing recalculation when we need to get back on track. Jesus came to search out and save those who are lost. Just as we trust a GPS device to guide us to our destination, we must place our trust in Jesus, believing that his teachings will provide trustworthy guidance, even when it seems counterintuitive or leads through unfamiliar territory.

2 Maccabees 6:18–31
Psalm 3:2–3, 4–5, 6–7
Luke 19:1–10

Wednesday

NOVEMBER 17

• ST. ELIZABETH OF HUNGARY, RELIGIOUS •

Hide me in the shadow of your wings. . . .
But I in justice shall behold your face;
on waking, I shall be content in your presence.
—PSALM 17:8, 15

Scripture is replete with metaphors for God, referring to God as rock, shepherd, potter, king, and bridegroom. One of the most poignant metaphors for God is that of a bird protecting her young with her wings. Some ancient cultures associated winged birds with divinity because of their ability to transcend the earth. This image is one of shelter, protection, and nurturing and reminds us of God's loving and protective care, warmth, and guidance. To seek refuge in the shadow of God's wings is to find security and peace in God's presence during difficult times by placing trust in God's protection and power. Seek refuge in the shadow of God's wings and find a contentment that the world cannot provide.

2 Maccabees 7:1, 20–31
Psalm 17:1bcd, 5–6, 8b and 15
Luke 19:11–28

Thursday

NOVEMBER 18

• THE DEDICATION OF THE BASILICA OF ST. PETER AND ST. PAUL, APOSTLES
* ST. ROSE PHILIPPINE DUCHESNE, VIRGIN •

With complete assurance and without hindrance he proclaimed the Kingdom of God and taught about the Lord Jesus Christ.
—ACTS 28:31

Some forces, like water, seem unstoppable. For years, despite my unprofessional attempts to seal cracks in my home's foundation, water continued to seep in. Similarly, the power of God's word is also unstoppable as attested to in today's reading from the Acts of the Apostles. Despite adversity, God's word continued to find a way to penetrate hearts and minds. Despite St. Paul's imprisonment, the message of the gospel continued to spread freely. Paul viewed his imprisonment not as a setback, but rather as an opportunity to show that the word of God cannot be chained, as he was. Don't let adversity hold you back. Rather, use it as an opportunity to show the unstoppable power of God's grace.

1 Maccabees 2:15–29 or Acts 28:11–16, 30–31
Psalm 50:1b–2, 5–6, 14–15 or 98:1, 2–3ab, 3cd–4, 5–6
Luke 19:41–44 or Matthew 14:22–33

Friday

NOVEMBER 19

My house shall be a house of prayer, but
you have made it a den of thieves.
—LUKE 19:46

We live in a transactional society, which means that we are accustomed to giving something in order to get something. Too often, we bring this mindset to prayer and worship. When Jesus cleansed the temple, he made it clear that our relationship with God the Father is not transactional. We do not need to give him something in order to get something. Rather, when we pray, we enter more deeply into a relationship. Prayer is a relational and transformative practice that leads us to intimacy with God. As you approach God today in prayer, do so without a wish list and without a desire to change God's mind but rather with a desire to know the will of God and to put on the mind of Christ.

1 Maccabees 4:3–37, 52–59
1 Chronicles 29:10bcd, 11abc, 11d–12a, 12bcd
Luke 19:45–48

Saturday

NOVEMBER 20

[God] is not God of the dead, but of the living,
for to him all are alive.
—LUKE 20:38

Throughout human history, people have based their identity on lineage, economic status, or both. In some cases, people have been known to exclaim, "Do you know who I am?" if they believed their lineage or status entitled them to special treatment. In today's Gospel, Jesus reminds us that our true identity is not tied to these earthly realities but to the fact that we are children of the eternal God. Our earthly lineage and economic status are fleeting realities. Our relationship with God is eternal. We live our fullest life right here and now by recognizing our status as children of God and giving thanks for the abundant grace that comes with this spiritual pedigree. We also recognize that everyone we meet is of the same pedigree and therefore worthy of respect.

1 Maccabees 6:1–13
Psalm 9:2–3, 4 and 6, 16 and 19
Luke 20:27–40

Sunday

NOVEMBER 21

• OUR LORD JESUS CHRIST, KING OF THE UNIVERSE •

Jesus answered, "You say I am a king. For this I was born and for this I came into the world, to testify to the truth. Everyone who belongs to the truth listens to my voice."
—JOHN 18:37

Benevolent kings who lived up to their responsibilities were hailed by their subjects, who in turn eagerly and loyally identified with them. The same is true of our relationship with God. When we refer to Jesus as our king, we are acknowledging that he brings order to our lives, unifies his people, does what is best for us, mends relationships, conveys truth, fulfills his word, protects us from danger, brings justice, inspires us to live to our full potential, affirms us, and is present among his people. Because Christ the King does all of these things, we hail him, follow him, and identify with him.

Daniel 7:13–14
Psalm 93:1, 1–2, 5 (1a)
Revelation 1:5–8
John 18:33b–37

Monday

NOVEMBER 22

• ST. CECILIA, VIRGIN AND MARTYR •

To these four young men God gave knowledge and proficiency in all literature and science, and to Daniel the understanding of all visions and dreams.

—DANIEL 1:17

Today's first reading from the book of Daniel describes how God bestows gifts upon his people and expects that they will use these gifts to serve the best interests of others. Gifts are always meant to be shared, not hoarded for personal gain. Think of all the people in your life who have generously and selflessly shared their gifts with you and how you have benefited from this. Give thanks to God for these people and for the gifts they've shared. Ask God for the grace you need to recognize your gifts and to share them with others, expecting nothing in return other than the knowledge that your actions have made God's grace present in this world.

Daniel 1:1–6, 8–20
Daniel 3:52, 53, 54, 55, 56
Luke 21:1–4

Tuesday

NOVEMBER 23

• ST. CLEMENT I, POPE AND MARTYR • ST. COLUMBAN, ABBOT •
BL. MIGUEL AUGUSTÍN PRO, PRIEST AND MARTYR •

He answered, "See that you not be deceived, for many will come in my name, saying, 'I am he,' and 'The time has come.' Do not follow them!"
—LUKE 21:8

People have been spreading falsehoods for as long as human beings could speak. Today, with the impact of social media, we are exposed to a proliferation of falsehoods. Jesus urges us today not to be misled. More than ever, we need to do our homework and verify the truth of what we read and what we spread on social media. Truth-telling is one of the Ten Commandments: Thou shall not bear false witness against thy neighbor. Jesus went as far as to identify himself as not only the way and the life, but also as the truth. May we commit this day to be truth-tellers and to discreetly but boldly call out untruth when we encounter it.

Daniel 2:31–45
Daniel 3:57, 58, 59, 60, 61
Luke 21:5–11

Wednesday

NOVEMBER 24

• ST. ANDREW DUNG-LAC, PRIEST, AND COMPANIONS, MARTYRS •

Suddenly, opposite the lampstand, the fingers of a human hand appeared, writing on the plaster of the wall in the king's palace.
—DANIEL 5:5

Today's first reading from the book of Daniel reveals the origins of the phrase "see the writing on the wall." We use this phrase to refer to moments when someone's fate is revealed to them, often as the consequences of their own actions. These consequences are also obvious to everyone. One of the ways that we judge the morality of our own actions is by anticipating the consequences before we act and then evaluating the consequences after we act. We do this primarily through prayer, asking God to help us see and properly deal with these consequences. In prayer, God reveals his will to us and helps us to see clearly so that we don't miss the *writing on the wall* that everyone else can plainly see.

Daniel 5:1–6, 13–14, 16–17, 23–28
Daniel 3:62, 63, 64, 65, 66, 67
Luke 21:12–19

Thursday

NOVEMBER 25

• ST. CATHERINE OF ALEXANDRIA, VIRGIN AND MARTYR •
THANKSGIVING DAY •

And now, bless the God of all,
who has done wondrous things on earth.
—SIRACH 50:22

Giving thanks is associated with joyfulness. When we are filled with joy, we recognize the source of that joy and respond with thanks. On this Thanksgiving Day, we pause to do in a profound manner something that we should do each and every day: recognize what we are joyful for and give thanks to the source of that joyfulness, our loving and generous God. Doing this creates a *virtuous circle* (as opposed to a *vicious circle*) because recognizing and giving thanks moves us to share with others. When we reflect upon this sharing with others, we are grateful and filled with joy, which in turn compels us to share even more. May God grant each of us this joy of heart.

Daniel 6:12–28
Daniel 3:68, 69, 70, 71, 72, 73, 74
Luke 21:20–28

PROPER MASS IN
THANKSGIVING TO GOD:
Sirach 50:22–24
1 Corinthians 1:3–9
Luke 17:11–19

Friday

NOVEMBER 26

Heaven and earth will pass away, but
my words will not pass away.
—LUKE 21:33

We sometimes use the phrase "timeless truth" to refer to a saying that has ancient roots but remains relevant today. Similarly, God's words are timeless because God is truth. What God has revealed about mercy, justice, compassion, forgiveness, and charity has not changed since the moment God first revealed them, even though circumstances and how we apply these truths have changed. It is up to us to learn these truths, take them to heart, and teach them to others, especially in a world full of falsehoods. Timeless truths are like family heirlooms: We hold on to them and pass them on to each generation, knowing that their value continues to grow with each passing year. Take the time each day to delight in God's timeless truths that come to us in Scripture.

Daniel 7:2–14
Daniel 3:75, 76, 77, 78, 79, 80, 81
Luke 21:29–33

Saturday

NOVEMBER 27

Be vigilant at all times and pray that you have the strength to escape the tribulations that are imminent and to stand before the Son of Man.
—LUKE 21:36

I'm not a morning person. When I wake up each morning, I remain drowsy for a while, and my brain doesn't seem to be ready to work. If I'm called on to make a decision or move into action shortly after awakening, I'm definitely not going to be at my best. This kind of drowsiness can seep into our spiritual lives, causing us not to be at our best when it comes to meeting life's challenges. Jesus urges us today to "be vigilant at all times" for the "tribulations" that will come upon us. The tribulations we face can strip away all distractions and bring us face-to-face with God. Pray today for the grace to stand before God with nothing to hide.

Daniel 7:15–27
Daniel 3:82, 83, 84, 85, 86, 87
Luke 21:34–36

Sunday

NOVEMBER 28

• FIRST SUNDAY OF ADVENT •

In those days Judah shall be safe
and Jerusalem shall dwell secure;
this is what they shall call her:
"The LORD our justice."
—JEREMIAH 33:16

In the early days of rock and roll, the Beach Boys produced many hit songs including the youthfully optimistic "Wouldn't It Be Nice," which expresses the longing of a young couple to finally be together forever with no obstacles in their way. Such longing for a better future is not limited to youth—it is part of the human character. As we begin Advent, the prophet Jeremiah talks about a hoped-for future when all God's people will be safe and secure, living faithfully according to the Lord's justice. During this season of hope, we are called to live according to the Lord's justice, bringing light where there is darkness, hope where there is despair, joy where there is sadness, and faith where there is doubt.

Jeremiah 33:14–16
Psalm 25:4–5, 8–9, 10, 14 (1b)
1 Thessalonians 3:12—4:2
Luke 21:25–28, 34–36

Monday

NOVEMBER 29

Come, let us climb the LORD's mountain,
to the house of the God of Jacob,
That he may instruct us in his ways,
and we may walk in his paths.
—ISAIAH 2:3

Throughout life, people seek guidance and instruction from experts, coaches, gurus, mentors, personal trainers, financial advisors, and so on. We seek instruction that will guide us in a new way of thinking, speaking, or acting—a new way of living. The season of Advent is an invitation to seek instruction in a new way of being human, following the instruction that comes to us from God through his prophets and ultimately through his Son, Jesus Christ. This instruction is not imposed upon us. Rather, it is something that we seek and readily invite, knowing that our way of being human is lacking. Pray today and throughout Advent for the grace to walk in the light.

Isaiah 2:1–5
Psalm 122:1–2, 3–4b, 4cd–5, 6–7, 8–9
Matthew 8:5–11

Tuesday

NOVEMBER 30

• ST. ANDREW, APOSTLE •

As it is written, "How beautiful are the feet of those who bring the good news!"
—ROMANS 10:15

Feet are not normally considered to be the most attractive feature of human anatomy. And yet, today's first reading tells us that the feet belonging to those who announce good news are quite beautiful. Today, we celebrate the Feast of St. Andrew, whose feet were indeed beautiful because they belonged to one of the apostles who announced the Good News of Jesus to the world. Take a moment today to think of where your feet will carry you and how you can beautify your feet by allowing those journeys to be characterized by the announcement of good news to others: hope, joy, mercy, compassion, forgiveness, joy, and justice. May our feet be like Andrew's, carrying us without hesitation and with boldness to share our faith with others through our words and actions.

Romans 10:9–18
Psalm 19:8, 9, 10, 11
Matthew 4:18–22

Wednesday

DECEMBER 1

On this mountain he will destroy
the veil that veils all peoples.
—ISAIAH 25:7

Celtic tradition speaks of *thin places*,referring to the belief that God's presence is normally veiled from human awareness except for certain places or moments where or when that veil is quite thin. In today's first reading, Isaiah speaks of a day when God "will destroy the veil that veils all peoples." The Gospels of Matthew, Mark, and Luke all speak of the temple veil being torn when Jesus died on the cross. The message of Scripture is that the veil has been destroyed, and as St. Paul famously wrote, nothing can separate us from the love of God in Christ Jesus. God's grace is not veiled from you—God is near to you at all times. And through your words and actions, you can bring God's nearness to others to whom God seems distant.

Isaiah 25:6–10a
Psalm 23:1–3a, 3b–4, 5, 6
Matthew 15:29–37

Thursday

DECEMBER 2

Jesus said to his disciples: "Not everyone who says to me, 'Lord, Lord,' will enter the Kingdom of heaven, but only the one who does the will of my Father in heaven."
—MATTHEW 7:21

Institutional Christianity provides us with beliefs, morals, and rituals that create order and stability in individuals' lives and in society as a whole. It is possible, however, to engage in those rituals and external expressions of faith while ignoring and even rejecting some of the core beliefs and morals of the Christian faith. Jesus calls out such hypocrisy when he says that only those who do the will of the Father will enter the kingdom of God. If we want to know what the will of the Father is, we need only look at the selfless love, mercy, compassion, and justice that Jesus embodied. Each day, we live the Father's will by serving the needs of others.

Isaiah 26:1–6
Psalm 118:1 and 8–9, 19–21, 25–27a
Matthew 7:21, 24–27

Friday

DECEMBER 3

• ST. FRANCIS XAVIER, PRIEST •

Those who err in spirit shall acquire understanding, and those who find fault shall receive instruction.
—ISAIAH 29:24

Today, many people are working to bring about what is known as *restorative justice,* which seeks to go beyond punishment, while holding offenders accountable, and repair the damage and harm caused by crime. This is characteristic of God's justice, summed up in today's first reading from Isaiah, which speaks of providing instruction for those who err. God's justice is not like the vengeance portrayed in many movies, which show the hero blasting the bad guys out of existence. Vengeance may feel good, but it is not God's way. Justice requires much harder work, but it begins with each one of us being grateful for the ways God has shown mercy to us and provided us with instruction to mend our ways. We, in turn, are called to do the same for others.

Isaiah 29:17–24
Psalm 27:1, 4, 13–14
Matthew 9:27–31

Saturday

DECEMBER 4

• ST. JOHN OF DAMASCUS, PRIEST AND DOCTOR OF THE CHURCH •

At the sight of the crowds, his heart was moved with pity for them.
—MATTHEW 9:36

Jesus was no magician. He did perform numerous acts that mystified and baffled the crowds; but unlike magicians, who perform to draw attention to themselves, Jesus's mighty deeds were performed out of compassion for others. Likewise, while magicians closely guard and conceal the secrets of their power, Jesus sought to reveal the source of his power—his Father in heaven. And not only that, but Jesus also sought to share that power with others. Still today, Jesus seeks not to attract fans but to form apprentices and empower others to perform similar acts. Such acts won't in most cases be spectacles, but rather reassurances that God is near to those who suffer. The fact is, a small act of kindness, mercy, or compassion that you show today may very well be the miracle someone has been praying for.

Isaiah 30:19–21, 23–26
Psalm 147:1–2, 3–4, 5–6
Matthew 9:35—10:1, 5a. 6–8

Sunday

DECEMBER 5

• SECOND SUNDAY OF ADVENT •

In the fifteenth year of the rule of Tiberius Caesar, . . . the word of God came to John the son of Zechariah in the desert.
—LUKE 3:1–2

Today's Gospel reminds us that we are to approach Jesus with a reversal of expectations. To get the full effect, imagine verse one through the names Annas and Caiphas in verse two being announced with a loud booming voice like boxing ring announcer Michael Buffer's "LLLLLet's get ready to rumble!" Now, imagine the booming voice suddenly halting followed by a quiet, almost bewildered voice announcing, "the word of God came to John the son of Zechariah in the desert"—cue the crickets and tumbleweeds. God bypassed the highest leaders and powers that be and instead sent his mighty word to a "nobody." May this passage remind us that God calls ordinary people like you and me to bring his word to others.

Baruch 5:1–9
Psalm 126:1–2, 2–3, 4–5, 6 (3)
Philippians 1:4–6, 8–11
Luke 3:1–6

Monday

DECEMBER 6

• ST. NICHOLAS, BISHOP •

The wilderness and the parched land will exult;
the steppe will rejoice and bloom.
They will bloom with abundant flowers,
and rejoice with joyful song.
—ISAIAH 35:1–2

Cartoonists have great imaginations. Think how many times Wile E. Coyote had an anvil flatten his head while chasing the Road Runner, only to see him get back up, wiggle his flattened head, and have it snap back to normal. Imagination and hope are closely tied together: In order to hope, we must have an imagined future. Isaiah was able to paint a portrait of a hoped-for future—deserts transforming into streams of water and flowers blooming in abundance—that inspired the people of Israel to envision a better future for themselves and their children. Pray today for the grace of imagination, to see light and hope where there is darkness and despair and to bring that light and hope to others.

Isaiah 35:1–10
Psalm 85:9ab and 10, 11–12, 13–14
Luke 5:17–26

Tuesday

DECEMBER 7

• ST. AMBROSE, BISHOP AND DOCTOR OF THE CHURCH •

Comfort, give comfort to my people,
says your God.
Speak tenderly to Jerusalem, and proclaim to her
that her service is at an end,
her guilt is expiated.
—ISAIAH 40:1–2

After a long period of exile in Babylon, the people of Israel needed encouragement. God directed his prophet, Isaiah, to speak words of hope, comfort, and encouragement to his people. Today, many people experience a type of exile—feeling estranged and displaced from all they once held dear. Such loss needs to be mourned. However, after a time, that loss can and must be transformed by hope lest despair gain the upper hand. Many people you will encounter today need the comfort and tender words that Isaiah speaks of. You yourself may be mourning a loss. Pray for the grace you need to embrace hope and to extend that hope to those you encounter.

Isaiah 40:1–11
Psalm 96:1–2, 3 and 10ac, 11–12, 13
Matthew 18:12–14

Wednesday

DECEMBER 8

• THE IMMACULATE CONCEPTION OF THE BLESSED VIRGIN MARY
(PATRONAL FEAST DAY OF THE UNITED STATES OF AMERICA) •

The man called his wife Eve,
because she became the mother of all the living.
—GENESIS 3:20

The biblical story of Adam and Eve tells us that the first humans chose to cooperate with evil in an effort to place their own wills over God's will. Today, on the Feast of the Immaculate Conception, we celebrate Mary as the "New Eve" who cooperates with God's will to bring our Savior, Jesus Christ, into the world. We refer to Mary as our spiritual Mother, again echoing the role of Eve as the mother of all the living. Mary, like all the saints, points the way to her son, Jesus. We do not worship her, but we honor her and learn from her how to be disciples of Christ since she was the first to believe in Jesus, to accept God's will, and to direct others to do whatever he says.

Genesis 3:9–15, 20
Psalm 98:1, 2–3ab, 3cd–4
Ephesians 1:3–6, 11–12
Luke 1:26–38

Thursday

DECEMBER 9

• ST. JUAN DIEGO CUAUHTLATOATZIN, HERMIT •

Whoever has ears ought to hear.
—MATTHEW 11:15

Jesus spoke very highly of his cousin John, known as the Baptist, comparing him to the prophet Elijah. The life of a prophet is hard because people often don't like being confronted with the truth. Prophetic messages challenge us and require discernment on the part of the listener to determine how the prophet's words apply to us. This is why Jesus told the crowds to truly hear the messages they heard. To truly hear is to ponder, reflect, and discern in order to hear God's truth. This Advent season is a good time for discernment since it is a season of patient waiting and hopeful anticipation that is conducive to slowing down and reflecting. Take advantage of this season's invitation to slow down and heed carefully what God is saying to you in prayer or through the prophets present in your life.

Isaiah 41:13–20
Psalm 145:1 and 9, 10–11, 12–13ab
Matthew 11:11–15

Friday

DECEMBER 10

Thus says the LORD, your redeemer,
the Holy One of Israel:
I, the LORD, your God,
teach you what is for your good,
and lead you on the way you should go.
—ISAIAH 48:17

I find it humorous when I come across TV programs, books, or podcasts that claim to explore "secrets of the Bible" while at the same time referring to Scripture as *revelation*—a word that is the exact opposite of a *secret*. God does not keep secrets. In fact, Scripture reveals account after account of God revealing his Word and his presence to his people, culminating in the Incarnation: Jesus Christ, the revelation of God in human flesh. Speaking through Isaiah, God reminds us once again that he goes out of his way to teach and to lead us, revealing his truth, goodness, and beauty, so that we might find our way into his loving arms.

Isaiah 48:17–19
Psalm 1:1–2, 3, 4 and 6
Matthew 11:16–19

Saturday

DECEMBER 11

• ST. DAMASUS I, POPE •

Then the disciples understood that he was speaking to them of John the Baptist.
—MATTHEW 17:13

John the Baptist had a very specific mission: to predispose people to open their hearts and minds to the Messiah, Jesus Christ. When his work was done, John said it was time for him to decrease so that Jesus could increase. In our own lives, we can think of people who were like John the Baptist for us—they entered our life for a short while, helped us to change our way of thinking, speaking, and acting, and then moved on. Take some time today to thank God for the blessings that these people have been in your life and pray for the grace to do the same for others, helping them to open their minds and hearts to the Good News and then stepping out of the way to allow the Spirit to work.

Sirach 48:1–4, 9–11
Psalm 80:2ac and 3b, 15–16, 18–19
Matthew 17:9a, 10–13

Sunday

DECEMBER 12

• THIRD SUNDAY OF ADVENT •

Rejoice in the Lord always. I shall say it again: rejoice!
—PHILIPPIANS 4:4

Is it really possible to *rejoice always*? St. Paul seemed to think so, and he backed up his words by expressing joy even in the midst of the greatest hardships, including imprisonment. That is not to say that he enjoyed the experience of being chained in a prison cell. What it does mean is that such hardships helped him recognize ever more deeply that God's grace alone sustains us and that we are never separated from the love of God we find in Christ Jesus. Paul teaches us that joy—a deep-down gladness—is a deliberate choice to trust and delight in God—unlike happiness, which is a feeling that depends on our circumstances. In the midst of your challenges and frustrations today, embrace the joy that you carry within, knowing that God's grace will sustain you.

Zephaniah 3:14–18a
Isaiah 12:2–3, 4, 5–6 (6)
Philippians 4:4–7
Luke 3:10–18

Monday
DECEMBER 13

• ST. LUCY, VIRGIN AND MARTYR •

The chief priests and the elders of the people approached him as he was teaching and said, "By what authority are you doing these things? And who gave you this authority?"
—MATTHEW 21:23

When children at play begin to argue and one child exerts authority, it's common to hear another child ask, "Says who?" In essence, this is the same question that the chief priests and elders asked of Jesus: *Says who?* They wanted to know where Jesus's authority came from. They wanted to know if Jesus was *authentic*—a word that comes from the same root as *author*—the Greek word *authentes*, which means "one who acts on their own authority." As you approach God in prayer today, do so with supreme confidence that Jesus, our Lord and Savior, is authentic and can be trusted since he, with the Father and the Holy Spirit, is the author of life.

Numbers 24:2–7, 15–17a
Psalm 25:4–5ab, 6 and 7bc, 8–9
Matthew 21:23–27

Tuesday

DECEMBER 14

• ST. JOHN OF THE CROSS, PRIEST AND DOCTOR OF THE CHURCH •

But I will leave as a remnant in your midst
a people humble and lowly,
Who shall take refuge in the name of the LORD:
the remnant of Israel.
—ZEPHANIAH 3:12–13

With nine children to provide for and little money, my mom became expert at sewing patches on hand-me-downs. To do this, she always maintained a supply of remnants—leftover pieces of fabric that could be used to extend the life of worn-out clothing. Today's first reading speaks of God providing a remnant among his people Israel whose faith had frayed. This remnant is not some sort of rapture that selects a group of elites while leaving others behind. Rather, we are told that this remnant will pasture, protect, and care for their flocks. This Advent, pray to be used by God like a remnant of fabric that restores those who are worn out and whose faith has become frayed.

Zephaniah 3:1–2, 9–13
Psalm 34:2–3, 6–7, 17–18, 19 and 23
Matthew 21:28–32

Wednesday

DECEMBER 15

Go and tell John what you have seen and heard.
—LUKE 7:22

In his book *The Power of Habit,* Charles Duhigg tells the story of how, in the early twentieth century, a marketing person persuaded the makers of Pepsodent toothpaste to add an ingredient that would create a tingling sensation when people brushed their teeth. As a result, brushing teeth caught on as an important part of personal hygiene. It seems that people need some kind of a sign that a product they are using is having some effect. Disciples of John the Baptist asked for such evidence from Jesus, who responded by telling them to report what they had seen and heard. In a similar way, we are called to report what we have seen and heard in our own lives—evidence of lives transformed by Jesus Christ, beginning with our own life stories.

Isaiah 45:6c–8, 18, 21c–25
Psalm 85:9ab and 10, 11–12, 13–14
Luke 7:18b–23

Thursday

DECEMBER 16

Your redeemer is the Holy One of Israel,
called God of all the earth.
—ISAIAH 54:5

In sports, it is common for players who have had a bad game to talk about redeeming themselves. This means that they are looking to restore their reputation and prove their value and worth. In the spiritual life, we learn that we are not capable of redeeming ourselves from sin without the grace of God, who Scripture tells us is our *redeemer*. In ancient times, people taken into slavery could be redeemed by someone who paid the price of redemption. Jesus paid that price for us by dying on the cross, thus setting us free from the slavery of sin. Ask God to restore you to a life of grace. Give thanks to God today for this redemption and strive to help others recognize their true value, which God restores through his saving grace.

Isaiah 54:1–10
Psalm 30:2 and 4, 5–6, 11–12a and 13b
Luke 7:24–30

Friday

DECEMBER 17

The mountains shall yield peace for the people,
and the hills justice.
He shall defend the afflicted among the people,
save the children of the poor.
—PSALM 72:3–4

Today's psalm response speaks of peace, a word that becomes somewhat ubiquitous during the Christmas season as we sing about "peace on earth, goodwill toward men." In Scripture, peace is not simply the absence of war—it is the result of God's will intersecting with the human heart. The Incarnation is the establishment of peace because heaven and earth are joined through the birth of Jesus. As we journey through these last few days of Advent, let us pray that God's will be done on earth as it is in heaven. The traditional Christian hymn "Let There Be Peace on Earth" states clearly, "let it begin with me." Today's psalm, likewise, reminds us that if we want peace, we must work for justice.

Genesis 49:2, 8–10
Psalm 72:1–2, 3–4ab, 7–8, 17
Matthew 1:1–17

Saturday

DECEMBER 18

Such was his intention when, behold, the angel of the Lord appeared to him in a dream.
—MATTHEW 1:20

It is interesting to note that the New Testament has very few references to dreams as opposed to the many references in the Old Testament. Three of these references, including today's Gospel, are connected to the birth and childhood of Jesus. Matthew is clearly emphasizing God's active role in the fulfillment of his promise. In his book *Dreams: God's Forgotten Language*, John Sanford reminds us of the importance of *interiority* in the spiritual life, of which dreams play a part. While our dreams may not be direct communications from God, they draw our awareness to our hopes, fears, joys, desires, anxieties, and pain. During these days of diminished sun, we can use the darkness to draw our attention to our interior life—the place of dreams—where God is seeking to get our attention.

Jeremiah 23:5–8
Psalm 72:1–2, 12–13, 18–19
Matthew 1:18–25

Sunday

DECEMBER 19

• FOURTH SUNDAY OF ADVENT •

Mary set out and traveled to the hill country in haste to a town of Judah, where she entered the house of Zechariah and greeted Elizabeth.

—LUKE 1:39–40

It is often noted that Mary pondered many things in her heart. She was indeed contemplative. Today's Gospel, however, reminds us that Mary used her contemplation as a catalyst for action. As soon as Mary found out that she was called to be the mother of Jesus, she leapt into action, setting out *in haste* to visit her cousin Elizabeth. This was not easy for Mary since she herself was pregnant and was traveling through hill country. We can imitate Mary by showing our missionary zeal—moving eagerly into action, even in the face of obstacles, to bring the Good News of Jesus to others. We can stir the life that is within others as Mary's greeting stirred the baby in Elizabeth's womb.

Micah 5:1–4a
Psalm 80:2–3, 15–16, 18–19 (4)
Hebrews 10:5–10
Luke 1:39–45

Monday

DECEMBER 20

Mary said to the angel, "How can this be, since I have no relations with a man?"
—LUKE 1:34

Throughout Scripture, people who are asked by God to play a special role in his plan of salvation experience a moment of hesitation, if not actual doubt. Abraham felt he was too old. Jeremiah felt he was too young. Moses insisted he couldn't speak well. Isaiah confessed to having unclean lips. Jonah flat out said no! In today's Gospel, Mary asks "How can this be?"

During these dark days of winter, we can sometimes experience doubt and anxiety. Author Abraham Verghese, in his novel *Cutting for Stone*, says, "Doubt is first cousin to faith," explaining that faith is simply the *suspension* of our doubts. Let us pray for the grace to suspend our doubts as Mary did and to place our faith in the Lord, even in the face of the unknown.

Isaiah 7:10–14
Psalm 24:1–2, 3–4ab, 5–6
Luke 1:26–38

Tuesday

DECEMBER 21

• ST. PETER CANISIUS, PRIEST AND DOCTOR OF THE CHURCH •

For see, the winter is past,
the rains are over and gone.
—SONG OF SONGS 2:11

In the spring of 1969, in the middle of tensions ripping apart his famous rock band, The Beatles, George Harrison took a much-needed day off and visited his friend Eric Clapton. As he walked through Eric's garden, the sun came out, and within moments, George sat down and wrote the classic song "Here Comes the Sun," in which he sings of ice melting after a long, cold, lonely winter. Today's first reading is lush with similar imagery, even as, all around us, winter is just beginning! With all four candles of our Advent wreaths lit, we know that the light—our Lord and Savior, Jesus Christ—is coming to dispel the darkness. May this knowledge melt our hearts and dissolve the clouds that prevent the light of Christ from shining within and around us.

Song of Songs 2:8–14 or Zephaniah 3:14–18a
Psalm 33:2–3, 11–12, 20–21
Luke 1:39–45

Wednesday

DECEMBER 22

He has cast down the mighty from their thrones
and has lifted up the lowly.
He has filled the hungry with good things,
and the rich he has sent away empty.
—LUKE 1:52–53

It has been said that we have *domesticated* Jesus, or reduced his message to something less challenging as opposed to one that confronts the status quo. We sometimes do the same with Mary as we emphasize her acquiescence to God's will while glossing over the part of her Magnificat prayer that indeed challenges the status quo, using prophetic language to speak on behalf of those who are oppressed. As we step closer to the celebration of Christmas, let us remember that the coming of Christ is a call to upset the status quo and that our sharing of gifts is a sign that we are called to ensure that all people enjoy the abundance of God's creation.

1 Sanuel 1:24–28
1 Samuel 2:1, 4–5, 6–7, 8abcd
Luke 1:46–56

Thursday

DECEMBER 23

• ST. JOHN OF KANTY, PRIEST •

Immediately his mouth was opened, his tongue freed, and he spoke blessing God.

—LUKE 1:64

When it comes to sharing faith with others, we sometimes become tongue-tied. We don't know what to say or how to explain our relationship with the Lord. Today's Gospel shows us how this can be overcome: Speak in praise of God! Zechariah, the father of John the Baptist, had been without words since learning that his son would have a special role in God's plan of salvation. Once he accepted God's will, his tongue was loosened and he praised God. To praise God is simply to draw attention to his greatness. We can do this simply by telling others of the goodness of God in our own lives and helping them see the goodness of God in their own lives. We need not be great orators—we just need to speak in praise of God.

Malachi 3:1–4, 23–24
Psalm 25:4–5ab, 8–9, 10 and 14
Luke 1:57–66

Friday

December 24

Thus says the LORD*:*
Should you build me a house to dwell in?
I have been with you wherever you went.
—2 SAMUEL 7:5, 9

The forty-year journey of the Israelites through the desert is often depicted as one of a people who were lost. While they experienced many hardships on their journey, one thing in particular comforted them: Wherever they went, God went with them. God was in their midst. When David wanted to build a temple in Jerusalem, God reminded him that the Lord cannot and will not be confined to one location. On this Christmas Eve, we rejoice once again as we anticipate the coming of Emmanuel: God with us. And this Emmanuel we celebrate is not located in any one place but is nomadic and mobile—the Word made flesh goes with us always and everywhere. May we carry the Lord with us wherever we go.

2 Samuel 7:1–5, 8b–12, 14a, 16
Psalm 89:2–3, 4–5, 27 and 29
Luke 1:67–79

Saturday

DECEMBER 25

• THE NATIVITY OF THE LORD (CHRISTMAS) •

And the Word became flesh and made his dwelling among us, and we saw his glory, the glory as of the Father's only Son, full of grace and truth.
—JOHN 1:14

The English translation of the Gospel of John differs from the Greek, which says that the Word made flesh "pitched his tent" among us. This is like saying that Jesus moved into the neighborhood with us. The Israelites placed the Ark of the Covenant, which was viewed as the presence of God, in a tent for safekeeping wherever they pitched camp. Today's Gospel reinforces that God is with us wherever we go, which is a good reason to sing "Joy To the World."

VIGIL:
Isaiah 62:1–5
Psalm 89:4–5, 16–17, 27, 29 (2a)
Acts 13:16–17, 22–25
Matthew 1:1–25 or, for shorter form,
Matthew 1:18–25

NIGHT:
Isaiah 9:1–6
Psalm 96:1–2, 2–3, 11–12, 13
Titus 2:11–14
Luke 2:1–14

DAWN:
Isaiah 62:11–12
Psalm 97:1, 6, 11–12
Titus 3:4–7
Luke 2:15–20

DAY:
Isaiah 52:7–10
Psalm 98:1, 2–3, 3–4, 5–6 (3c)
Hebrews 1:1–6
John 1:1–18 or, for shorter form,
John 1:1–5, 9–14

Sunday

DECEMBER 26

• THE HOLY FAMILY OF JESUS, MARY, AND JOSEPH •

Brothers and sisters: Put on, as God's chosen ones, holy and beloved, heartfelt compassion, kindness, humility, gentleness, and patience, bearing with one another and forgiving one another.
—COLOSSIANS 3:12–13

Pope Francis referred to the family as a "school of deepening humanity" (*Amoris Laetitia*). Indeed, families are capable of providing the kind of love, care, and connection not easily found elsewhere. Within families children can learn about compassion, kindness, humility, gentleness, and patience, as St. Paul wrote in his Letter to the Colossians. As such, families can realistically become change agents in a world where so many of these virtues are lacking. On this Feast of the Holy Family, we pray that families, beginning with our own, truly become schools of deepening humanity as we strive to transform the world to more fully embrace and reflect the reign of God.

1 Samuel 1:20–22, 24–28 or Sirach 3:2–6, 12–14
Psalm 84:2–3, 5–6, 9–10
1 John 3:1–2, 21–24
Colossians 3:12–21 or, for shorter form, Colossians 3:12–17
Luke 2:41–52

Monday

DECEMBER 27

• ST. JOHN, APOSTLE AND EVANGELIST •

Then the other disciple also went in, the one who had arrived at the tomb first, and he saw and believed.
—JOHN 20:8

The Gospel of John refers occasionally to an unnamed disciple many Scripture scholars believe was a literary device St. John the Evangelist used to refer to himself in his Gospel account. Today's Gospel recounts how this "other disciple" ran to the tomb first but did not enter, allowing Peter to enter first. Whereas Peter seems to have seen the evidence that a body once was laid here, we are told that John saw *and believed*. John was the first male disciple to believe in the Resurrection. The lesson for us is to pray for the grace to see not only what is right before our eyes, but also the possibilities that lie beyond. Faith is based on evidence, not proof. Like John, may we *see and believe*.

1 John 1:1–4
Psalm 97:1–2, 5–6, 11–12
John 20:1a and 2–8

Tuesday

DECEMBER 28

• THE HOLY INNOCENTS, MARTYRS •

If we say, "We are without sin," we deceive ourselves, and the truth is not in us.
—1 JOHN 1:8

Twelve-step programs teach us that healing from any addiction begins with honesty, acceptance, and admitting powerlessness, recognizing that life has become unmanageable. Only a higher power can help one move from denial to a willingness to change. Sin is an addictive behavior, and today's first reading reminds us that we have the tendency to live in denial when it comes to sin, believing in our total innocence. We *deceive* ourselves. On this Feast of the Holy Innocents, we pray for the grace to be honest with ourselves, admit our sinfulness, and turn to God who alone can rescue and restore us. At the same time, we pray for the protection of all innocent victims, especially children, for the sanctity of life, and for ourselves to have the courage to defend the vulnerable.

1 John 1:5—2:2
Psalm 124:2–3, 4–5, 7b–8
Matthew 2:13–18

Wednesday

DECEMBER 29

• ST. THOMAS BECKET, BISHOP AND MARTYR •

The way we may be sure that we know Jesus is to keep his commandments. Whoever says, "I know him," but does not keep his commandments is a liar, and the truth is not in him.
—1 JOHN 2:3–4

When someone speaks surprisingly bluntly, it is not unusual to hear another person respond sarcastically, "Tell us how you really feel." This might well be our reaction to the words St. John shares with us in today's first reading. John tells us bluntly that if we claim to be followers of Christ but do not love our neighbors, we are liars. Boom! Sometimes we need such bluntness to wake us up to the fact that we ourselves may claim the mantle of disciple while still withholding love or even holding grudges against others. Today, we pray for the grace to be brutally honest with ourselves, to love our neighbors, and to truly know the Lord.

1 John 2:3–11
Psalm 96:1–2a, 2b–3, 5b–6
Luke 2:22–35

Thursday

DECEMBER 30

There was a prophetess, Anna, the daughter of Phanuel, of the tribe of Asher.
—LUKE 2:36

Luke wastes no time in his Gospel introducing us to unexpected characters—people we wouldn't normally expect to see as significant. Anna is a woman and a widow—not someone with great status in Jewish society. However, she is named (in Scripture, names reveal identity, purpose, and destiny) and identified as a prophetess—someone who speaks on God's behalf. Despite her seeming insignificance, she was among the first to recognize Jesus as the long-awaited Messiah. After encountering Jesus, Anna declared Christ's coming to others who longed for redemption. Anna's life exemplifies how faith can sustain us through long periods of waiting and grief, reminds us that our life's purpose can unfold at any age, and inspires us to do significant work on God's behalf even if we consider ourselves to be less than significant.

1 John 2:12–17
Psalm 96:7–8a, 8b–9, 10
Luke 2:36–40

Friday

DECEMBER 31

• ST. SYLVESTER I, POPE •

Children, it is the last hour.
—1 JOHN 2:18

With the new year upon us, many of us are undertaking New Year's resolutions. Unfortunately, many of our resolutions fall by the wayside within a few weeks for a variety of reasons, not the least of which is that many of them are simply unrealistic! When it comes to changing our habits, the changes need to be realistic and incremental, lest we become overwhelmed and give up before we really get going. It is always a better idea to celebrate small successes along the way instead of waiting to celebrate a monumental achievement. As my friend Gary Jansen reminds us in his book *Microshifts: Transforming Your Life One Step at a Time*, it helps to make small changes (microshifts) that help us emerge gradually from unhealthy behaviors and move into healthier ones. God be with us!

1 John 2:18–21
Psalm 96:1–2, 11–12, 13
John 1:1–18

About the Author

Joe Paprocki, DMin, is a Master Catechist, author, speaker, and pastoral/catechetical minister with more than forty-five years of experience. He has authored more than twenty-five books on catechesis and pastoral ministry, and has presented in more than 200 dioceses internationally. Joe earned his Master's degree in Pastoral Studies from the Institute of Pastoral Ministry, Loyola University of Chicago, and his Doctor of Ministry Degree from the University of St. Mary of the Lake, Mundelein Seminary. Joe, who is retired, lives with his wife Joanne in Evergreen Park, IL.

A Special Excerpt from Joe Paprocki's

***8 Steps to Energize Your Faith*.**

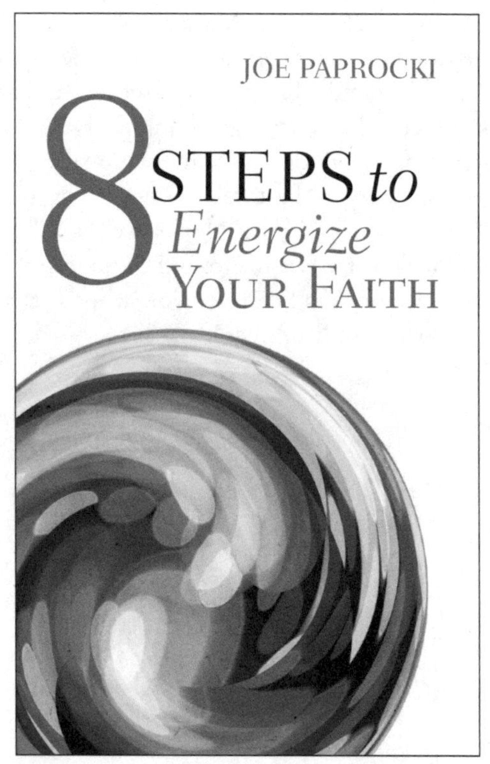

I Wanna Live Again!

The glory of God is a man [or woman] fully alive.
—St. Irenaeus

An Angelic Intervention

After suffering serious financial setbacks, George Bailey (*It's a Wonderful Life*) comes to the realization that he is worth more dead than alive (life insurance). Standing on a bridge over turbulent waters, George is prepared to jump in and end it all. Instead, his angel, Clarence, intervenes and dives in first, thus prompting George to save him instead of taking his own life. Clarence goes on to show George just what a wonderful life he really has, which brings George to the point of begging, "I wanna live again!"

Like George Bailey, the prophet Elijah had a wake-up call. He concluded that, despite all the powerful works God had accomplished through him, he (Elijah) was a failure whose only reward was a bounty on his head and a life as an outcast, on the run from his enemies. He decided that he wanted to go to sleep under a broom tree and never wake up again. That is, until an angel intervened, tapping him and saying, "Get up and eat." Elijah got up, had some bread and something to drink, and went right back to sleep. So, his angel had to work overtime and rouse him a second time, saying, "Get up and eat, for the journey is too much for you." This time, Elijah got up, ate and drank, and found the strength to travel forty days and forty nights until he reached Horeb, the mountain of God (1 Kings 19:3–9).

Both George Bailey and the prophet Elijah were in such despair that they lost their will to live, and both regained their desire to live again because of the intervention of an angel.

"I Wanna Live Again!"

The truth is, sometimes life is too much for us, just as it was for George and Elijah. And, like them, we sometimes feel as though we are burned out and don't have the wherewithal to keep going. In such cases, we need an angel to intervene; in other words, if we hope to get up and be spiritually reawakened, we need help from beyond ourselves or what we call a "divine intervention." The presence of an angel in each story signals that, when confronted with the meaning of life, we enter the spiritual realm. Like Clarence, Elijah's unnamed angel intervened to prompt Elijah to "get up" and to want to live again.

Lord knows we continue to endure turbulent times the likes of which few of us have experienced before. Our spiritual lives have been taking a beating in recent times (in our civil communities as well as in our parish/church communities), as we have attempted to navigate unprecedented experiences of a pandemic, racial strife, economic uncertainty, political divisions and acrimonious elections, rampant incivility on social media, and ideological polarization, to name a few. As a result, many of us now find that, like George Bailey and Elijah, we are losing our zest for life. This spiritual lethargy manifests itself in a variety of ways, including a tendency to withdraw, joyless recreation, feelings of despair, a sense of cynicism and negativity, spiritual disconnection, doubt, feelings of being overwhelmed, emotional and physical fatigue, and an increasing desire to "anesthetize" through overindulgence in various pleasures.

While we all experience some of the above from time to time, it is spiritually unhealthy when these feelings become chronic and our spirit is no longer able to "get up." It is when we reach that point that we are in desperate need of an angel: an intervention from God. Luckily for us, *intervening* is what God does best; it is God's "MO" to insert himself into the lives of his people. Such interventions are typically not as dramatic as George Bailey's or Elijah's, and our angel often turns out to be a friend, coworker, neighbor, or stranger in the most unlikely time or place. The good news is that, through the Holy Spirit, we have access to divine energy—not just human energy that we try to generate ourselves but God's own life!

Claiming Your Inheritance

Imagine that, after a long period of being down on your luck financially, you discover that you are the sole heir of an insanely wealthy relative who is the owner of a wildly successful corporation that has borne the family's good name for generations. Now that this relative has decided to retire, she has intervened in your life and announced that you will now take over control of the corporation and share in its abundance. There's only one stipulation: you must agree to continue upholding the company's long-standing credo, which she insists has been the key to its success. You would no doubt "do your homework" to learn your relative's philosophy and values embodied in that credo so that you could put them into practice. You would strive to live up to the family's name and emulate your relative's way of proceeding to ensure continued success for yourself and for the company. In other words, you would want this relative to reveal her mind and heart to you so that you could, in turn, embody those same values, beliefs, and principles in your role as successor.

The above scenario is an apt metaphor for how God intervenes in our lives and prompts us to "get up," reawaken our faith, and tap into divine energy. The key to this transformation comes from beyond ourselves, and we can do nothing to earn it; however, we must do some serious work to hold up our end of the bargain.

The Good News of Jesus Christ is that we are heirs to the abundant riches (graces) of God's kingdom and that we are called to begin sharing in this inheritance NOW. This is what St. Paul tells us in his letter to the Romans when he says that "we are God's children. Now if we are children, then we are heirs—heirs of God and co-heirs with Christ" (Romans 8:16–17) and again in the letter to the Ephesians when he says that we are sealed with the Holy Spirit, "guaranteeing our inheritance" (Ephesians 1:14). We are literally called to start a new life filled with an embarrassment of riches. This is the essence of discipleship: to live as an heir of God's kingdom and to invite others to share in its abundant riches.

We Have Some Work to Do

This new life, which is freely given to us, also calls us to respond in a particular manner. If we want to keep this inheritance—if we want to tap into divine energy—we have some work to do. We are called to emulate the One who bestows this gift upon us. And to emulate God, in whose image and likeness we are made, we need to ask God to reveal his heart and mind to us. Luckily, God has already done so; we see this so clearly throughout sacred Scripture and through the work of the Holy Spirit. Scripture is not so much about following rules as it is about imitating someone, namely, our Creator. This imitation of the Divine is the key to reawakening our faith and tapping into divine energy so that we can become more fully human.

This book explores the ways you can see God's "intervention" in your life, enabling it to be infused with divine energy that will make you want to get up and live again! You can do this by, first, recognizing that you are a child of God and an heir to God's abundant graces and, second, freely responding with a commitment to emulate God's "way of proceeding" as revealed in Scripture, so that you might flourish in this endeavor. In doing so, you will be able to venture further into the reawakening of your faith, which opens a path to a new or deeper relationship with God and others. In this book, we will focus on eight of these divine attributes.

Divine Attributes (God's Way of Proceeding)	What We Must Do to Emulate God
God is a creator: God's first act is to create all of reality.	Create something.
God delights in his creation: God states that everything he made is "good."	Delight in nature and all of creation.
God appreciates simplicity: God asks us to unclutter our lives and get rid of anything that makes it hard to encounter him.	Simplify your life.
God is relational: God *is* community (Father, Son, and Holy Spirit).	Build and celebrate relationships.
God is compassionate: God's primary characteristic is compassion for those who are suffering or vulnerable.	Show compassion.
God fixes things: God seeks to mend, heal, and rescue.	Make repairs.
God is generous and selfless: God's love is expressed most powerfully in Jesus, selflessly laying down his life for us.	Share generously and selflessly.
God is—he just IS!	Be still.

By engaging in the above actions, we emulate God and act as his true heirs (disciples), which enables us to enjoy the fullness of his inheritance and tap into divine energy. You'll notice that the actions I describe are not very "churchy." It is unfortunate that the notion of living a spiritual life is so often measured solely by the amount of time one spends in church or in performing pious religious practices, worthy as these practices are. After all, spending time in church doesn't make you a Christian ("holy") any more than spending time in a garage makes you a car. While I make a case for participation in the life of the Church as part of a healthy spirituality, my main focus is to illustrate how a healthy spiritual life must be cultivated and practiced in ordinary daily living, because even weekly churchgoers spend 167 of 168 hours per week in the details of everyday life.

To truly embrace the potential of divine energy to which we are heirs, we must break down the compartmentalization of faith that has led to an unfortunate and artificial separation between the sacred and the so-called "secular" and, instead, recognize the presence of God in all things, in all people, and in all of creation. It is in our daily living that we need to focus our attention; it is in daily living that the energy and direction of God need to take hold. Tapping into this divine energy gives us the ability to integrate all our life through a new vision and allows us to reflect God's life more fully.

Now Is the Time

When it comes to "getting up," renewing our spiritual life, and tapping into divine energy, we cannot simply wait for the negative circumstances around us to change so that they bother us less. That rarely happens. Rather, we must change our hearts and minds so that we more closely emulate God, who wants us to begin enjoying our inheritance now.

Don't be lulled into thinking that God's plan is for us to grit our teeth and endure this messy world to earn some kind of eternal "reward" in the afterlife. Although this sentiment too often pervades Christian thinking (as revealed by this verse of the evangelical spiritual "I'll Fly Away": "Just a few more weary days and then, I'll fly away; to a land where joy shall never end, I'll fly away"), you will not find such sentiment in the Bible! Instead, we are called to embrace the words of St. Paul, who recognized that we don't have to wait to begin enjoying our inheritance: "Now is the time of God's favor, now is the day of salvation" (2 Corinthians 6:2). With the help of the Holy Spirit, let's get up and start living—tapping into divine energy—NOW!